ANTARCTIC
EYEWITNESS

CHARLES F. LASERON'S SOUTH WITH MAWSON

AND

FRANK HURLEY'S SHACKLETON'S ARGONAUTS

INTRODUCED BY

TIM BOWDEN

Birlinn

This edition first published in the UK in 2002 by
Birlinn Limited
West Newington House
10 Newington Road
Edinburgh
EH9 1QS

www.birlinn.co.uk

South With Mawson first published in 1947 by
Angus & Robertson Publishers
Shackleton's Argonauts first published in 1948
by Angus & Robertson Publishers
Combined edition first published in 1999 by
HarperCollins*Publishers* Pty Ltd, Australia

ISBN 1 84158 220 4

British Library Cataloguing-in-Publication Data
A catalogue record for this book is available from the British Library

Printed and bound by Creative Print and Design, Wales

Contents

INTRODUCTION

by Tim Bowden

Of all the early nineteenth-century expeditions that took place in the so-called 'Heroic Era' of Antarctic exploration, two stand out in terms of raw, sustained survival and the triumph of the human spirit set against seemingly impossible odds.

One is Sir Douglas Mawson's 1911–14 Australasian Antarctic Expedition (marked by his own odyssey of endurance), and the other is Sir Ernest Shackleton's unsuccessful attempt to cross the Antarctic continent from 1914–16 and the extraordinary survival of his entire party after the expedition's ship *Endurance* was crushed and sunk in pack-ice.

Both expeditions were superbly chronicled by the indomitable Australian photographer Frank Hurley.

Hurley's stunning black-and-white images – he was one of the first and the best of the twentieth-century's photo-journalists – would be reason enough for HarperCollins to combine two polar classics in the one volume.

At the end of the twentieth century, the 'Heroic Era' is being revisited with the benefit of hindsight. A major photographic exhibition based on the *Endurance* saga opened in New York in April 1999, with previously unpublished Hurley images; a new book on the Shackleton 1914–16 expedition has been published; and at last, a definitive biography of Sir Douglas Mawson is in the pipeline. So the publication of *Antarctic Eyewitness* gives the polar enthusiast and general reader (can the two be separated?) a welcome opportunity to contrast first-hand accounts against retrospective scholarship. As well, these two books give us an insider's account of what it was like to be there – the smell, feel and flavour of high adventure and sustained, icy terror.

While there has been a welcome facsimile edition of Sir Douglas Mawson's *Home of the Blizzard* published in 1996, his is by definition the view from the top. Charles Laseron's *South with Mawson*, the first of the journals included here, not only gives us informal insights into

Mawson's personal and leadership style as the AAE members shelter from the blasting blizzards in the hut at Commonwealth Bay, but we also have some wonderful descriptions of Frank Hurley, humorist and practical joker extraordinaire, fearless expeditioner, and the man who would do absolutely anything to get film or still photographic images he considered in the realm of the possible.

With Laseron's affectionate descriptions of him fresh in our minds, we can read Hurley's own narrative in the second part of this compendium, *Shackleton's Argonauts*, with added insight. Hurley combined his genius with the camera with a vivid, engaging prose style. From him, as with Laseron, we get the view from 'under the boat' – literally in the case of the miserable situation on Elephant Island when, after escaping from the pack-ice, twenty-two men huddled under two overturned dories for nearly five months. They subsisted mainly on the oily flesh of elephant seals and penguins, until Shackleton returned to rescue them after his desperate 1200-kilometre voyage to South Georgia in an 7.5-metre open boat.

Laseron's *South with Mawson* was first published in 1947, and again in 1957 – three years after Australia's first permanent continental station (named after Sir Douglas Mawson) was established, and on the threshold of the International Geophysical Year involving a massive international effort to combine coordinated scientific observations in Antarctica. In his preface to the 1957 edition, Laseron (who was a zoologist on Mawson's 1911–14 expedition and survived Gallipoli shortly afterwards) modestly disputes the use of the term 'heroic' to describe the efforts of the explorers of his generation:

> *Though methods have improved, enabling more to be done in a given time, Antarctica is still the same inhospitable land, and requires the same human effort to overcome its rigorous and treacherous climate and the hazards of its approach and conquest. If 'old style' be substituted for 'heroic' this may more fittingly describe the difference between expeditions of the early twentieth century and today.*

Laseron said he wrote his personal impressions to 'perpetuate memories of a splendid lot of fellows', and makes a claim he believed was unique:

Introduction

During the whole of our stay in Antarctica there was not one serious quarrel, nor even any serious friction among our members. Yet we were no band of angels, only a typical group of young Australians, with one Swiss, one New Zealander, and two Englishmen, with the average variation of temperament.

From Laseron we get informal glimpses of Mawson. During the unloading and hut-building at Commonwealth Bay in January 1912, a case was lost overboard. It was thought to contain a vital part of the hut's stove, so Mawson told Laseron they should try and recover it. The case was visible in about 2 metres of water, and, after grappling for it without success, Mawson said to Laseron: 'There is only one thing for it.' The egalitarian leader stripped off and dived into the ice-strewn sea, managing on his second attempt to lift it up. As soon as they reached the shore, he sprinted for the hut, ice already forming on his bare skin. The case turned out to contain tins of jam only. The missing piece of the stove turned up shortly afterwards, beneath some other gear.

There was no dedicated cook in the AAE, and the expeditioners took turns. Hurley, Laseron and several others formed 'The Secret Society of Crook Cooks'. Those so nominated could only be promoted to the rank of 'chef' if they produced a dish voted worthy of that title by everyone present. Sadly, there were some who delighted in the title of 'crook cook' right to the end.

In a chapter titled 'Twenty-Four Hours in the Hut', Laseron gives a wonderful informal description of what it was like to live in 'The Home of the Blizzard'. Accustomed to the continuing howl of the katabatic wind, a sudden calm had a disturbing effect on those in the hut. Says he:

In the middle of lunch we become aware of something strange. Our ear-drums commence to throb as with a great noise. Somebody speaks and his voice cracks like a whip on the stillness. For the wind has stopped, and, accustomed as we are to its howl, the silence can literally be felt. For a while we speak almost in whispers, our heads are ringing and we feel very uncomfortable.

Frank Hurley met every situation with humour. According to Laseron he would:

…joke in the face of death. The rougher things were, the more cheerful he became, and the more he poked fun at anything and everything. Powerful physically, he was an ideal mate for such a trip [sledging journey]. His fertile brain and imagination made a comedy of the most desperate situation…he composed fantastic and absurd poems…One could never be downhearted with Frank, even when things were at their worst.

Laseron's observations of Mawson in his book were respectful and affectionate. Only his private diaries (recently read by Mawson's biographer Philip Ayres) show a glimpse of another side of 'The Doctor'. On 4 February 1913, four days before Mawson returned alone from his disastrous sledging expedition and believing him to be dead, Laseron wrote: 'The poor old chief – we loved him with all his faults.' A year earlier, on 18 February 1912, he confided in his diary that Mawson was:

…very popular, and though sometimes stern as billy, oh! he is far more of a comrade than any of us thought he would be…we now like him much better than at first. This is of course all in spite of his faults, of which he undoubtedly has a good many. One of his worst is a nasty sneery way he has of saying things at times, though perhaps he doesn't mean all he says and evidently forgets it soon after.

Regardless of these criticisms, there is no doubt Sir Douglas Mawson had the respect and affection of his team.

So did Sir Ernest Shackleton, of whom Hurley writes with great regard. As Hurley succinctly summarises in the introduction to *Shackleton's Argonauts*:

Here we were, a small coterie of scientists and seamen, poles apart in learning, culture, beliefs and creeds, banded together with the one common impulse – to survive. We "suffered, starved and…grovelled down". Suffering is a mighty leveller, and suffering welded us into a united brotherhood – a brotherhood inspired by the invincible spirit of our leader.

Contemporary opinion is that Shackleton's party might not have survived the attempt to cross Antarctica with the equipment and logistics available to them. So while it is hard to think of the saga of the Shackleton expedition as lucky – after the *Endurance* was trapped for ten months in the ice before sinking and the remarkable survival of all on board, living on the ice and escaping by small boats to Elephant Island – it could have been a better option for survival than the original plan.

That they survived at all is a triumph of leadership and group solidarity. That we also have both moving footage and still photographs of it is simply miraculous. Hurley disobeyed Shackleton's orders and rescued his film, which was still on board the *Endurance* and underwater after the ship was abandoned. Hurley reports that he and a sailor hacked their way through the splintered timbers to reach the film canisters. 'After vainly fishing in the ice-laden waters with boathooks, I made up my mind to dive in after them,' he reports. 'It was mighty cold work groping about in the mushy ice in the semi-darkness of the ship's bowels, but I was rewarded in the end and passed out the three precious tins.'

As Seaman How was massaging Hurley vigorously to restore his circulation, 'the vessel began to shake and groan ominously' under more intense ice pressure. 'We sprang for our lives and leaped on to the ice – almost into the arms of the astonished leader, who demanded "What the hell are you up to?"'

Shortly afterwards Shackleton had to assist Hurley in an awful but necessary act of historical vandalism. The expedition could not possibly carry 500 of Hurley's heavy glass-plate negatives during their escape across the pack-ice from their stricken ship. Hurley writes: 'I had a painful hour. Sir Ernest and I went over the plates together, and as a negative was rejected, I would smash it on the ice to obviate all temptation to change my mind.' Hurley was able to retain 120 glass-plate negatives as well as his cinecamera film. He abandoned all his photographic gear except for one small pocket camera and three spools of unexposed film. In something of an understatement, Hurley wrote: 'I wonder if three spools of film ever went through more exacting experiences before they were developed.'

Many of those images, together with the narrative of two truly 'heroic' participants in extraordinary Antarctic events, are combined in this timely and immensely readable volume.

SOUTH
WITH MAWSON

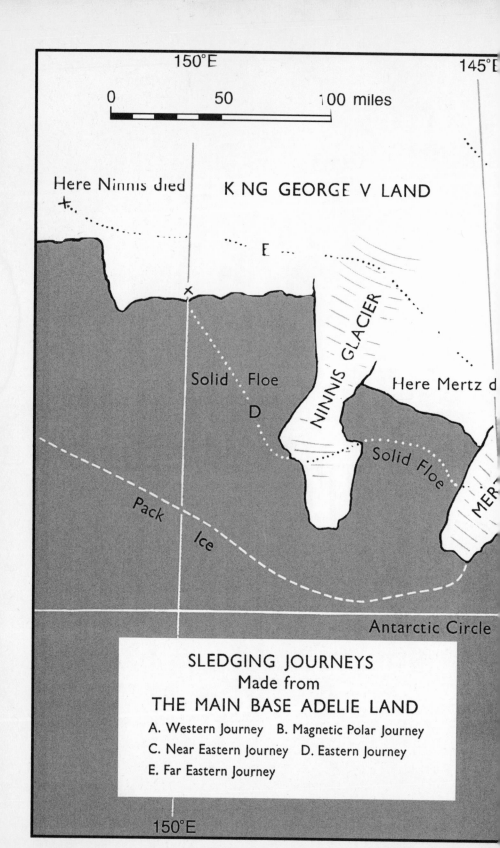

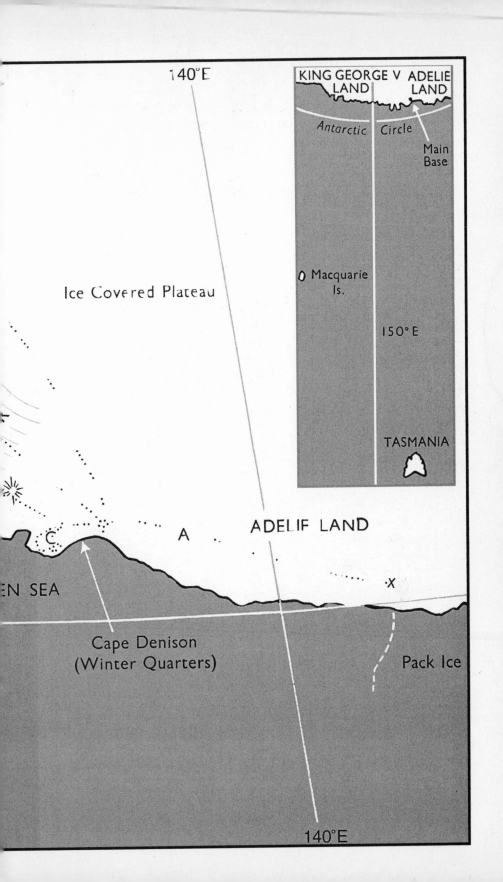

140°E

Ice Covered Plateau

KING GEORGE V | ADELIE
LAND | LAND

Antarctic Circle

Main
Base

○ Macquarie
Is.

150°E

TASMANIA

A ADELIF LAND

C

x

EN SEA

Cape Denison
(Winter Quarters)

Pack Ice

140°E

CHAPTER 1

SOUTHWARDS BOUND

With youth at the helm and youth at the prow,
And the spirit of youth within,
What matter the shadows of after years
When ours is the world to win.

At the beginning of 1911 the organisation of the Australasian Antarctic Expedition was well on the way. It is not within the scope of this book to detail the whole of the events which previously led to the idea of a purely Australian expedition. Sir Douglas Mawson, then Dr Mawson, had been a member of Shackleton's expedition in 1909, and was a member of the sledging party that first won a way to the magnetic pole. It will be remembered that on this expedition, Sir Ernest Shackleton, with the main party, successfully climbed a huge glacier on to the main plateau and reached a point only 87 miles from the geographical pole, to that date the most southern limit attained by any expedition. In 1910 he was planning a further expedition with the object of finally conquering the Pole itself. Circumstances, however, forced Sir Ernest Shackleton to postpone his own plans, and it was Captain Scott's expedition which set out for this purpose, reached the Pole, only to find itself forestalled by Amundsen. Scott died on the return journey; this, of course, is now history.

In the meantime Dr Mawson was busy organising his own expedition, one that was to be essentially Australian – or rather, Australasian, as our sister dominion, New Zealand, was to have her share in the enterprise, and be linked with Australia, as she was at a later date, with all that the word 'Anzac' implies. The object of the expedition was generally to explore the sector of the Antarctic continent immediately to the south of Australia. No ships had visited these waters since before 1842. Within a short interval prior to this date, Commander Wilkes of the United States' exploring expedition and a Frenchman, Dumont d'Urville, had both explored in these longitudes, but owing to the stormy conditions, had not stayed long. Wilkes reported a number of landfalls, but many of these have since been rather open to doubt. This is not to disparage the great navigator, as the conditions were peculiarly difficult, the proximity of the magnetic pole made the compass practically useless, sights were often difficult on account of the incessant blizzards, and, most of all, gigantic icebergs, covered by large dome-shaped accumulations of snow, often have a distinct appearance of ice-covered land. Merely to attain these latitudes in the old days of sailing ships, with neither proper clothing nor equipment, in face of the ever-present dangers of pack-ice and icebergs, of continual storms and adverse winds, was in itself a remarkable feat of navigation and courage, and all credit is due to the few who pioneered the way for the properly equipped expeditions of later years.

D'Urville actually sighted land at a point almost due south of Tasmania, and landed on a small rocky islet off the coast. The mainland, which he could see to the south, he named Adélie Land in honour of his wife.

Following these expeditions a very long interval elapsed before the area was again approached, and it was not until 1902 that a German expedition landed a party on an extinct volcano, the Gaussberg, some 1500 miles farther to the westward. The land adjoining this to the south was named Kaiser Wilhelm II Land. With these exceptions, practically the whole of the coast as far eastwards as Cape Adare was *terra incognita*, that is to the point where the coast bends southwards to form the western shore of the Ross Sea.

To the north-west of Cape Adare lie the ice-covered Balleny Islands, and it was to the south of these that Mawson intended to establish the first winter base on the mainland itself. This was to consist of twelve men. Two other bases were to be established farther to the west – the second of six, the third of twelve men – and by sledging journeys it was hoped to link up and complete the mapping of the whole of the coastline. Subsequent events were to modify these plans considerably, and ultimately only two bases were established in Antarctica proper, in addition to the intermediate base on Macquarie Island, one of the chief functions of which was to act as a wireless and meteorological station.

The early organisation of the expedition was attended with many difficulties, the chief of which was finance. After many vicissitudes, the Australasian Association for the Advancement of Science came partially to the rescue, and then all the Australian governments gave financial support, so that at last all preliminary obstacles were overcome, and the expedition was able to make a start. A full account of these early troubles appears in the official history of the expedition.

Ultimately the *Aurora* left England under the command of Captain J.K. Davis, and after a protracted voyage arrived in Hobart, where the final preparations were made. On board were several members of the land parties who had been selected by Dr Mawson when in England. Among these were Frank Wild who had already served on both the earlier Scott and Shackleton expeditions. Other Englishmen were Bickerton, an engineer, and Lieutenant Ninnis. The only non-Britisher was Dr Xavier Mertz, a Swiss, who, with Ninnis, had charge of a number of sledging dogs. On board also was an aeroplane which was to be used for exhibition flights in Australia and the engine adapted afterwards for the purposes of motor traction in the south. Unfortunately, however, the machine was smashed on a trial flight in Adelaide, but the engine was salved and afterwards used in the way originally intended.

Dr Mawson had in the meantime returned to Australia and busied himself with the completion of the personnel of the land parties and with other details of the final organisation. Up to this time the idea of becoming a member of such an expedition seemed beyond my rosiest dreams; nevertheless, with the vaguest of hopes, I put in an application, and implored all my scientific friends to state what a fine fellow I was. At the time I was employed as collector at the Technological Museum, and fortunately for myself had always been keen on the collection of marine life. Among the many applicants there was a dearth of those with the necessary experience in this direction, and my hopes were advanced a stage when I was granted an interview with Dr Mawson himself. I well remember the occasion. I felt rather nervous, and his somewhat abrupt manner did not put me at my ease. His first question was not as to my scientific attainments, but as to whether I could cook. I admitted that I had made dampers on various camping excursions, but confessed that my first efforts at least were probably still in the bush in a state of semi-petrification. For some reason this admission seemed to please him, but after a very short interview I was dismissed without any definite promise of inclusion.

In fact, I never did receive official notification of any appointment. The next intimation I had was a letter from Dr Mawson from Melbourne, telling me to get in touch with John Hunter, then demonstrator in zoology at the Sydney University, and enclosing long lists of stores and equipment that had to be collected in Sydney and shipped to Hobart. Among other instructions were orders to see Mr Grant, the taxidermist at the Australian Museum, and take lessons in the art of skinning birds.

It was thus that my dreams were realised, and for the next few weeks I trod on air. To a young fellow leading a more or less humdrum existence, the sudden prospect of embarking on a great expedition, the first in the history of his country, the prospect of travelling into new lands and encountering who-knows-what wonderful adventures, was almost overwhelming. Our last few weeks were one whirl of excitement, the necessary leave, incidentally without pay, was granted me by the department, and, even before this came through, my chief, R.T. Baker, curator of the Technological Museum, was exceedingly kind, and allowed me every latitude during museum hours. Consequently I was free to devote my time to the affairs of the expedition.

Day by day Johnnie Hunter and I rushed about the city in a hansom cab, from office to office, warehouse to warehouse, and from shipping company to wharf. During this time it was brought home to us the enormous amount of organisation necessary to fit out a polar expedition, and later, when actually in the South and cut off from all civilisation, we realised how complete that organisation had been. Whether we needed a sewing machine or a toothpick, every want seemed to have been anticipated.

Many of the Australian firms had been very generous with gifts of provisions and equipment, and it was our duty to take delivery of these and see them shipped. One of the huts that were to form our winter quarters in Antarctica had been built in Sydney, taken to pieces, and the timbers numbered, quite a little cargo in itself. There were sledges and skis locally made from spotted gum and mountain ash. There were cases of bacon, tobacco, biscuits, hams, and a hundred other sorts of provision. Added to this, Johnnie and I had to check and complete the lists of all that was necessary for the collection and preservation of zoological specimens at four bases. There were dredges and sieves, skinning knives and forceps, collecting jars and boxes, stocks of alcohol, formalin, arsenical soap, and other preservatives, everything, in fact, that we thought might be needed. Betweenwhiles we spent hours at the Australian Museum learning how to prepare the skins of birds and animals for museum purposes. It was a great trouble to get dead birds to practise on, and the keepers of bird-shops no doubt felt very surprised at the sudden demand for deceased pigeons and canaries, and, what is more, they never forgot to charge us for what must otherwise have been consigned to the dirt-box.

The last week was a tremendous rush, and it was only by the utmost courtesy of the shipping company that we were able to complete the loading in time. Wharf space is, of course, valuable, but we were granted space for a depot, and for the last day or two were on constant duty, checking the innumerable cases, or rushing away to hurry others that had been delayed. At last our cargo, some 50 tons or so, was safely on board, documents all in order, and only at the last moment were we free to make a final farewell and board the *Paloona* on the first stage of our adventure.

There is little need to describe our voyage to Hobart in the *Paloona*, except to mention that for the first time we met several other members of the expedition. For another thing, we scored distinctly over the officers, particularly the minor officers, of the *Paloona*. There were several pretty girls on board, and no mere ship's officer had a chance against a polar explorer, even if only an explorer in the making. The weather was comparatively calm, but, alas for my social success,

I succumbed to those pangs of sea-sickness that were later to be suffered in an aggravated form. Consolation came, however, when, after some hours of misery, I crawled on deck and found a chair beside a pretty little brown-haired girl who was also a victim. I wonder, whoever she was and wherever she is, if she remembers how, in the intervals of our confidences, we wandered to the side and were sick together.

In Hobart we saw for the first time the *Aurora*, which was to take us to the South, and here we linked up with those members who came from the other states, and two, Webb and Dr Whetter, from New Zealand. Here also were those who had accompanied the *Aurora* from London, Wild and Bickerton, Ninnis and Mertz. Ninnis, who was a lieutenant in the Royal Fusiliers, we at once christened 'Cherub', partly on account of his complexion, which was as pink and white as that of any girl. He was tall and rather ungainly in build, and had more boxes of beautiful clothes than seemed possible for one mere man. He took our chaff good-naturedly enough, and afterwards we learned to love him for the thoroughbred he was. Together with Mertz he had one of the dirtiest jobs on the trip, that of the charge of the dogs, but he never complained; in fact he was the personification of keenness, and revelled in his part of the expedition right through.

Xavier Mertz deserves a paragraph to himself. He was a Swiss, a doctor of laws, and a magnificent athlete, having won the world championship in ski-running in Switzerland just prior to leaving. We took Mertz to our hearts at once. His Christian name did not sound well to Australian ears, and was soon abbreviated to 'X', by which he was known to the end. His English was a little shaky when we first knew him, and I understand he had rather scandalised a young lady in a stationer's shop in Cardiff by asking for some 'bloody' paper, when he meant blotting-paper. One of his sayings became quite a gag on the expedition. Someone had played some harmless joke which momentarily aroused his ire. He almost tore out his hair as he sought for adequate English.

'*Sapristi*,' he cried at last, '*sapristi*! Too much ees enough.'

Our days in Hobart were spent in sorting and checking the thousands of packages that littered the wharf, and wheeling them to

the ship, where they were taken on board. Here wharf-labourers
stored them into the hold. Much had to be unpacked and divided
into four parts, and then repacked to supply the wants of four
separate bases. Coloured bands were then painted around the cases,
and they were then packed into the hold so as to be available as
required; those of the last base being at the bottom, and so on. At
one stage a strike was threatened, as objections were taken to some of
our members encroaching on what was considered trade-union
ground. The grumblers were, however, told that we were quite
prepared to do the whole work ourselves, and nothing further was
heard of the impending trouble.

Then at last, on 2 December 1911, we stood on the wharf with a
vast throng and waved a temporary farewell to the *Aurora* –
temporary, because about twenty of us were to leave the week after in
an auxiliary steamer, the *Taroa*, and join the *Aurora* at Macquarie
Island. The last six days were a complete relaxation, and spent in an
endless round of gaiety, and on the 8th we, too, said farewell to
civilisation for a long sixteen months. Even then we were not quite
away. As we pulled out into the bay, the glass was falling rapidly, and
we were evidently in for a stiff blow. As a result the anchor of the
Taroa was let go, and for two days we kicked our heels waiting for the
weather to moderate.

Finally, on 10 December, our bow was pointed southwards, and at
last we were truly on the way to the Antarctic. I cannot say that I
enjoyed this part of the journey. There are some fellows, like Frank
Hurley, who do not mind crawling to the end of a yard-arm when the
ship is rolling 40°, and whose appetite actually improves under the
circumstances. For myself, when there occurs that sudden slide down
into the trough of the waves, I always feel that a vital part of me has
been left in the air, so to speak. I like to think that, even in a state of
extremis, some spark of levity remained. To quote Johnnie Hunter,
who was in the next berth to mine: 'I shall never forget poor Joe in
the middle of a particularly violent spasm, turning and gasping, "Well,
there goes my liver at last."'

Joe, by the way, was my nickname acquired a little later on the
trip. On the strength of having belonged to a musical society I rather

fancied myself as a singer, though long since I have awakened to the fact that I never was a Caruso. I was very fond of old negro songs, but the others considered that my rendering of 'Old Black Joe' was particularly mournful. Though I was quickly disillusioned as to musical genius the name stuck, and to this day I am greeted by old members as Joe, and nothing else. Strange to say, though it carries a story of vanished hopes, I like it.

To return to sea-sickness, the greater part of my time on the *Taroa* was spent in my bunk, and it was only as we neared Macquarie Island that I found my sea-legs, and began to think life worth living again.

This experience was rather a pity, because I missed much of what was happening aboard. The *Taroa*, in fact, had come straight from a yarn by W.W. Jacobs. She was a small iron steamer, and had been previously engaged carrying freight and passengers to the west coast of Tasmania. If the skipper had a proper name we never heard it, as he was known, not only on board, but in shipping circles generally, as 'Roaring Tom'. A rather burly personage with a black beard and a habit of shouting at the least provocation, his ways were, to say the least, very casual. When the last of the stores was being loaded in Hobart, the Plimsoll mark was nowhere to be seen, so Roaring Tom, swearing that someone had been playing a joke, had himself lowered over the side in a bo's'n's chair and personally painted in a new one. Later, at Macquarie Island, when the *Taroa* was steadily rising in the water, as the stores were unloaded, the old Plimsoll mark reappeared from beneath the water where it had been submerged to a depth of some 2 feet.

The mate was deaf and a Christian Scientist. His hobby was to argue on every conceivable subject, even if he had never heard of it before, and as he never heard any replies he won all arguments to his own satisfaction. The crew, consisting of boys, cheeked him incessantly with competitive obscenity, but he never heard a word.

How we fluked Macquarie Island is a mystery. The mate could navigate, but the skipper never believed his results, and the skipper himself, from day to day, forgot on which side the variation of his compass lay. The course he set tended naturally to wobble a bit. One day he took Hoadley and Dovers into his confidence. He had just determined his position, but was puzzled at the result. According to his figures the *Taroa* was in the centre of India. It sounds incredible, but is quite true.

His final achievement was well worthy of his previous record. Having just taken a shot with the sextant, he proudly announced that we would strike Macquarie Island about sundown on the following day, and no sooner were the words out of his mouth than there was a cry of 'Land on the port quarter'. Sure enough, dimly discernible, was the misty outline of distant mountains from which we were steaming away. The skipper, for once, was distinctly abashed, and said nothing for a long time.

Putting about, we approached our rendezvous, the north end of the island. Drawing nearer, a tall hill, some hundreds of feet high, looking like an island, detached itself from the mainland. Actually, however, it was a peninsula, connected with high land to the south by a low, narrow strip of land, only a few feet above sea-level. In the bay thus formed lay the *Aurora*, at anchor about a mile and a half from the shore. These waters were, of course, quite uncharted and full of hidden reefs, but our skipper was not to be deterred, and seemed anxious to recover the remnants of his prestige. 'If those blighters can go in, we can,' he said, and with engines at full speed, we went straight in, luckily missing anything that might have been in the way, and dropped our anchor about half a mile inshore from the *Aurora*.

CHAPTER 2

MACQUARIE ISLAND

A lonely island in a distant sea,
Upon its reef the endless combers roar;
While writhes and twists the brown kelp in their lee,
And bones of ships lie rotting on the shore.

Macquarie Island is a speck in the vast Southern Ocean, the only land between Tasmania and New Zealand far to the north and the Antarctic continent far to the south. East and west the waters stretch in an unbroken expanse encircling the world, save where a few other sub-Antarctic islands, such as the Kerguelens and the Crozets, poke their jagged peaks above the level of the sea. There are few shores so inhospitable and out-of-the-way. The island itself is about 20 miles long and 4 across. It is rugged and mountainous, the backbone composed of black, volcanic rocks that rise in peaks 1400 feet in height. There are no trees or shrubs, but the flats and slopes are covered with large grassy tussocks between which are treacherous patches of oozy swamp. The only method of progress is to jump from tussock to tussock, and a false step means plunging into black mud up to the armpits.

There are no harbours, but according to the direction of the wind several anchorages are available on either side of the island. During our stay, which lasted nearly a fortnight, the prevailing wind was from the north-east, an unusual occurrence, but it enabled us to anchor in comparative shelter on the western side of the peninsula that forms the northern extremity of the island. The climate is cold and bleak for the greater part of the year. Westerly gales sweep without interruption completely round the world, and pile their burden of rain, sleet, snow, and fog on the barren shores.

When the *Taroa* was still some miles from shore, our attention was attracted by a boat pulling towards us. On approach it proved to be full of hard-bitten sea-dogs, looking as if they had stepped straight from the days of Captain Kidd and the *Jolly Roger*. They hailed us, and we learned that they were the crew of a sealing vessel, the *Clyde*, which had been wrecked some time before on the eastern side of the island, and who, when the *Aurora* arrived, were getting very short of provisions. Their relief was great when they learned that the *Taroa* was going back to Hobart and would give them a passage. Later they showed their gratitude by helping themselves to most of our shore clothes which were being sent back, but that is another story.

The peninsula at the north end of the island is very steep and precipitous, particularly on its seaward sides. It is separated from the mainland by a tussocky and very marshy flat, about half a mile long, flanked by rough beaches of black waterworn stones. This peninsula was selected as a site for the wireless station, and five of our chaps were to remain there for the forthcoming winter. Their job was to survey the island completely, examine it geologically, and make collections of the bird and animal life as well as marine life from the surrounding waters. The party was led by Ainsworth, who was also meteorologist; Blake was geologist and surveyor; Hamilton was zoologist; and Sandell and Sawyer were in charge of the wireless.

Immediately the *Taroa* anchored we were met by the whaleboat from the *Aurora*, and the unloading of stores for the Macquarie Island base commenced. It was now that we took a not-unwilling farewell of the cramped and unsavoury quarters of the *Taroa*. The last sight of Roaring Tom was typical. He was busily engaged in clearing boxes and bags of flour from the bath which apparently had not been used for many years. The unwonted exercise was not due to a sudden love of cleanliness, but, as the boat returned from the first trip ashore, it had brought back a couple of live penguins which he intended to sell to the Hobart zoo. As far as I know, this commercial venture was not successful.

It was now our turn to go ashore. With all our dunnage loaded into the whaleboat, we picked a way through a labyrinth of half-sunken rocks and treacherous reefs. Great masses of kelp swirled under the motion of a slight swell, rolling and twisting like myriads of brown snakes. There was something peculiarly fascinating in this endless motion – sinister also. The writhing tentacles seemed more animal than vegetable, and appeared ever reaching for some invisible prey. It was easy to realise how dangerous was this coast in any kind of sea, and how fortunate we were that the weather was kind. We landed on a beach of black, round, basalt pebbles, and crossed the isthmus on a rough track which had been made by sealing parties which regularly visited the island.

On the eastern side was a small wooden hut, and in this we camped throughout the whole of our stay.

With almost the first step ashore there was evidence of animal life. Our first experience of sea-elephants was rather startling. No sooner had we entered the tussocks on the edge of the beach, when a terrific roar, seemingly underfoot, caused the whole of our party to jump hurriedly back. These gigantic creatures, some of which attain a length of 20 feet and a weight of over 2 tons, are regular inhabitants of the sub-Antarctic islands, coming ashore to breed and rest. They lie and wallow in the mud between the tussocks, and cannot be seen until almost trodden upon. Fortunately they are very sluggish on land, for the old bulls are exceedingly bad-tempered and have formidable jaws. In repose they look like huge slugs, and owe their name to the proboscis-like snout developed in the old males. The cows are very much smaller, not above 6 or 7 feet in length, and are quite timid and gentle. When disturbed, the bulls raise themselves on their front flippers and give an overwhelming roar, floundering forward in a clumsy attempt to reach the intruder. We soon got used to their presence, and as they were so easily avoided, took no further notice of them. Like the walrus in the north, all the males are covered with scars, for in the breeding season they fight bitterly and inflict dreadful wounds on each other.

The sea-elephant is the game of the modern sealer. The old days of hunting for the fur seal are long since gone. A hundred years ago the islands of the far south netted fortunes for the intrepid navigators who dared these stormy seas. In one year alone some 30,000 skins were taken from Macquarie Island, with the result that the fur seal is now nearly extinct. A few, I believe, still exist on an inaccessible reef about 7 miles north of the island, which makes a natural sanctuary for the survivors. Nowadays the sea-elephant is killed for the thick layer of blubber that lies beneath the skin. This is melted down in tanks and the oil is shipped away in casks.

There are usually several sealers on the island, and they live a lonely and hazardous life. On more than one occasion a sudden change of wind has caught one of their vessels on a lee shore, and it has been wrecked with loss of life. All down the east coast are the remains of these old wrecks. In one place is a cave in which for two years nineteen castaways, including one woman, lived on penguins, seals, and a plant known as native cabbage. On the day of rescue the woman died of malnutrition and exposure. The wreck of the *Clyde*, whose crew has already been mentioned, lay just in front of the hut in which we camped. Already she was smashed nearly to pieces by the heavy seas, and only her bones lay bleaching on the treacherous rocks. A little farther to the south lay all that was left of another sealer, the *Gratitude*, a portion of the bow high and dry upon the beach. About her were hundreds of penguins who passed to and fro through the broken timbers between their rookeries and the sea.

The next few days saw us hard at work. The site chosen for the hut of the Macquarie Island party was just at the foot of Wireless Hill. The immediate problem was, however, to haul all the wireless masts, dynamo, and equipment to the top of the hill, which was exceedingly precipitous.

Luckily the weather held, and we were able to use a small boat harbour on the western side. Here a long cable had been erected by the sealers in the form of a flying-fox which had fallen into a state of dereliction, and needed much repair before it could be used. The rocks at the foot were inaccessible from the shore side, and as many sea-elephants congregated here, the sealers had devised this method of hauling the blubber to the top, and then dragging it down the farther side. After strengthening, the flying-fox proved quite adequate, and eventually, to the tune of many a chanty, the whole of the heavy spars for the wireless masts and all the other gear were safely hauled up this precarious way.

It was now we began to really know one another, for in the evenings, after the day's toil was done, we yarned and sang to our hearts' content. Two of our number were always left to clean up the hut and prepare the evening meal for the crowd of hungry, returning men. There were no professional cooks on the expedition, and many and varied were the achievements of our budding amateurs – which leads to Archie Hoadley's great experiment. For some days the disappearance of our roast mutton was a source of great mystery, and it was only after the *Aurora* was well on its way southwards that it was learned why fried penguin had been substituted on the evening in question. The story eventually leaked out. Seeking fat in which to roast the leg of a sheep newly killed, Archie asked one of the sealers remaining on the island and was told that there was plenty in a tin in the hut. Unfortunately he helped himself to a cask of soft soap, and the dish was actually sizzling before he discovered his mistake. The result was buried secretly before the others returned.

Day by day we followed a regular routine. In this latitude in the middle of summer the hours of darkness are very few, and we had daylight until after 10 p.m. Setting off, after an early breakfast, we climbed Wireless Hill, and spent the day in digging holes for the wireless masts and for anchorages for the stays, in hauling gear to the top, and in other labours.

Each morning at the foot of the hill, we ran the gauntlet of a rookery of skua gulls. These birds are the scavengers of the south seas, and are also great enemies of the eggs and young of other birds. When nesting they are very savage and at times rather terrifying. We always knew when we were in the vicinity of the nest of a skua gull. The adult birds would hover overhead, uttering loud raucous cries, then without warning swoop down straight at the head of the intruder. Instinctively an arm was raised to protect the face, and they would then swerve just sufficiently to pass a foot or so overhead. So close would they come that it was possible to strike them with a stick in mid-flight.

Macquarie Island is the natural breeding-ground of countless sea-birds. As it is the only land within a vast area of sea, they naturally congregate from far and wide. Albatross, terns, cormorants, petrels, and seagulls of all descriptions are found all over the island. Each species generally keeps together and, as a result, nests are found in well-defined rookeries, which may contain only half a dozen or so families, or, as in the case of the penguins, many millions. Penguins are such a feature of the southern seas that no account of a voyage is complete without some mention of them. Except in the winter months on the Antarctic continent itself, there was no time during the expedition when we were not in touch with them. Even when hundreds of miles from the nearest land we met schools or shoals (the term 'flock' could hardly be used) of them porpoising through the water, sometimes pausing a moment to eye, as if with wonder, this great floating monster that trespassed in their seas.

All the species we met with in Macquarie Island differed from those farther south. In the neighbourhood of our hut were a number of rookeries of the crested penguin, a pretty little chap of about 15 inches in height, with two tufts of yellow feathers on either side of the head. Generally speaking, they were much more timid than the other species, but at this time they were sitting on the nests and were very irascible when disturbed, making a hideous din, and fluffing their feathers and pushing out their yellow tufts until they looked like the moustaches of a retired Indian colonel.

But by far the commonest penguin on the island is the royal, a bird somewhat larger than the crested penguin, and without the crests at the side of the head. Some of the rookeries of the royal penguin are of incredible extent. Imagine a shallow valley about a mile square in which every square yard is occupied by a nest. The nest consists, if the owner is fortunate, of a ring of small stones. There are many such rookeries on the island, each of which must contain some millions of individuals. The din is frightful, as every bird seems to be quarrelling ceaselessly with its neighbour. Apart from those on the nests, thousands of others are always passing to and fro, and their passage is a continual source of argument, vilification, and pecks. The domestic life of the penguin is a dual affair, the female and male taking it in turns, first to sit on the egg, and after the egg is hatched, to go to sea in search of food.

How each bird found its nest among all that number puzzled us greatly. The presumption is that they do find the correct domicile; though if not, the movie-like domestic tangles could easily account for part of the noise. Penguins undoubtedly have a wonderful sense of orientation. The unerring manner in which, at the same period of the year, they find their way from all over the trackless ocean to such an isolated spot as Macquarie Island proves this. On their nests they get very angry when disturbed, and viciously strike with their flippers, or peck at the intruder; but on the beach a mild curiosity seems their only emotion. No doubt they took us for merely bigger penguins. There were always some thousands of royal penguins gathered on any individual beach, for here they seemed to pause awhile on their way both to and from the rookeries. It was very amusing to watch one of these concourses, and the scene was quite comparable to the crowd on Manly beach on a summer Sunday afternoon. With their little white breasts looking like well-starched shirt-fronts, some bustled about their business, others gathered in groups and appeared to discuss the latest scandals of the rookeries. Some dozed in the sun, while still others continually came in and out of the surf. They all looked very human.

Some of the rookeries were close to the beach; others were high on the hillsides or even far inland. The beds of numerous creeks formed regular highways for the constant stream of pedestrians, as the birds might well be called. Considering their short, stumpy legs, they made astonishing progress, jumping with great agility from rock to rock.

The largest species of penguin on Macquarie Island is the king penguin, a close relation to the emperor which is the largest of all, but which lives only in the extreme south. The king penguin stands about 3 feet in height, has a long beak and a patch of golden yellow on either side of the head. We saw a few later at Caroline Cove on the south end of the island, but they were not as common as the other species.

Our labours on Macquarie Island lasted for over a week, and for the whole of this time we were blessed with fine weather, a most unusual occurrence. One or two minor accidents occurred in the operation of the flying-fox. On one occasion a heavy piece of machinery carried away just before it reached the top, and rolled over and over to the bottom, striking Frank Wild on the thigh and bruising it badly. He was incapacitated for a couple of days, but still superintended the unloading and transhipment of gear.

In the meantime we were joined by Frank Hurley and Harrison, who had made a rather adventurous traverse of the island. It appears that when the *Aurora* first made it to Macquarie Island a landing was effected at the extreme south end, and, after she had left, Hurley found that he had left a valuable cinema lens on the rocks. Accordingly Dr Mawson gave him permission to make the journey overland to recover it and, with Harrison and one of the sealers who volunteered as a guide, he fought his way over the rough country for 20 miles to the south and back again. It was a very arduous journey, as the way lay over rocks, mountain, and bogs, and when they arrived back at the northern end all were much exhausted. Hurley had sprained his ankle slightly, but was anxious to obtain photos at the top of Wireless Hill, so he allowed himself and his camera to be hoisted on the flying-fox, a giddy and nerve-testing exploit that no one was tempted to emulate.

Our stay was rapidly drawing to a close. The wireless masts were erected, and the island party had all their equipment ashore, most of which had been carried in the *Taroa*. Their hut was not built, but it was all assembled ready for them to start. Time was drawing on, and it was necessary to move to the south before the brief summer drew to its close. There was much ashore that had to be transferred to the *Aurora*, and on 23 December we started to embark. There were signs that the weather was breaking, the barometer was falling, and the sea was rising fast. The last trip of the whaleboat was anything but pleasant. It was crowded with passengers and every variety of dunnage. Several sheep which had been landed to feed and rest, and a number of sledge-dogs which had also been taken ashore were included in the list. What with the overloading, the choppy sea, and the difficulty of keeping the dogs from the sheep, the situation for a time looked serious, and it was with great relief that eventually we got under the lee of the *Aurora*. Considerable difficulty was experienced in manoeuvring alongside, and in unloading the various impedimenta. Wild was at the steering oar, and it is a tribute to his skill that no accident occurred. Once on board we waved farewell to the little group just visible on the beach and at once turned southwards on the next stage of our journey.

CHAPTER 3

POLAR SEAS

From sapphire caves, where surged the lifting swell,
The echoes came to speak the parting knell
 Of dying bergs which drifted slowly by,
 Their wave-worn sides uptilted to the sky
And still beyond, the cohorts of the pack,
With flanks far-stretched, would turn invaders back,
 Until the ice-floes, parted by the breeze,
 Their portals opened to uncharted seas.

After the whaleboat it was a relief to feel a fairly steady deck underfoot, though there was still a little too much up and down for my own comfort. It is time a word was said about the *Aurora* herself. Although we had helped to load her in Hobart, this was the first time most of us had taken up our quarters on board. It seemed at first impossible to squeeze us all in. The room aft was very limited, and, apart from the ship's officers, there were twenty-six in the land parties to find berths. A steep companionway led to the small saloon, where the restricted space necessitated all meals being taken in three relays. Off the saloon were a number of small cubicles, which could hardly be called cabins, and into each of these were crammed from three to five men. Fortunately we were already in fairly cold latitudes, and the overcrowding was gratefully warm.

Washing had already been practically dispensed with. We were indeed short of water for cooking and drinking purposes, and one cup of tea each was all that was allowed at meals. For anything else, the only way was to get on the right side of Gillies, the engineer, and beg a little warm, oily water as distilled from the engines. It is a curious thing about washing that when the facilities are denied the desire rapidly disappears. At a dinner given by the Royal Society just before our departure from Sydney, one of the speakers, who had explored in central Australia, stated that the least of all hardships was the inability to wash and bathe regularly. His remarks created much amusement, but we found them quite true.

The *Aurora* herself was a barquentine-rigged auxiliary steamer of some 600 tons, and had previously been a whaler in northern seas. On one occasion she had been used in the search for the ill-fated Greely expedition. She was a stout old ship, massively timbered and strengthened to withstand ice pressure, and throughout gave to all on board a satisfying feeling of security.

Already those who left Hobart in her had had evidence of her sea-going qualities. The gale that had caused the delay to the *Taroa* had caught the *Aurora* with its full force. Mountainous seas had swept her from stem to stern, and had even carried away part of the bridge. She was not only fully laden, but carried a large deck cargo, including the timber for the huts, and it was feared at one stage that part, if not all, of this would be lost. However, by a great effort on the part of all hands it was made secure and all was saved. The ship herself came through splendidly, though those on board had experienced a most uncomfortable time. A further experience tested her thoroughly. While cruising near the south end of Macquarie Island, she ran onto a submerged reef, balanced for a few minutes, then slid into deeper water. An iron steamer would probably have had the bottom torn out, but the stout old whaler was quite undamaged.

There was very little room to move about on deck. The deck cargo was everywhere. It included the large case containing the aeroplane engine, the timber for three huts, innumerable cases containing benzine and methylated spirit, and other gear for which there was no room in the holds. Over all this were tethered some forty dogs, several of which died before we reached the land, and also a number of sheep which were later killed. The mess the dogs made was indescribable, and though the timber was washed down occasionally with salt water, filth lurked in unexpected places, and was a constant source of profanity or amusement, according to the viewpoint of victim or onlooker.

The dogs were a mixed lot, varying much in size and power, but mostly very friendly. One savage brute, with which nothing could be done, was left at Macquarie Island, where he could find abundant food and worry nobody. None of the dogs could bark, no doubt owing to the strong strain of wolf in their breeding. Sometimes they would howl, and when one started the others generally took it up in chorus. Forty dogs howling in concert, if not in harmony, made a terrible row in the confined quarters of a small ship, and the watch below anathematised them on many occasions.

It was late on 23 December 1911 when the bow of the *Aurora* was finally turned from the old anchorage, and all that evening we steamed southwards along the coast. The glass had risen again, and the threatened storm had not eventuated. It was beautifully calm. The morning of Christmas Eve saw us anchored in Caroline Cove, right at the south end of the island. Here a small basin of water was enclosed by high, precipitous rocks, with deep water right to the shore. A large rock partially closed the entrance, and it was with considerable care that the *Aurora* felt her way in and dropped the main anchor. The kedge was also dropped to prevent undue swinging. All hands immediately set about the task of watering ship. A small gully led down to the head of the cove, down which flowed a small stream polluted by the hundreds of penguins that wandered up and down from their rookeries farther inland. Clean water was, however, found by digging in a small branch gully, a short way from the beach, and a chain of men with buckets was formed. In this way the casks that had been towed ashore were filled, and again towed out to the ship. It was monotonous work, but by the evening more than half of our requirements were safely on board. We turned in with the idea of completing the job on the morrow, and the prospect of Christmas Day on shore was pleasing to everybody.

It was not to be, however. My next recollection was a violent bumping somewhere beneath that nearly shook me from my bunk. Half-asleep, the conclusion flashed on me that we were still ashore, and that this was one of the earthquakes to which Macquarie Island is subject. Geological instincts were strong, and I called to Stillwell who was a geologist and also my cabin-mate.

'Wake up, Frank! It's most interesting. There's an earthquake.'

Much chaff came my way later in consequence.

With complete wakefulness came realisation that something was happening. Beneath, the bumping still continued, and above on the deck feet were hurrying backwards and forwards, and a voice was shouting commands.

Then came a stentorian bellow: 'All hands on deck!'

So, slipping on some clothes, we rushed up. What had happened was simple enough, though it might have had disastrous consequences. The officer on watch had left the bridge for a few minutes, in which time a breeze had sprung up. The first puff of wind caused the anchor to drag, and before anything could be done the ship had swung and was bumping broadside on to the rocks. Fortunately the light kedge-anchor held and kept the stern offshore, thus saving the rudder and propeller. As it was, a handy billy was hurriedly rigged on the kedge-rope, and with everybody putting their backs into it, the ship swung free from the rocks. Then the engines started, and the *Aurora* backed slowly into deep water again, to the great relief of all. Nor was she at all damaged, proving again her wonderful staunchness, for an ordinary vessel would have been badly holed in similar circumstances.

But gone, alas, was the prospect of an easy Christmas Day exploring ashore. Captain Davis had had enough of the treacherous possibilities of this coast, and decided there and then to proceed south straightaway. So that when we woke again from our interrupted sleep the ship was once more heaving uncomfortably up and down on the open ocean.

That Christmas Day is a hazy memory. Efforts were made, I know, to provide a special dinner, but I took little interest in the matter of food. As a sort of duty I ate it – and lost it, which was a sheer waste of good provisions. Incidentally, the cooking on the ship left much to be desired, even when the inclination to eat returned. So bad was it that on several occasions one of our number, Walter Hannam, volunteered for the job. Walter, fat and cheerful, was physically cut out for the part, and was a thorough success. There was the case of the salmon rissoles. The only trouble was that there did not seem to be enough of them. Strange, however, is the point of view of the real shellback. A deputation, led by the bo's'n, who, a good man at his job, was yet something of a sea-lawyer, waited aft on the captain, with the complaint that salmon rissoles were not fit food for sailormen.

It was the first time that we had seen the skipper handle men. Up to this time we only knew him from the outside. He was tall, and one of the thinnest men I have seen, with ginger hair and beard. We thought him old; indeed he looked more than his years, which were then little more than thirty. His taciturnity and seriousness had led to the nickname 'Gloomy', but not to his face. Afterwards we realised what a great responsibility was his, that of the safety of the whole ship and company in uncharted waters. If it rested rather heavily upon him, who can blame him? He had our confidence, that was the main thing, and when we returned in 1913 we found him the best of company ashore.

Reverting to the deputation, Gloomy listened in silence, but his short red hair seemed to bristle, as it always did on such occasions. There was an impressive pause, while the members of the deputation began to shuffle and move restlessly under his stony eye. Then he spoke, and his voice at best could be heard above any hurricane.

'What in the hell do you want, angel's wings? Get the bloody hell out of this!'

The deputation got.

In January 1915, on the troopship *Ulysses* in Colombo, I was sergeant of the guard on the occasion of the visit of the Governor of Ceylon. All the captains of the fleet of transports accompanied him, among them Gloomy Davis himself. It was an unexpected meeting, and we had time only for a hurried handshake and greeting, but it brought back a vision of a tall thin figure, crowned by a woollen cap, seemingly never leaving the bridge, on which he paced up and down, night and day. And of the same figure in 1913 in Hobart, when we had a final dinner before dispersing to our homes, roaring endless verses of 'Rolling Home' in a voice that lacked nothing in carrying power.

Christmas Day had come and gone, and every mile brought the *Aurora* nearer to the ice-capped lands that lay ahead. The bright sun and the calm seas made the voyage at this stage almost picnic-like, added to which was the knowledge that we were now in uncharted waters, and any moment might bring forth who-knows-what discovery – the first sight of an undiscovered island, perhaps!

Day after day the hours of darkness dwindled, and the sun, instead of rising in the east, rose almost in the south and swept in a great circle about the horizon, sinking at last in almost the same spot from which it was to emerge but a few minutes later.

On 29 December we saw our first iceberg, irregular, hummocky pieces, the remnants of once-larger bergs, corroded by the warming seas as they drifted northwards. Then a soft mist shut us in, and we steamed slowly forwards in a narrow white world, indescribably eerie. Now and again a hollow, booming sound on either side announced the near presence of icebergs; and once a great white wall suddenly loomed through the mist ahead, causing the wheel to be put hard over just in time. Generally the air was filled with sound, and it was impossible to tell in which direction danger lay.

At last the mist parted, and we beheld a beautiful sight. About half a mile away on the port side was a great, flat-topped berg, about three-quarters of a mile long and about 150 feet high. Framed in fleecy masses of rolling mist, its outlines were softened, and it seemed to be suspended in a mysterious element of its own. As the mist cleared it became more defined, and we could see the great caves worn by the waves, into which the swell rushed with a ceaseless, hollow roar. Every crack, every crevice was outlined in the purest sapphire blue.

We gazed spellbound for a while; then the silence was broken by someone asking the old sailmaker what he thought of it. 'Sails', like any true old salt, was not to be impressed.

'Huh!' he said. 'Yon wee bit o' berg? Why, it's ther smallest berg I ever see.'

That night we hardly lost the sun at all, and at midnight it was light enough to read. Truly we were in Antarctic waters.

Ice was now all about us – bergs, or loose bits of pack from the ice-fields farther south. Then, far ahead, the horizon became illuminated with a white glow, and at once the old hands recognised true iceblink.

This phenomenon is a useful sign to navigators in polar seas, indicating what may be expected ahead. Even if a ship is surrounded by heavy pack-ice for as far as the eye can see, a dark band on the horizon, or what is known as a 'water sky', points to the presence of open water in that direction. On the other hand, an illuminated horizon, or iceblink, shows that there is nothing but ice ahead.

Soon we came up with the first of the pack, isolated pieces of the winter's floe, from 20 to 40 yards across, and floating a foot or two out of the water. Upon these, here and there, seals could be seen basking at their ease in the sun, either the white variety known as the crab-eater, or the savage and voracious sea-leopard. Little groups of Adélie penguins, too, their white waistcoats gleaming brilliantly, stood and curiously watched us go by.

Presently the pack grew thicker, the pieces of the floe larger, the lanes between them narrower. The *Aurora* now showed what she was capable of. Striking a large piece of floe full on, she would recoil from the shock, only to move forwards and strike again. Often on the second or third blow the floe would split across, or else would be forced away, to go grinding and swirling along the side of the ship.

Here in the centre of the pack a sea-leopard was shot on the ice beside the ship. The companionway was lowered, and with the aid of a block and tackle the carcass was soon on board. To my lot fell the task of skinning it – not a difficult job in the first place, but long and laborious when it came to removing the layer of blubber, some 3 inches thick, that lined the whole of the pelt. The flesh was fed to the dogs, giving them a change from the biscuits which constituted their daily ration.

But the ice blocks grew larger and larger, and at last were so thickly packed as to constitute practically one solid mass. A brilliant iceblink filled the horizon ahead, and it was obviously useless to try and penetrate farther. Reluctantly the *Aurora* was put about, and after a bit of a struggle reached open water again.

Blocked in our intention to go due south, we changed course to the westwards, and for several days we skirted the edge of the pack, looking in vain for a way through to the land that lay somewhere beyond. Gradually it became evident that the limited amount of summer left would not permit the landing of more than two bases, so the parties were again rearranged, the first land party consisting of eighteen men, the second of eight. Frank Stillwell and I had particularly chummed up. It had been intended that he should do the geology and I the zoology on the third base; now we were both attached to the first.

By this time we were all beginning to feel a bit anxious as to our prospects of getting to land at all, when, at 5 a.m. on 3 January 1912 our luck changed. Quite unexpectedly the pack thinned, and beyond it appeared a long, even wall of ice, stretching on either hand as far as the eye could see. At its base the water was practically clear of pack-ice.

What was it? Was it a monster iceberg? Or the seaward limit of ice-covered land? Or a portion of one of the great floating ice-barriers of the south?

For a couple of hours as we steamed along the trend of the ice-wall was east and west, then, quite abruptly, we turned the corner and open ocean lay before us directly to the south. Great now was the jubilation of all on board at the prospect of seeing lands that none had ever seen before. On our left the ice-wall now ran north and south as far as could be seen, and it seemed obvious that it was a barrier, or glacial tongue, joined to the land somewhere to the south.

To understand the nature of these barriers it is necessary to know something of the general physiography of Antarctic regions. Antarctica is a continent bigger than Australia, but approximately the same shape. At about the centre is the geographical South Pole, on a plateau over 10,000 feet above sea-level. The whole of the continent is intensely cold – so cold that, winter or summer, the temperature never rises to freezing point. As a result there is no rain, and the snow that falls accumulates through the ages, and has solidified into a vast ice-sheet that covers the whole land to a depth of thousands of feet. So thick is this ice-sheet that only the highest mountains remain unburied.

The weight of the icecap is enormous, and as it accumulates in the centre it is squeezed outwards into an ever-moving flood of ice. The movement is slow, a few inches – a few feet – a year. Where the coast is steep the comparatively warm water laps at the base of the ice-sheet and it melts, or the tide breaks it away in small, irregular icebergs. But where the slope is gradual, as at the mouths of valleys, the ice-sheet will sometimes be pushed hundreds of miles from land, floating, but still attached to the shore ice. These are the great barriers of the south. On top of them fresh snow is forever accumulating, compensating for the corrosion by the sea-water below, thus keeping the height approximately uniform. Thus, on their seaward edge they generally consist of fairly recent, stratified snow, as distinct from the hard, glacial ice of the interior.

Occasionally the movement of ocean currents or the stress of storms causes huge pieces to break off, sometimes miles in diameter, and these form the flat-topped bergs so characteristic of the Antarctic.

Steaming southwards for several hours, the ice-wall continued unbroken on our left, occasionally receding into bays or projecting into headlands, but keeping a general north and south trend. Then suddenly it changed direction again, and veered away to the south-east, so that open water lay on the port side as far as the eye could reach. Away to our right now appeared a high dome-shaped island of ice – an iceberg probably – but so similar in appearance to land that it might easily be reported as such. No doubt some of the landfalls reported by the early explorers were of this nature, only to be disproved by later expeditions sailing across the actual positions on the chart.

It was now that we got our first touch of an Antarctic blizzard. Though the sun still shone, a sudden blast of wind from the south rose rapidly to gale force, against which the *Aurora*, with difficulty, made headway. The barrier made a nasty lee shore, so the *Aurora* put about and steamed under the lee of this ice island, steaming up and down slowly for the next twenty-four hours. We thought at the time that this was quite an experience, little realising that, severe as the wind was, it was a mere suggestion of the mighty hurricanes we were to face during the next year. Beyond the regret at the delay, it was a pleasant enough time for the land parties, for there was nothing we could do on deck, so we stayed below in the snug cabin, played bridge, held singsongs, and otherwise enjoyed ourselves.

On the afternoon of 5 January the wind began to drop, and then it seemed, quite suddenly, we were once again steaming south over a calm, blue sea, with the sun shining brightly down from a cloudless sky. It was not long before we picked up the ice-barrier again, now trending across our course in a south-westerly direction. We concluded that we had crossed a large bay, and it was not until a year later that we learned our mistake. For then the *Aurora*, coming to pick us up, steamed in open sea right across the position of the 'barrier', and then a few weeks later, with the land party on board, picked it up again about 100 miles to the west. So that it was really a gigantic iceberg, over 40 miles across, broken away from the main ice-sheet, and slowly drifting to the west – surely the largest iceberg ever seen by human eyes.

A sounding now gave only a little over 200 fathoms, proof that we were on a continental shelf, and not far from land. Further evidence was afforded by the presence of an occasional Weddell seal, asleep on floating ice. These are the littoral seals of the Antarctic, and are never found far from the shore.

The weather was misty and we proceeded with caution, picking a way between numerous icebergs which studded the sea. All hands were on the lookout for the first sight of land. Late on the evening of 6 January there loomed far ahead a high misty outline of white, at first barely distinguishable from the sky into which it merged, but becoming more defined with our approach. As we came still nearer, lofty cliffs of ice appeared right across our course. We were in a broad bay, flanked everywhere by unscaleable white walls. Beyond, in a gradual slope, the surface rose to a far and faint skyline, relieved in one place by a swelling dome some 1500 feet above sea-level.

It is a wonderful sensation, this first sight of new and untrodden lands. A little exultation and great deal of awe were, perhaps, the chief ingredients of our emotions. For myself, the first impression of the great plateau was one of hostile beauty. It seemed so bleak, so absolutely desolated, so lifeless. Later, when sledging over its surface, these characters seemed to merge into a relentless, resentful, and definite personality, which ever waited implacably for the single false step that would hand the intruder into its power. One had the impression of fighting, always fighting, a terrible unseen force.

The hour was 11.30 p.m., and it seemed curiously fitting that our first sight of Adélie Land should be by the light of the midnight sun.

Landing was now the problem. Here and there, at the foot of the ice-cliffs, were black patches of rock, but nowhere was a spot from which it was possible to ascend to the cliffs above. Consequently the course was again changed, and we steamed slowly along the new coastline to the west. As 7 January wore on, prospects were a little more favourable. Rounding a headland, the coastline was more broken, and several rocky promontories looked as if they might be possible landing-places. Everywhere the sea was studded with icebergs and small rocky islets, the contrast of pure white against the vividly blue water being indescribably beautiful.

This day we had a small snow-storm, which covered the ship with a mantle of white. It cleared very quickly and the sun shone again. Everyone was in the best of spirits and in a frolicsome mood, and some of the chaps indulged in mild snowballing. Hodgeman was on the bridge, sketching the outline of the new coastline, and Cecil Madigan took the opportunity to have a shot. At that moment Gloomy put his head round the corner of the wheelhouse and received a snowball right in the eye. The change of scene was miraculous. One moment all was bustling humanity, the next nothing but a deserted deck. An hour later a notice appeared in the saloon stating that gentlemen of the land parties were requested to refrain from such frivolous pursuits, as it set a bad example to the crew.

A number of sheep were now killed and their carcasses hung in the rigging out of reach of the dogs. There is practically no decomposition in the clear, cold air, and to the end of the winter we had roast mutton that was still quite good.

So another day passed. On the 8th we steamed into a wide moon-shaped bight, which was afterwards called Commonwealth Bay. Far away to the west it terminated in a cape that corresponded with land seen by d'Urville in 1840 and named Cape Decouverte. There, then, was the Adélie Land he had named in honour of his wife. About the centre of Commonwealth Bay a patch of black showed at the base of the steep slopes that led to the interior, and towards this the *Aurora* steamed. Coming closer, the black patch resolved into rocks, and when about a mile away the *Aurora* hove to, and the whaleboat was lowered to investigate. An hour or so later the advance party returned to report that the rocks we saw were really islands off the coast, but that beyond them was a rocky peninsula, eminently suitable for the establishment of a base.

So, feeling her way round the extremity of these islands, the *Aurora* at once cast anchor between them and the shore. The weather was beautifully calm and no time was lost. The launch was also lowered, both boats loaded with stores, and with the whaleboat in tow, set off for the shore. The sun shone brightly and there was not a breath of wind, so none of us who went on the shore with this trip worried about extra clothing or even mitts, a detail that well showed our inexperience of the treachery of the climate.

It was 8 p.m. as we landed to find a light wind blowing a mist of fine snow off the edge of the ice. Almost in a moment we were chilled through and through. The landing of the stores seemed interminable, as all of us were bitterly cold and miserable. Hoadley, perhaps, suffered most, as he had three fingers slightly frostbitten. As we chug-chugged back to the *Aurora* the wind was steadily rising, and it was a cold and sorry crowd that dived below to the warm shelter of the messroom. It now began to blow really hard, so the *Aurora*, leaving her anchorage, steamed under the lee of the high ice-cliffs that flanked the peninsula on either side. There was no time to take the boats inboard, so with several hands in each to keep them bailed, they were taken in tow. It was a tricky business anchoring the *Aurora*, owing to the possibility of hidden reefs. The sea-bottom was very uneven, and soundings jumped from 30 to 10 fathoms in a few yards. Eventually the anchor was dropped within 500 yards of the shore, and we waited for the blizzard to subside.

In the meantime some of the party had a hazardous adventure. Suddenly the launch broke away, and before anything could be done was drifting rapidly towards a rock on which the sea broke heavily. Aboard were Bickerton, Whetter and Hunter, and while Bickerton tried desperately to start the engine, Hunter bailed, and Whetter tried to rig a jury rudder to replace the other which had been unshipped. Fortunately, just as their position looked desperate, the engine started, and soon all were on board again, the launch hoisted, and all made snug.

For forty-eight hours this blow continued, waxing in intensity until it seemed impossible for the anchor to hold. It was barely possible to stand against the force of the wind, and everybody, except those on duty, kept below. The wind was directly offshore, but although we were under the immediate shelter of ice-cliffs 150 feet high, quite a sea was running, and the crests of the waves were torn into sheets of driving spray.

At last, on the morning of 10 January, the gale moderated sufficiently for us to lower the boats again and resume unloading. From now until the 19th there was no time to consider anything except the urgent need to get all our goods ashore while the weather held. It was eight hours on and eight hours off for all hands, hauling coal briquettes, boxes of provisions, bags of potatoes, and what-not from the hold, lowering them to the boats, hauling them ashore, and sledging them about 100 yards inland to the site chosen for the hut. Even during this time there were several more intervals in which the gales, which we were already learning to accept as a regular feature of this region, descended upon us from the south.

One incident showed how easily fires can occur at sea. While shifting coal in the lower hold we came on a number of sacks of potatoes that had accidentally been buried before the ship left London. They were not only rotten, but the heat engendered by their decomposition had caused them to boil, and the surrounding coal was also very hot. As each bag was unearthed the fumes filled the hold with a sickening stench, and we had to wait until they cleared somewhat, then to rush in and drag the fermenting mass to the open air. It took some time before all the bags were removed.

It was hard and laborious work, but on 19 January the last parcel was ashore, and we gathered in the wardroom to say goodbye to the ship's company and to those of the second base who were to land somewhere to the west. Mawson made a short speech which we all loudly cheered. Then came the toast of the expedition, drunk in wine with a history. This was some Madeira, presented by Buchanan who had been hydrologist on the *Challenger*, and it had travelled round the world on this famous expedition in 1873 to 1875, and crossed the Antarctic circle slightly to the west of our present position.

There were seven, beside Frank Wild, to constitute the second base: Andy Watson, George Dovers, Moyes, Doc Jones, Kennedy, Arch Hoadley and Harrison. Last letters home had already been written, so with a handshake with these good fellows, and mutual wishes for good luck, we crowded into the whaleboat for the last trip ashore.

An hour later the *Aurora* was a patch of smoke on the northern horizon, and we were left to our resources in a world of our very own.

CHAPTER 4

EARLY DAYS IN ADÉLIE LAND

The white untrodden hills in lonely splendour lay
Beyond the cliffs of ice which girt the azure bay,
Through clouds of silken mist by fairy fingers spun,
The snowy slopes reached up and kissed the midnight sun.

A smudge of smoke faded on the horizon, and with the smudge the last link with civilisation. On some barren rocks were eighteen men, surrounded by piles of dunnage. East, south, west, lay eternal fields of ice; north a blue sea sprinkled with icebergs, and beyond – some 2000 miles away – home.

It was well, perhaps, that in these early days we had no leisure to ponder on our isolation – an isolation so complete that those who have not been in Antarctica can hardly realise. There are few remote regions in the world that have not some link with inhabited areas. Even far within the Arctic circle there are forests and flowers, and tribes of human beings find a sustenance in this environment. But in the Antarctic the explorer must depend entirely on the resources he has brought with him.

In the brief summer, it is true, penguins and seals come onshore to breed, but for the rest of the year it is a dead continent, perpetually frozen and swept by terrible blizzards. There is no food, no timber, no help of any sort for those who venture into the icy wastes. They must depend for life itself on what they bring with them, and their sole hope of ultimate rescue lies in a small wooden vessel, even now battling somewhere in the stormy uncharted waters to the north.

Not that we brooded on these matters. There was so much that was new and interesting, and so much to be done, that there was no time for introspection. The immediate problem was to build our hut and make ourselves secure against possible emergencies.

We now took stock of our surroundings. As it happened, we had been very fortunate in the discovery of this spot for a base. The peninsula itself was about three-quarters of a mile wide and half a mile deep, and consisted of a number of rocky ridges, behind which, during the brief summer, melted snow formed several small, clear lakes. A small and nearly enclosed boat harbour made an excellent landing-place. The spot chosen for the hut was about 40 yards from the water's edge, and here a fairly level expanse of rock made a good foundation. Just to the south a large pile of rocks was fortunately placed so as to afford some protection from the blizzards we now knew to expect.

On either side of the peninsula, now called Cape Denison, the shores of Commonwealth Bay stretched in a great semicircle, bordered everywhere by high ice-cliffs, with here and there a patch of black rock showing at the base. Inland a steep slope led upwards to the plateau directly behind the hut, and up this slope sledging parties would ultimately find a way to explore the new lands, east, west, and south.

During the erection of the huts a temporary shelter was formed of benzine cases, piled in a double row to make the walls, and roofed over with sections of the large case that had contained the aeroplane engine. This housed most of us, and a couple of sledging tents provided for the overflow. We slept in sleeping-bags of reindeer skin with the hair inside, and after a working day of some sixteen hours did not need rocking.

The huts had originally been built and put together in Australia, and the parts numbered to facilitate erection. This saved an immense amount of time, just when time was of the greatest value. With the union of the first and second bases two huts were available, and it was decided to erect them together, making one the main living-room, the other the workroom and store. The largest of the huts was 24 feet by 24 feet inside – not a very big room when it is remembered that it had to serve as bedroom, kitchen, dining-room, and living-room for eighteen men. Still we managed to pack in. Bunks were arranged in double tiers round the walls. A small cubicle in one corner, 6 feet square, housed Dr Mawson, as well as the chronometers, barometer, and other scientific instruments. The roof of this made a platform useful for storing gear. In the adjacent corner was the darkroom, 4 feet by 4 feet, and adjoining this the stove, a kitchen bench and shelves. A large table, with hinged flaps at each end, occupied most of the remainder of the floor, and above it an acetylene generator provided us with light. The two small windows were near the apex of the low-pitched roof.

In the small hut or outer room, 16 feet square, was the dynamo and wireless outfit, a lathe, a stove, carpenter's bench, and a bench for the zoologists. Taken all in all, if the desire had come to swing the proverbial cat, it would have been hard on the cat.

Outside the main rooms the pitch of the roof was continued downwards, the space thus enclosed forming a useful storehouse and a shelter for the dogs. Again, to the windward of this, cases of provisions were piled, so that nowhere could the wind exert a lifting pressure against the walls or roof. Adjoining the west side of the hut a structure of benzine cases was erected, and here throughout the winter Bickerton worked at every available opportunity, fitting the aeroplane engine to a large tractor sledge, which afterwards did yeoman-like service in drawing heavy loads of sledging provisions up the steepest slope to a depot 5 miles inland.

Later on, snow accumulated until all of our buildings were nearly completely buried. This was a fortunate occurrence, for though the huts were specially built to withstand wind pressure, it is doubtful if they would otherwise have survived the winter hurricanes. Means of ingress and egress became somewhat complicated as the snow deepened.

Only one door led from the inner to the outer hut, and from here another door led to the veranda, and a further door opened outside. This rapidly became blocked, and then a curved tunnel was dug through the snow to the outer veranda. From here a hole in the snow in one corner was so windswept that it was clear throughout the winter, and was the only place where one could enter or leave the hut.

The building of the hut was not without minor incidents. The memory of Walter Hannam's cooking exploits on the *Aurora* secured ready acceptance of his offer to act as temporary cook. There were no frills at this stage. The menu was limited – stew and more stew – but varied in its ingredients, according to what Walter could rummage from the provision cases. Hard tack, butter, jam, cocoa, and tea were the etceteras, all in abundance, and hearty appetites did the rest.

So far I have said little about the other members of the expedition. Mertz and Ninnis I have already described, but during the voyage events crowded so fast, one on the other, and the scene changed so rapidly, that memory is filled with things rather than people. Now that we were thrown so closely together and were so interdependent in all things on each other, personality became the predominant factor in our life. To this day faces on the ship are hazy, but every detail of the hut, every feature, every mannerism of the other seventeen, makes a mental picture as clear and vivid as it was thirty-six years ago. It is a happy picture with no discordant tone. As my story develops each member must inevitably appear in turn, and if one treasures the occasional laugh we had at another's expense, it is not with malice, but with the undying affection engendered by good comradeship.

The smallest qualification became of value if it administered in any way to the general welfare. Frank Stillwell could play the piano, therefore, in the manipulation of the small folding organ, which was our one musical instrument, he became exceedingly popular. Herbert Murphy was a born raconteur, and he was worth a place on the expedition for this alone, even if his yarns were occasionally stretched. To be able to cook, to ply a needle and threat with some skill, to work a lathe, to figure out a mathematical calculation – everything had its value, often relatively much greater than the same quality in civilised life. The humorous side of small accidents became greatly exaggerated. Dad McLean, when fixing the chimney to the stove, lost his footing and rolled to the ground, chimney and all, while Ninnis, holding the pipe inside, was covered with soot. There were shrieks of delight from everybody. Mertz, nailing slats on the inside of the roof with his usual emphasis, drove a long nail home with one blow, to the discomfiture of Bickerton, who sat on the outside fixing the rubberoid covering in position. More universal joy. Someone dropped a hammer on Hannam's head. Mertz, always polite, though innocent, thought it was up to somebody to apologise and did so, thus reaping the full flood of Walter's invective, to his own great astonishment, and everyone else's amusement.

About this time I had evidence of our leader's quality. A part of the stove was missing, and as a case had dropped overboard in the boat harbour, it was concluded that this probably contained the lost part. One day Dr Mawson said to me: 'Come on, Joe, let us see if we can get it.'

Getting into the whaleboat, we pushed out from the shore. The case was clearly visible in about 6 feet of water. For some time we angled with a boathook, but without success. Presently Mawson remarked, 'There is only one thing for it,' and straightaway stripped off and dived over. His first effort was unsuccessful, but at a second attempt he was just able to lift it up, and I got it on board. The temperature of the sea was at the time about 30°F – that is below the freezing point of fresh water – and the air was much colder. Ice was already forming on his body as he raced for the hut to dry himself and get into his clothes again. And the case contained … tins of jam. The missing piece of the stove turned up shortly after beneath some other gear.

As the hut neared completion we were able to turn our attention to other matters. Hunter and I were very anxious to begin our collecting, so the whaleboat was requisitioned, and a number of fish-traps set about half a mile from the shore. When we raised these the following day we had quite a fair haul, all of one species of fish, a big-headed cod-like type called *Notothenia*, besides a few starfish and marine worms. There was a considerable argument with the cook of the day, who wanted the fish for dinner, but a compromise was reached. Science made a selection for specimens, and the balance proved very good eating, though not quite enough for a big helping all round.

This was one of the few hauls we made. A blizzard intervened, and when it was calm enough to pull out again all the traps had been swept away. The next casualty was the whaleboat itself. For safety it was taken out of the water and securely tied, as we thought. Again the blizzard came, this time the most severe we had felt, and a few hours later all that was left was a broken rope to show where the boat had been. Lifted bodily by the great force of the wind, it was somewhere on the way to Australia. It was a big disappointment, as we hoped, before the sea froze for the winter, to visit the outlying islands and do some dredging in the neighbouring waters.

A red-letter day was 30 January 1912, for on this date we were finally domiciled under our own roof. It was an occasion for rejoicing. We all gathered in a group on the rocks to the side of the hut, and Dr Mawson made a brief speech. The Union Jack and the Australian flag were hoisted side by side, and while we uncovered, he took possession of the land in the name of the King and the British Empire. We gave three cheers, then put our helmets on as quickly as we could, for a nasty wind was blowing that nipped our ears.

We had been indeed lucky, for though we had several hard blows, the skies had kept clear and no snow had fallen. Yet on the very first night we slept in the hut it snowed hard, and Murphy, whose bunk was nearest the door, woke to find himself covered with a thick mantle of white.

In the high winds it was indeed hard to keep the snow out. Though the walls of the hut were double, with a layer of malthoid between, the wind found almost imperceptible cracks and forced the fine drift through. Much of our leisure was spent at this time in pasting newspaper, nailing slats or otherwise repairing the weak places above our bunks.

Not that we had much leisure. There seemed a thousand jobs that had to be done before we were secure for the winter. For the purpose of magnetic observations, a small hut was erected some 400 yards away from the main hut. Here were installed the instruments that recorded the slightest variation in the earth's magnetic currents. So delicate were these instruments that copper instead of iron nails were used in the hut's construction, and it had to be kept quite away from the main hut. Even the observer had to be careful not to take a knife or anything else of iron when he entered to obtain the records.

The magnetic observations, which were the charge of Webb, a New Zealander, were one of the most important objects of the expedition. The close proximity of the base to the magnetic pole, only some 300 miles away, made every fact discovered of the utmost scientific importance. The magnetic pole, unlike the geographical pole, is not a fixed point. Actually the area of attraction towards

41

which all magnets point is situated at a depth of hundreds of miles within the earth, and the pole is that part of the surface above, on which a free-swinging magnet will point vertically downwards. Never exactly vertical, for, from day to day and minute to minute, the dip, as it is called, varies, sometimes for a degree or more. At the base, the dip averaged around 87°, and though generally steady, sometimes fluctuated wildly for several hours, producing what are called 'magnetic storms'. These are not appreciable to the senses, but as the winter darkness deepened, and we witnessed displays of the aurora australis, it was found that these always corresponded with magnetic storms as recorded on the instruments, and evidently have some connection.

The high magnetic dip near the pole has one peculiar effect, a rather inconvenient one for explorers. The ordinary compass becomes absolutely useless for steering purposes as the horizontal needle swings aimlessly in any direction. For this, when sledging, substitutes had to be found, the best being the constant direction of sastrugi or wind-carved ridges, and sun-compasses, which were made by Bage, the astronomer of the party.

Webb, who was in charge of the magnetic work, was a tall, athletic chap, who took life and his job very seriously. From azimuth, a word which figured largely in his conversation, he acquired the nickname 'Azi', and as Azi Webb he was always known. Naturally rather quick-tempered, he was inclined at first to bite a little bit at the ceaseless chaff, but, to his great credit, he again and again curbed his wrath, and was one of the best chaps of the party. He was conscientious to a degree, and his job was, during the winter months, very unpleasant. Day by day he had to fight his way to the magnetic hut and secure records automatically made during the previous twenty-four hours. Periodically he made what is termed a 'quick run' – that is, for four hours the readings would be personally noted, checked, and recorded. On these occasions one of us always accompanied him as recorder. The four hours seemed interminable.

In a temperature of from 10 to 20°F below zero, there was no chance of movement in the cramped space of the magnetic hut. It was impossible to write with mitts on, so the hand had to be kept uncovered, and got so stiff and cold that the pencil could hardly be held. In fact a quick run always meant that two individuals struggled back to the hut in a half-frozen condition.

With our establishment in the huts, it was necessary that our domestic economy should have some organisation, and some sort of routine be established. Up to this time Walter Hannam had acted as cook, but he had his own work to attend to, and naturally wanted some relief. For a day or two I acted as his assistant, and then took over for a week, after which a regular roster was made, and each took his turn.

In addition to cooking, we also all took a turn as cook's assistant or messman, whose duty was to sweep out the hut, see that plenty of ice was melted for the cook's requirements, help wash up, and generally do all the dirty work. Another job which came in rotation was that of nightwatchman. Owing to possible danger from fire, it was necessary that someone should be awake all the time. Then the stove had to be stoked, meteorological observations taken, and records kept. This turn of duty gave the opportunity, if so desired, to wash out a pair of socks or so, or even to have a bath in the small folding canvas bath provided for the purpose.

Dr Mawson made a great feature of the cooking, and having had previous experience, was not averse to having a turn himself. His habit of butting in, however, made him somewhat unpopular with the cook of the day, particularly as we gained in skill and began to fancy ourselves.

The first day that the stove was in commission he said to me, 'Joe, come here and I will show you how to make blancmange.'

I looked on for a while and the Doctor explained the process, until, happening to look at a packet, I remarked: 'Why, here are the directions on the packet.'

'Oh, yes,' remarked the Doctor airily, 'those are what I am following, but what is most important is the technique of the thing.'

Later, when the blancmange wouldn't set, the Doctor discovered that instead of boiling it for ten minutes, as the directions stated, he had simply brought the stuff to the boil. Hannam came to the rescue with some cornflour and made a good job of it. But I must say the Doc's scones were excellent, and between us all we had a very good dinner that night.

For my week's cooking I had Ninnis as messman, and in the intervals between providing for the wants of eighteen hungry men, we swapped reminiscences. In quaint idiom, he spoke of social life in London, of the messrooms of swagger regiments, of his own people and friends, all with the greatest simplicity and no suggestion of snobbery. He was a friendly soul with a simple outlook on life, but terribly keen on the expedition. He was very proud that he had met Pavlova, the famous dancer, on the *Aurora*, just before leaving London, and treasured a signed photograph she had given him. In her honour one of the sledging dogs had been named Pavlova but, unfortunately for reputations, she always ate her pups. In return I told him something of bush life in Australia, of dances in far-back towns, and of my experiences as museum collector.

Talking of Ninnis reminds me of his famous cooking exploit, which, though it came later in the year, can be told at this stage. Mrs Beeton was our great authority on all culinary matters, so when Ninnis one day decided that salmon kedgeree would be a good dish for lunch, he looked up the recipe. This read something as follows: 'Take 1 tin of salmon, 2 oz of butter, 2 oz of flour, pepper and salt to taste.'

'That's all right,' he thought; 'as there are eighteen of us, I will need four times the quantity.'

So he took 4 tins of salmon, 8 oz of flour, 8 oz of butter, but instead of pepper and salt to taste, he read 8 oz of pepper and 8 oz of salt. He confessed afterwards that it seemed rather a lot. The funny thing is that the dish looked all right as it came nicely browned from the oven. I had been nightwatchman the night before, and did not rise for lunch, but was aroused by the howl of anguish that followed the first mouthful. Ninnis never heard the last of this, and for a while it quite soured his usual sunny disposition.

Modesty prevents my dilating on my own reputation as a cook. Personally I think I was a great success, and I certainly was very proud of my pastry. All I will say is that Cecil Madigan said to me one night after dinner, 'There is one thing about your cooking, Joe. A fellow always feels he has had a square meal.'

Frank Hurley was a success in this direction, and always went in for very elaborate menus. His fault was that he would at times sacrifice tastiness for effect, deliberately making pastry tough, so that it would stand up in the form of a ship or some grotesque shape. Early on, Hannam, Hurley, Hunter and I formed The Secret Society of Unconventional Cooks, classing the others under the plebeian stigma of 'crook cooks'. As each in turn produced a worthy dish he was elevated with due ceremony to this aristocracy of chefs, until most of the party were admitted, and the sense of individual superiority disappeared. But even to the end there were a few who still ranked as 'crook cooks', and even gloried in the title.

At this time we tried out our prowess at skiing. The main difficulty was the lack of suitable surfaces. The slope at the back of the hut consisted of hard glacial ice, but some distance higher up there were patches of *névé* snow, somewhat uneven, but with a surface that gave some grip to the skis. Mertz gave a first demonstration, and it was wonderful how he exercised control even on the ice surface, coming down the slope at express rate, then suddenly turning. Then we all tried, mostly with disastrous results. Even when we learned to balance fairly well, there was no way to stop except by falling, and many a bruise resulted. Walter Hannam, with his 17 stone, partially solved the problem by using the skis as a sledge, on which he lay full length; and great was the delight of all when they separated from beneath him and he continued on his way for a considerable distance before he could pull up.

The following day we made another attempt, but Dr Mawson considered that the pastime was unnecessarily dangerous on the unsuitable surface, and it was deferred until such times as fresh falls of snow made conditions more favourable. Unfortunately this never happened, so throughout our stay our skis were of very little use.

So far I have said little about those other important members of the expedition – the dogs. We had some twenty of these to start with, huskies from northern Siberia. Many of them were practically purebred wolves, but nearly all were friendly, and several became great pets. Their instinct for sledge work is marvellous, comparing with the instinct of the sheep dog. Even in puppyhood – and we had several pups born in Adélie Land – they will pull if harnessed to anything. And once going they seldom shirk, but will pull, if allowed, until they drop dead from fatigue.

Basilisk was the king of the pack. He was a fine, dignified old chap, and carried himself with a certain air of responsibility. Yet he loved to romp, and would play like a puppy with any of the chaps. He was not the largest dog by any means, but quick as lightning when it came to a scrap. He ruled very strictly, and never allowed promiscuous fighting among the others. But for real gameness I doubt if there was ever the equal of Jack Johnson. He was a mongrel with a small body and a big heart. In turn he had tackled every dog bigger than himself, and been duly licked. He even went for Basilisk himself, which was courting disaster. He was covered with scars. Until winter set in properly the dogs were kept tethered at intervals to a long rope, just in front of the hut. Numbers of Adélie penguins were still about, and the dogs, if loose, harried them ceaselessly.

One day Bickerton rushed into the hut to say that a huge beast had come ashore and was approaching the dogs. Someone grabbed the rifle, and we went out to investigate. Surely enough, there was a huge sea-elephant, very rare in these latitudes, laboriously dragging itself over the rocks, and only a few yards away from the nearest dog, which happened to be Jack Johnson. The dogs were terrified, and dragging at their chains away from the threatened danger. That is, all but Jack Johnson. With every hair erect, he snarled and growled, and likewise strained at his chain, but towards the monster, which he defied to mortal combat. A couple of shots ended the career of the sea-elephant, and the next job was skinning it. It weighed nearly 2 tons, and it was very awkward to turn and manipulate the rapidly freezing pelt in a biting wind. Ultimately it was done, and the skin removed into the hut, where, for a week or more, I cleaned away the thick layer of blubber. Then the skin was packed with plenty of salt into a cask, but it did not arrive in Australia in the best of condition. The blubber and carcass gave us a fine supply of feed for the dogs, and Jack Johnson got an extra ration for his pluck.

A few days later a white seal, or crab-eater, was shot near the hut. It was a pretty creature, about 6 feet long, with a beautiful skin, but very savage, and tried hard to get at us as we surrounded it. We were rather glad to get a specimen of this seal, as it is not nearly as common as the other species. Properly stuffed and mounted, this chap now forms one of an Antarctic group in the Australian Museum, Sydney.

Weddell seals were very abundant on the rocks and ice near winter quarters. Beyond killing a few to augment our fresh meat, and also provide an additional supply for the dogs, we did not interfere with them. These are the commonest seals on the coast, and are the most harmless creatures imaginable. From 6 to 9 feet was the usual size, and they had a very small head with a blunt nose, and a face something like that of a pug-dog, with large, mild, round eyes. When disturbed, they made no attempt to move beyond half rolling over and gazing at the intruder with an expression of mild alarm. Then, if no further movement was made, they simply dropped their heads and went to sleep again. In the water they are hunted by the voracious sea-leopard and killer-whales, so to rest they come onshore or onto floe-ice, where long immunity from danger has instinctively removed any fear of strangers. We never killed them unnecessarily, but when required we always tried to get one that had just come out of the water. Often these had just fed, and the stomach contained undigested fish and small crustaceans, which made useful additions to our zoological collections.

When shooting a Weddell seal one day, John Close took the matter very seriously, rather as if he was facing a lion in the African wilds. He stalked it very cautiously, much to the amusement of several onlookers – and, of course, this was too good an opportunity to be lost. On 17 February, after dinner, the Doctor introduced Hurley to the gathering, and said that Hurley had an announcement to make. Hurley, for the occasion, had donned an old football jersey and a pair of pants over his Antarctic clothes, and with an old straw hat he looked a typical bottle-oh! In a rather rambling speech, with much studied and picturesque metaphor, he presented a medal, made of aluminium in the form of a cross and suitably inscribed. On the obverse it bore the words 'For Valour', also 'Design, C.L. Hoil', and on the reverse, *'Bravado Killus Terror Weddelli Seallus Pro Bono Publichouso'*. The latter phrase, Hurley explained, meant 'For the good of the public in their homes'. A favourite saying of Hurley was 'according to Hoyle', and Hoyle became his nickname, by which he was always known.

It was a night of medal presentations, for Herbert Murphy was also given one, in the form of a Maltese cross, made from his own bread, into which he had forgotten to put baking powder.

Thus February 1912 came and went. Already we had slipped into this new life as if it had always been. Day by day the outside world faded farther from our thoughts. It was indeed hard to imagine we had ever been puppets tied to the routine of cities. Even thoughts of home came as memories of a remote past. We lived in a world of our own, a primitive world, in which the only standards were efficiency and utility, and in which, in an all-satisfying way, we made our own news, devised our own pleasures, and were busy with our own work.

CHAPTER 5

THE COMING OF WINTER

Snow-laden from the south, from sunless waste
Which girds the pole, and frozen plateau bare,
There came a wall of wind in angry haste
To merge in spume the shattered wave and air.

In a land where the shade temperature never rises above freezing point, it seems strange to speak of winter; nevertheless the contrast between the calm, sunny days in which, even if the thermometer points to zero, there is no discomfort, and the long, bitter nights, when the snow-laden hurricane rages and howls in a ceaseless crescendo, is so great, that the coming and going of the sun is watched with intense interest.

In February the sun was already dipping below the southern horizon for an hour or so each night, but in March every day made an appreciable addition to the period of darkness. Away to the south, at the Pole itself, the land was already entering on its long six months' night; but here, practically on the Antarctic Circle, we never completely lost sight of the sun. Even on a midwinter's day, at noon, for a brief half-hour, its golden disc would emerge just clear of the northern horizon, to subside again for another twenty-four hours. Theoretically, from a point situated right on the Antarctic Circle, the sun at noon in midwinter should appear exactly half above the horizon; but actually refraction, or the bending of the light rays through layers of the atmosphere of different density, causes it to appear in a higher position, so that its disc is wholly visible, thus adding somewhat to the precious period of sunlight.

The sunrises and sunsets at this time were sights that will be remembered always. For five or six hours the sea to the north was a blaze of colour – blues, greens, purples, with here and there a touch of vivid fire. Icebergs, silhouetted against the light, were magnified into an infinity of weird shapes, often lifted by mirage so that they floated right in the air itself. To the south, the ice slopes leading to the plateau would be bathed in a flood of rosy pink. As the sunlight faded, the tones deepened, to lighten again to shining silver as the moon slowly rose.

This was, of course, on those occasions when the air was sufficiently clear of drift snow to allow objects more than a few yards distant to be seen at all. Reference has already been made to occasional blizzards, which hampered our work from the first day of landing. We anticipated wind, as the early voyagers in these seas had experienced gale after gale, and it was this fact which had, to the time of our expedition, kept Adélie Land a sealed book to the world. During February the wind blew with an intensity varying from a full gale to nearly a hurricane for about half the time, attaining continuous velocities up to 60 miles an hour. With the coming of the equinox it was anticipated that these conditions would be maintained, probably throughout March, but we looked forward to a period of winter calms, during which the frozen sea would provide a highway east and west.

The main sledging journeys would be made in the following summer, but it was intended that parties should go out even in the winter months, lay down depots, and pave the way for further exploration in the spring. Temperatures would be cold, but, even when well below zero, unless the wind blew there would not be any extreme discomfort.

Already we were becoming acclimatised to the cold. Our clothing consisted of thick jaeger cloth, soft and comfortable, much lighter than the furs that are usually considered part of a polar explorer's equipment and equally warm. The suits were made in one piece, were very roomy, with flaps at the front and back that buttoned at the waist. Underneath these we wore heavy woollen underclothing, and on our feet two or three pairs of socks. Large leather boots, with nails to grip the ice, were generally worn about the hut, but finnesko, or dog-skin boots with the hair outside, were used if out for any length of time. To resist the wind we had outer trousers and blouses of the very finely woven material known as burberry, and these were very efficient. Woollen balaclavas were our headgear, and, over these, helmets of burberry covering all but the centre of the face, with a funnel-like front which made a sort of calm air pocket when out in the wind. In bad weather it was necessary to adjust the burberries very tightly at the neck, waist and ankles, as drift snow found its way through the slightest gap.

In the hut itself the temperature was kept uniformly at slightly above freezing point, and we found that at 38 to 40°F it was quite comfortable to write or do any other sedentary work. The maintenance of the temperature was difficult at first, for the cold air found its way in, in spite of our attempts to close the slightest crevice. As the hut became buried deeper and deeper in the accumulating snow-drift, draughts ceased, and the contrast between the snug interior and low temperatures outside became very marked. Even then, some careless soul on entering would leave the door open, to be greeted with a chorus of: 'One, two, three – CLOSE THAT DOOR!'

This ultimately had the desired effect, and even to this day closing doors is a confirmed habit with most of us.

To keep the hut warm the stove was kept going night and day, and for fuel we depended on some 20 tons of the best Welsh briquettes, which had been landed from the ship. To eke this out we occasionally used seal blubber, which burns so fiercely that it often made the top of the stove red-hot.

With the advent of March the weather became steadily worse, and the calms between blizzards fewer and fewer. Apart from the wind, the almost ceaseless drift snow made things still more uncomfortable. To step from the entrance of the hut was to disappear into a white chaos in which it was often impossible to see more than a few feet. Journeys away from the hut became more and more hazardous, though we became used to even these conditions, and learned to recognise the shape of individual rocks and to keep a course by the constant direction of the wind.

The anemometer, which was the instrument for recording the velocity of the wind, was located on a ridge of rocks about 200 yards from the hut. This instrument consisted of a horizontal cross-piece, each arm terminating in a cup-shaped bowl. It revolved with the wind, and registered the actual number of miles blown in an hour. By means of a revolving drum, worked by clockwork, a needle traced a continuous record in 100-mile units, dropping to the bottom of the drum again as each 100 miles was completed. The drum revolved once in every twenty-four hours, when it had to be rewound and a new record substituted. The anemometer was in the charge of Madigan and Hodgeman, and each day they had to visit it and obtain the result of the previous day's record.

On one occasion they became separated on the way back to the hut, and Alfie Hodgeman was lost for about two hours, wandering around trying to pick up some landmark by which he might find the way back home. During the whole of this time he was, apparently, never more than 100 yards from the hut. Thinking he might have met with an accident, all hands were out searching for him, but at last he found his way in unaided. He came in for a lot of chaff on this occasion, but really everyone was greatly relieved, for it might have been much more serious.

It was, perhaps, this incident that gave rise to the legend of Hodgeman's third leg. In some mysterious way Alfie became linked in the folklore of the expedition with the Isle of Man, and taking inspiration from the well-known crest, we confidently asserted that he was possessed of a third leg. In spite of his expostulations the legend grew into an accepted fact, and a third leg he had to have until the end of the trip. Any member might casually remark, for instance, how convenient it was in blizzards to be built in a tripod form, so that one leg could always be stuck out to leeward, to act as a prop. Alfie bit once or twice, but soon learned to accept philosophically such things as a technical biological discussion on the matter, bringing in such subjects as comparative anatomy, missing links, aberrant races of mankind, pre-natal influences, magic and the stars. It was all very absurd, but good fun.

Any personal idiosyncrasy was always seized on with great gusto. Thus Close was a great reader of Nansen, and quoted him repeatedly. Nansen, under extreme conditions, had acquired a taste for raw seal blubber, so Close perforce had to try it, and pronounced it excellent, though we all noticed he did not tackle it again. From this grew the legend that he had an inordinate appetite, and was capable of devouring seals and penguins alive. As a result he was variously known as 'Hollow-leg' or 'Terror'. From arguments that rose on one occasion when Whetter and Close were cook and messman respectively, likened to an eruption between the volcanoes Erebus and Terror, to be corrupted to Terribus and Error, by which names these two were often known. Archie McLean had a habit of calling everybody 'Dad', so he became 'Dad' himself, and was never known as anything else. He was a chap of high ideals, therefore, by the law of contraries, he was credited with a very amorous disposition and assumed to be partial to nurses. Correll was the 'baby' of the expedition, being only nineteen at the time, so this was exaggerated, and he was never considered in conversation as being more than a babe in arms. A phrase of his own, 'Little-Willie-Smith-so-high', was often applied to him. Hurley was our comedian, and poked so much fun at everything and everybody, including himself, that jokes at his expense were apt to misfire. Madigan and Stillwell were fine chaps and popular with everybody, but somehow had no eccentricities on which to pin nicknames. They were called 'Madi' and 'Frank' respectively, and nothing else.

With references to nicknames, it is curious how in some individuals a nickname will stick, while with others, either the Christian name or surname is abbreviated, or in other cases is used in an unabridged form. There seems no rule to govern the matter. For instance, below is a list of those at the main base, with their pseudonyms, generally used in the second but occasionally in the third person. For instance, Dr Mawson would always be called just 'Doctor', but when speaking of him he would be referred to as 'D.I.', from *dux ipse*, 'the leader himself'. Here is the list:

Dr Mawson	Doctor or D.I.
Madigan	Madi
Bage	Badget
McLean	Dad

Hodgeman	Alfie, Uncle or Uncle Alfie
Hurley	Frank or Hoyle
Hunter	Johnnie
Correll	Percy or Little Willie Smith
Bickerton	Bick
Murphy	Herbert
Hannam	Walter
Close	J.C. or Terribus
Webb	Azi
Stillwell	Frank
Whetter	Whetter or Error
Ninnis	Cherub or Ninn
Mertz	X
Laseron	Joe

Hurley's ingenuity in staging jokes often provided much amusement, and he spared no trouble in making them effective. There was one member of the party who was very nervous of fire, as indeed we all were, for a fire would have been disastrous. But he voiced his anxiety too often. Moreover, he had a deep-rooted distrust of the acetylene generator, which he was sure was always on the point of blowing up. One night this member was nightwatchman, so Frank took the long length of rubber tubing that always seemed to play a part in his schemes, and immersing one end in the water for the generator, carried the other to his bunk. Here at intervals through the night, and at the expense of his own rest, he blew hard, creating a most satisfactory bubbling. It was too much for the nightwatchman. After climbing up several times to investigate and finding nothing to reveal the cause, he at last woke the Doctor. D.I., annoyed at being disturbed, at once spotted the trouble, but did not give the show away. He merely remarked that it certainly was dangerous, but even if it did blow up, nothing could be done before morning, and calmly went back to his bunk again. The nightwatchman spent the rest of the night in anxious misery, and it was not until some days later that he came to understand the hilarity that greeted any discussion on the nature and habits of acetylene generators.

I shall never forget the occasion, either, when we found this same member fast asleep with his favourite book, Roosevelt's *Strenuous Life*, open on his chest.

A typical Hurley joke was the composition of a song describing the Doctor's prowess at shooting birds. At the critical moment, when he fired the little wooden gun he had made for the occasion, a bell rang at the target he had placed at the end of the table. There were also numerous loud bangs from beneath the table, where a little carbide had been brought into contact with water by pulling a string and inverting a number of small tins. The lids blew off with quite convincing reports. Moreover, from various points in the roof dead Antarctic penguins and skua gulls dropped in every direction on those sitting beneath, while the gramophone funnel descended as an extinguisher on Alfie Hodgeman's head.

In the month of March the wind averaged 49 miles an hour, which, up to this time, for a sustained velocity, was almost inconceivable, and far exceeded all world records. For days on end it had blown 70 miles an hour, not in gusts, but actually maintaining that velocity throughout. The force of the wind was such that if it had been let loose on the inhabited regions of the earth little would have stood before it.

At first it was found impossible to walk in these high winds. At 60 miles an hour, we crawled about like animals on all fours, fighting desperately to prevent ourselves being picked up and hurled bodily downwind. Then with practice we learned the knack of wind-walking, leaning always at an angle and bracing our feet against every projecting piece of rock and ice. In this way we could walk against a 70-miler, and could stand against 80, but when the 90 and 100 miles were reached we gave up, and were content to wriggle about like snakes.

Day by day throughout March we looked forward to the calmer days that were to come, and it was well, perhaps, that we were spared the knowledge that this was but a foretaste of what was ahead. As time drew on, our outdoor labours became more and more limited in scope. No trouble had been anticipated, for instance, in the erection of the wireless masts; now, every minute of comparative calm was of the utmost value. The two masts each consisted of three segments, and secure anchorages had to be found for the wire stays to hold them. At every opportunity all hands were thus employed, collecting rocks as weights, boring holes in the hard rock, or digging foundations for the masts themselves. Suitable projecting corners of solid rock, where possible, were used to fasten the stays. With all our labour we did not complete the work until September, and by this time the hours of darkness were not sufficient for proper wireless communication to be made. Of course, wireless at this date was comparatively in its infancy, and both transmitting and receiving had not attained their present efficiency. Ultimately, I believe, a few mutilated messages reached Australia, but of this we knew nothing at the time, as no answers came through.

One of these messages, we heard afterwards, caused some degree of anxiety. How it was sent is not known, but probably Hannam or Bickerton, practising morse, did not realise that their effort was actually going over the air. The origin of the message is also obscure, but it looks as if some would-be effort of humour on my part had gone flat, for the words as received were: 'We are sorry for poor Laseron.' Fearing some tragedy, Eitel, the secretary of the expedition, fortunately decided to wait for further particulars before informing my family. When the *Aurora* finally picked us up he was on board, and almost his first words were: 'How is Laseron?' We were greatly puzzled until he explained.

Hunter's and my own work, too, suffered from the weather conditions. The loss of the whaleboat destroyed any hope that we had of dredging in deeper water, and as yet the sea showed no signs of freezing. The temperature was quite cold enough, but the perpetual winds so churned up the water that it would never set. The sea made an impressive sight in a hurricane. The whole surface was literally swept off in a blinding sheet of spray, so that it was impossible to tell where water ended and air began. Up to a point we had some success in the boat harbour immediately in front of the hut. This was about 300 yards long by 100 wide, and the deepest portion was not more than about 3 fathoms. It froze over quite early in the winter, and the narrow entrance prevented the ice thus formed being blown to sea. The ice became thicker and thicker, and eventually was some 6 to 7 feet through, and formed a well-defined ice-foot, about 100 yards from the entrance. Most of our fish-traps had been lost in the early days, but, improvising others, we lowered these from the ice-foot. We lost some of them when the edge broke away, but obtained several species of fish, besides starfish, sea-spiders and other organisms. With the small hand-nets we also procured many of the surface animals, mostly small shrimps, jellyfish and a few of the beautiful little winged molluscs known as pteropods.

At every opportunity we took our dredge to the edge of the ice, and by lowering it near one shore were able to drag it right across the bottom to the other. We obtained a number of specimens in this way, but though the bottom was covered with a thick growth of kelp, it did not harbour much animal life. As soon as the dredge came up, its contents were emptied into a tube, and this raced up to the hut before it froze too hard. The freezing was apt to mutilate delicate organisms; nevertheless, we were able to add somewhat to our rather meagre collections.

It was a tricky business at times manipulating the dredge, for when the weather was dead calm all hands were wanted on the wireless masts, and we had to make our attempts in winds blowing up to 40 and 50 miles an hour, directly offshore. The surface of the ice was very slippery, and the greatest care had to be exercised to prevent being blown into the water. There were several very narrow escapes, but experience taught us always to have a rope handy to the grasp, and there was always someone to give the necessary assistance if required. The ice in the boat harbour got thicker and thicker as time went on, and the movements of the tide flung it into great folds. Ice, too, formed on the sea-bottom, and eventually made further attempts at collecting useless.

Of outdoor recreation there was practically none. Occasionally a few of us would take a sledge up the slope some distance and toboggan down – an exhilarating if somewhat dangerous pastime. On the hard ice it was practically impossible to steer, and just as difficult to pull up. We generally picked a spot where a mound of hard snow made a terminus, arriving at which we all fell off, though sometimes we would lose a passenger or two en route. One day the sledge bolted with us completely, and charged a heap of cases of benzine that formed a breakwind for a shaft in the ice. It was a terrific crash, and the corner runner went completely through two of the cases. Aboard were Hurley, Hunter, Correll and myself, and we were tossed in all directions, fortunately with no injury to the sledge or ourselves, beyond a minor bruise or two. This rather dampened our ardour, but we found a better ground some distance from the hut, where the slope terminated on the frozen surface of one of the small glacial lakes. Here we had a nice flat expanse on which to pull up. Moreover, we were out of sight of the Doctor, who rather frowned on our sport as unnecessarily imperilling both sledges and men.

Our other form of tobogganing was simple, and required only a smooth flat surface and a high wind, the former difficult to find, the latter always with us. Taking a small piece of board, with a piece nailed across the front on which to brace the feet, we would sit on it and be rushed downwind at a great speed. Sometimes the board would catch some slight irregularity on the surface and stop dead, while its passenger continued onwards in various attitudes; but this was part of the fun, particularly for the onlookers.

With the passing of March our hopes for winter calms vanished. The wind velocity for April averaged over 50 miles an hour, and during the whole month there were only three moderately calm days. The proportion of our time spent in the hut, therefore, perforce became much greater.

It might appear that in this narrative there is undue mention of winds and blizzards. I know that in every chapter, and in almost every incident, there is a repetition of the word 'wind'. Yet it is unavoidable, for the unceasing wind dominated the whole of our life; it dictated what we could do and could not do; circumscribed our outlook, and filled our conversations. Nothing could be planned, nothing undertaken without making allowance for it, from the day we landed to the day we were clear of the pack-ice on our return journey to Australia. In fact the terrific winds of Adélie Land can be considered as one of the major discoveries of the expedition. In their severer phases they are probably quite localised. As far as is known, an area of about 100 miles square of which our hut was approximately the centre, is the windiest region in the whole world. The wind is due to unique local conditions. Commonwealth Bay is one of the few parts, if not the only part, of Antarctica where an open sea throughout the year lies in direct contact with a steep shore. This produces a sharp contrast of temperatures within a very short distance. The sea is comparatively warm, never quite below freezing point, and has a marked effect on the temperature of the overlaying air. To the south the steeply rising plateau is intensely cold, and a few miles inland is from 15 to 20°F colder than at the coast. Except for a couple of months in the year, the thermometer is always well below zero. Above the warm sea the air is always rising, and into the vacuum thus created the cold air from the plateau rushes, making a continual vertical cyclone. The direction of the surface wind is remarkably constant, always within a point of south-south-east; but high in the air it is in exactly the opposite direction, as can be seen by the drift of clouds overhead.

Figures, at the best of times, make dry reading, but without them it is impossible to form any conception of the power of the wind. For purposes of comparison, it may be mentioned that the worst continuous blow ever experienced in Sydney since records have been kept, was on 6 May 1898, when for twenty-four hours the wind averaged 28.4 miles an hour. This would, of course, mean much higher gusts, attaining upwards of 60 miles an hour. This gale did much damage, and was considered, at the time, a very severe visitation of nature. In the light of these figures, those recorded in Adélie Land are almost unbelievable. The actual average velocity of the wind throughout the whole year, including calms and the milder summer months, was recorded on the anemometer as 48.5 miles an hour. Subsequently this had to be corrected slightly, as in very high winds the instrument obtains a momentum which slightly exaggerates the results; but allowing for this, the figures drop to about 44 miles. In April, as stated, the average was over 50 miles, and it never dropped below this figure until the following November. The following monthly figures speak for themselves.

1912

Month	Speed			
February	25 miles an hour			
March	49	''	''	''
April	51	''	''	''
May	61	''	''	''
June	57.9	''	''	''
July	56	''	''	''
August	60	''	''	''
September	55	''	''	''
October	56.9	''	''	''

For one hectic fortnight in May the average never fell below 70 miles an hour. The worst day actually experienced was 14 May, when for twenty-four hours the average was 90.1 miles. On this day and others a velocity of over 100 miles for a single hour was several times recorded. As the pressure of wind increases as the square of the velocity, its power during these periods was over nine times that of the greatest gale Sydney has ever known. A modern city would be levelled to the foundations before such a blast.

The day in question was literally an icy inferno. The hut itself, although almost buried, quivered under the strain, and the roof bent inwards beneath the weight of air. Outside, thick drift snow restricted visibility to a few inches, and the temperature was 28°F below zero, or 60° of frost. The daily trip to the anemometer on the part of Madigan and Hodgeman was an heroic achievement, and both were badly frost bitten as a result. Everybody at one time or another went out, if only to say they had experienced such conditions, but, except from urgent necessity, a minute or two quenched the most ardent thirst for adventure.

Fortunately the high winds were not always accompanied by snow. Often the skies were clear, and it seemed strange, while a hurricane raged, to see the stars shining brightly overhead. When the moon shone the reflection from the ice made it almost as bright as day. On clear, dark nights the northern sky was often aflame with the aurora australis. Pale masses of greenish light flickered like distant lightning beyond the horizon, or else appeared like luminous clouds suspended in the heavens, waning one moment, then glowing brilliantly the next. Then curtains of fire would form, one above the other, from the northern horizon right to the zenith. Five or six curtains would be in sight at the same time – real curtains suspended across the sky as if on invisible wires, and winding in and out in intricate folds. Pale green above, below they were banded with yellow, heliotrope and pink, while from end to end waves of intenser light raced in and out of the folds in a wild hide-and-seek, until the eye was dazzled by the rapidity of the motion. This would last for half an hour or so, and then the curtains would gradually fade and merge once again into uniform green nebulae, at last dying out altogether. The displays of aurora we witnessed were always in the north, reaching from the horizon to the zenith, but never beyond. We seemed, indeed, to be on the fringe of a well-defined auroral belt, encircling the magnetic pole. In support of this, at the second base, away to the west, they were always seen in the east. Again, in lower latitudes, such as Macquarie Island and the south coast of Australia, though displays are not so common, they invariably appear in the south.

That there is a definite connection between the aurora and the mysterious force known as 'terrestrial magnetism' seems beyond doubt. Our base, situated so close to the magnetic pole, was an excellent point to observe these phenomena, and invariably on the occasions of an auroral display the magnetic needle oscillated violently. Thus the careful records compiled by Webb, linking up with the work of magnetic stations throughout the world, have a double value. Helping to throw some light on this as yet little-known branch of physics, they constituted by no means the least valuable part of the scientific results of the expedition.

CHAPTER 6

TWENTY-FOUR HOURS
IN THE HUT

A day in a life, the spendthrift said,
There is time for nothing but play.
But a day to the wise is twenty-four hours,
And enough for a life in each day.

It is nine o'clock on a typical evening in midwinter. Outside the hut there is the unending shriek of the blizzard, and inside the air pulsates as the roof bends inwards beneath the pressure of the fiercest gusts. Ears are so attuned, however, that it passes unheeded. The day's tasks are ended, and all amuse themselves in various ways. At one end of the table Bickerton, Hannam, Hunter and I are engaged in a game of bridge, while Madigan, Murphy and the Doctor look idly on. Farther down the table sits Mertz, choosing a record for the gramophone, while Bage, with his favourite old pipe, its stem mended with adhesive tape, offers his advice. Stillwell is reading a book, and Close is writing something in his diary. Lying on his bunk, Whetter has his nose in a medical treatise, and on the other side of the hut Hurley, with facetious remarks, is cutting Correll's hair, and doing a job that would cause any self-respecting barber to have a fit.

The gramophone is wound and the record goes on. It is a band piece beginning quietly, but accelerating to a stirring crescendo in which the loud clash of cymbals comes faster and faster, to reach the climax in a resounding crash. Then the music dies away in a soothing melody. It is Mertz's favourite record, and peculiarly suited to his personality. Long since it has become known as 'Mertz Killing Seals', and is very suggestive of his emphatic methods.

Next comes a chorus from *The Mikado*. Argument arises as to the exact words, and the needle is put back again and again to try and distinguish them. 'Something, something, the Lord High Executioner', goes the refrain. What are the words? For months we have worried over them, but they still elude the ear. The missing part sounds like 'Japara', the material of which our tents are made, and 'Japara' it has to remain throughout our stay. The following year, on board the *Aurora*, there is a general rush for the libretto of *The Mikado*, to discover that the first part of the phrase is 'Defer to'. It is a great problem solved.

One by one the party breaks up and goes to bed. The last, generally Bage, who is a nocturnal animal, finishes his sewing or the latest gadget on which he has been working, says goodnight to the watchman and retires.

The nightwatchman rises from the table and puts some coal on the fire. Then he makes a saucepan of cocoa to last him the night and settles down for a quiet read. From one corner comes a snore, barely distinguishable above the sound of the wind. It is Walter Hannam, his blanket thrown aside, and his round face cherubic in the innocence of sleep. The watchman makes a mental note that Walter's nickname shall be 'Cupid' from thence on.

It is nearly midnight, and preparations must be made to take the usual observations. It is a serious business this, though the weather screen is but a few yards from the hut on the eastern side. First of all he draws on his burberry trousers, which he ties tightly with tapes round ankles and waist. Then comes the balaclava, and over it the burberry helmet. Woollen mittens come next to protect the wrists, and over, all the blouse, which is tied at the waist, neck, and wrists to prevent the entrance of snow. Finally, finger-less woollen gloves complete the outfit. The barometer is read, and the result noted in the record book; then the main adventure begins. Passing into the outer room, from thence to the porch, he crawls through the snow tunnel into the veranda of the main hut. Bracing himself for the shock, he climbs through a gap beneath the corner of the roof and is outside.

A howling, whirling wall of grey hits him, and he does not rise from his hands and knees lest he should be blown away. It is not quite dark, reflection from the white snow producing a faint luminosity, yet of visibility there is none. The hand held 6 inches before the face is hidden behind the drift that fills the air. Ice at once begins to form on the face, and in a few seconds small icicles dangle from the eyebrows and eyelashes, and bind the beard to the helmet. Carefully he rises to his feet, bracing himself against the wind, and step by step guides himself along the slope of the hut roof. Now he is round the corner, a few yards and he has turned again and is fighting his way upwind. He now calculates his distance – 1, 2, 3, 4, 5 yards. Now comes the plunge into the unknown. At right angles he makes a rush, and his hand gropes blindly about him. Here it is at last – a thin strand of wire, vibrating shrilly in the wind. As his fingers make contact with the wire blue sparks spring forth, and the metal rim of his helmet also glows with blue flame. This is St Elmo's fire, an electric discharge caused by the friction of the particles of snow. But at this moment he is not concerned with the superstitions of the old-time mariners, but instead hauls himself carefully upwards, his mind on the immediate task. As he clings to the screen with one hand, the wind plucks at him and tries to tear him away, but he hangs grimly on, and at last with his free hand successfully prises open the door. He inserts his head in the aperture and fumbles for the electric switch connected to a battery in the hut. A flicker of light falls on the thermometer, but first he must break the ice from his eyes and peer forward to within a couple of inches before he can read the temperature. He mentally notes the result, switches off the light, closes and fastens the door, and prepares to return.

Retracing his steps presents the same difficulties, but at last, after what seems an age, he finds the entrance and plunges through with a feeling of relief. In the porch he takes off his burberries, shakes the snow from them, and with his hand melts the ice from his eyes. His balaclava he leaves on until he is in front of the fire, for it has become frozen fast to his beard, and it is apt to be painful to pull it off too suddenly. In the warm hut again, his cheek feels rather numb, so he looks at himself in the glass and sees a round, shrivelled patch about the size of a shilling. It is frostbite, and he rubs it gently to restore the circulation. It tingles a bit as feeling comes back, and an hour later there is a blister in the place. He takes the record book and makes an entry, curiously similar to other entries for many pages back:

Twenty-Four Hours in the Hut

'12 midnight. Temp. −18°F, wind about 80, thick drift.'

He is now free until 6 a.m., when a further observation must be made. He decides to have a bath. The folding canvas arrangement that serves for the purpose is spread on the floor, the fire is stoked, and the front of the stove left open. Even then the temperature seems cold when stripped, so he hurries through his ablutions, taking one section at a time, for there is only room to squat in the bath, and care must be taken or the whole precarious contraption will upset on the floor.

Having dressed, for a few hours he reads or writes; then at 6 a.m. he must face the blizzard again for another set of observations. The wind has eased slightly and the drift is lighter, so the difficulties are not quite so great. This done, he begins to prepare for breakfast. The two boilers on the stove are replenished with ice from the veranda so that the cook of the day will have plenty of water; the porridge is put on and the cook called. At 7.30 he winds up the gramophone and, if he is a considerate chap, puts on a soothing violin solo, such as 'Humoresque', to be followed by others that become gradually louder. This is a great refinement by which the sleepers gradually wake to the strains of music. To this day I cannot hear 'Humoresque' without a vivid mental picture of every detail of the hut and of every face within it. At 7.55 breakfast is nearly ready, and with a loud banging on a saucepan, and cries of 'Rise and shine', everybody is exhorted to rise. Jaeger blankets are thrown aside and, in various postures, pyjamas are discarded and clothes hastily donned.

No one washes, except in dire necessity – the cook guards his supply of water too zealously for that; there is no shaving, so the morning toilet is only a matter of a few minutes. Conversation hums during breakfast, which consists of porridge, fried bacon, soda bread, butter and jam, with tea or a beverage. Breakfast finished, the messman clears the table, and all prepare for the day's work.

The weather is too bad for outdoor work, but Bickerton and Bage retire to the benzine hut or the hangar, as we ambitiously style it, and tinker all day on the aeroplane in a temperature still well below zero. Correll is in the outer room, working on his lathe and spinning aluminium sheets into a globe that will form part of a specially devised instrument to measure the velocity of single wind-gusts.

Hannam is busy adjusting the wireless sending set, in the hope that the aerial will soon be completed.

Herbert Murphy is on the veranda, filling the cook's order for the day. He has raised a trapdoor in the floor, and, armed with an ice-axe, prepares to extract the main joint for dinner. In the cramped space of this cellarette is a solid, frozen mass consisting of the remains of the mutton and a number of penguins killed in the early autumn. Penguin is the dish chosen, and presently muffled sounds of profanity come from the depths. An effort to loosen the topmost bird by a protruding leg has resulted in the leg's snapping off, and Herbert hitting his head against a floor-joist. There is nothing for it but to chip laboriously round and eventually undermine the carcass, which is at last dislodged and taken into the hut to thaw. This must be done thoroughly before cooking. There was one cook who neglected the process and served a leg of mutton, nicely done and sizzling on the outside, while the interior was still frozen hard.

Whetter, with an assistant, has donned his burberries and is fighting the blizzard in an endeavour to dig ice for the hut. This is not an easy job. One man has a box and hangs onto it like grim death, while the other, his feet braced against a small ridge, tries to wield a pick. Hampered by his mitts, and by the wind's catching the pick, it is difficult to hit twice within 6 inches of the same place. Consequently the chips of ice are small, and it takes a lot to fill the box. Moreover, unless grabbed at once, even big pieces are blown away, and much is lost in this way. The box itself, even when partially filled, is sometimes lost, wrenched from the hands and swept away to sea. No wonder Whetter sometimes growls at the cook's demands for ice, and the cook, in turn, resists request for water for such frivolous purposes as washing.

Mertz and Ninnis are on the portion of the veranda that has been walled off to house the dogs, for even these, though born in Arctic snows, could not live outside in Adélie Land. Later, if the weather moderates somewhat, they will be taken for a run, harnessed to sledges, and bring back a cache of geological specimens or a load of ice.

In the hut, Dad is examining a culture of bacteria under the microscope, while those who have no immediate task are sewing sledge harnesses, or helping the others. For my own part, I have taken down from a shelf above my bunk an Antarctic petrel, shot a couple of months before. It is partially thawed, and is now to be skinned to add to the collection. A small slit is made in the lower portion of the abdomen, and through this the body is gradually drawn, the tail, leg bones, wing bones and neck being severed from the inside, so that the skin is turned inside out. The brain and eyes are then taken out, the bones cleaned from flesh, all fat scraped from the skin, which is then painted with arsenical soap. The skin is turned right-side out again, feathers smoothed with a needle, the inside filled with cotton wool, and the one incision sewn up. A label with particulars of sex, date and other information, is attached to the leg, and the specimen is packed away, perhaps some day to be stuffed and mounted and grace the collection of an Australian museum.

Suddenly there is a terrific bang from the vicinity of the kitchen, and a few seconds later another one. All in the hut jump to their feet, and the cook rushes to the oven, flings open the door and jumps back. From everybody within hearing comes a gleeful yell of 'Championship', which, in the local vernacular, signifies that someone has blundered. The oven having cooled somewhat, the cook very gingerly approaches and removes two tins of salmon. There had been four, put in to thaw, but temporarily forgotten. Two have exploded and splattered the whole of the inside of the oven with fragments of salmon. Amid the ribald comments of the others, the cook perforce has to grin likewise, as he sets about the task of cleaning up the mess.

It is nearly twelve noon, and Madigan and Hodgeman are ready to set forth on their daily adventure to the anemometer to obtain the day's wind record. Azi Webb is down at the magnetic hut obtaining a quick run, and Johnnie Hunter is with him, acting as recorder, and no doubt wishing it was all over.

Presently, when all are returned, lunch is announced, and everybody sits down with anticipation. If the cook is ambitious, he has prepared something hot; otherwise it is sheep's tongue or ham, or some other cold dish, with tea and plenty of etceteras. In the middle of lunch we all suddenly become aware of something strange. Our eardrums commence to throb as with a great noise. Somebody speaks and his voice cracks like a whip on the stillness. The wind has stopped, and, accustomed as we are to its howl, the silence can literally be felt. For a while we speak almost in whispers. Our heads are ringing and we feel very uncomfortable.

No time is lost. Everyone hurries on burberries and gets outside as quickly as possible. There is much to be done, and for a while all are engaged on various tasks, making the most of the half-hour's daylight and the long twilight that follows. Outside the wind has indeed dropped, but scurrying clouds of drift snow a few hundred feet in the air show that the surface calm is but illusory. The wind plays queer tricks under these conditions. Gusts and whirlwinds come suddenly from all parts of the compass, strong enough to lift a man from his feet. These gusts are often very limited in width and on one occasion, while two of us were skinning a seal, the chap at the tail was nearly blown away, while at the head I was in perfect calm.

Presently, as the twilight fades, even the overhead drift ceases, and the moon comes out, bathing the plateau and sea in soft, blue light. It is too dark to work, so Hurley and I walk over to the far western edge of the promontory. Climbing a ridge of rocks, we come above the point where rock ceases and ice begins. The sea is at our feet, and to the left the great ice-cliffs tower, magnified in the moonlight to an abnormal height, while from their brink overhanging masses of snow shadow the deep caves beneath. The sea is already freezing, and pancakes of ice, with narrow ribbons of water beneath, produce a curious reticulated pattern, merging in the distance to a continuous sheet which shimmers with brilliant light. And the intense, utter silence – it seems as if the whole world is dead. The tinkling of a piece of ice falling in the distance rings out like a thunderclap. For a while we watch in silence, then the awe of it is too much for us. Without a word we turn away to that little haven in the void, where is the society of our fellows – and life.

Dinner is ready, and the cook has done himself justice. No 'crook cook' this, but one of the elite. The soup has not come from tins, but a ham bone, saved for the occasion, and with dried vegetables, a little emergency ration and other trimmings, it is tasty and hot. The soup finished, the cook gives the order, 'Pass bowls and lick spoons.' This is necessary, as spoons are short, and must serve for the pudding course. Fried breasts of penguin come next, in appearance not unlike very dark beef and, if carefully cleaned of all blubber, quite palatable. Next is the prize piece, baked jam roly-poly, nicely browned, light as a feather, and sizzling from the oven. There are loud cheers, for the cook has excelled himself. Dessert, figs or sweets, and coffee follow, pipes and cigarettes are lit, and a haze of smoke fills the hut.

But the calm is over. A sudden shriek of wind announces the return of the blizzard. As if to make up for the brief interlude it has granted us, it comes hurtling down the plateau with redoubled fury, and in a few minutes is blowing at 80 miles an hour. We shrug our shoulders and take no further notice, for is not this our normal weather?

Now is the time for the cook's chief effort. Custom has decreed that he shall amuse the company – sing a song, tell a story, read a composition or do a stunt of some sort. Songs are generally topical, written for the occasion. Here is one of them; the author, John Hunter; the tune, 'We've a Nice Little Farm' from *Our Miss Gibbs*:

I'm going to sing a little song about we, us, and co.,
The nicest lot of chaps that ever one could know.
There's Walter, for example, with his sixty-inch of girth,
Who never talks of anything, unless it's Mother Earth.
There's three-legged Uncle Alfie who is always getting lost,
But who's certainly our architecture boss.
While our champion dog experts
Are Cherub Ninn and Mertz,
And the Doc and Frank are searchers for the cherts.

CHORUS

We're a nice lot of chaps,
Some are thin and some are fat,
And our jobs are very varied, we must say.
For there's Madi with his annie*,
Who sometimes goes uncanny,
While Bick will fly his motor sledge some day.

* Anemometer

69

Then there's Joe with his skins
Of skuas and penguins,
And Baldy Bob, our champion gadget king,
And don't forget we beg
J.C. or Hollow Leg.
And here the chorus ends. Ting-ling-a-ling.

There is loud applause, and the cook, with becoming modesty, begins to gather the dishes for the washing-up. Then someone says, 'What about a yarn, Herbert?'

Herbert fidgets, looks nervously at the speaker, and deprecates his ability to tell anything that had not already been told. There is a general chorus: 'Go on, Herbert, tell us about Siberia, or Melbourne, or a visit to an English country house, or Cambridge, or anything you like.' So Herbert, importuned from every side, and with a diffident little cough, begins rather haltingly. A small boy or a dog comes into the tale, a sure sign of inspiration, and he brightens. He tells of social life in Melbourne, of one of his friends who proposed to two girls in one evening, and of how both accepted him, and of the complications that followed. From this he wanders to scandals in high places, hair-raising scandals with lurid details, of complicated domestic situations with ludicrous climaxes. When he personally figures in the story, it is always in a humble or absurd way. He holds himself up to ridicule as well as all his other characters. Yet he never loses his air of diffidence; his whole method is apologetic. His stories have a curious suggestion of truth; they are convincing and at the same time too impossible to be true. For Herbert is a genius, who from an ounce of fact can manufacture a mountain of entertainment. For an hour we rock with laughter, then the story, with a to-be-continued-in-our-next air, draws to a close.

The cook and his messman begin the washing-up, aided by a couple of volunteers, and as they start on the high sausage-like pile of soup bowls, the story of Walter's song comes to mind. I am sure he will forgive its repetition.

One day, when cook, Walter composed a song of which he was very proud, so he confidentially showed it beforehand to about half of the company, one by one. Now, though our songs were topical and intensely personal, care was always taken that real offence was not given, and in this case opinion was unanimous that is was somewhat over the line. Walter could not see this, so Frank Hurley prepared a counterattack. Adjoining the stove was a post that was invariably covered with burberries and other bits of clothing, hanging to dry. Taking advantage of Walter's absence from the hut, and with a couple of us keeping 'nit', Frank rigged up a length of acetylene tubing, attaching it to the post so that its end protruded just about the height of Walter's head. This end was filled with flour; the other, after a devious route, was in Hurley's bunk at the end of the table. Dinner was finished, and the company settled back for Walter's song. With the paper in his hand, and the stance of an opera singer, Walter, by the best of luck, stood about a foot away and slightly in front of the hidden tube. He began to sing, and Frank began to blow. Slowly, almost imperceptibly, Walter's head began to whiten. There was a suppressed guffaw and, heartened by this appreciation, Walter carried on with additional vim. The laughter became louder and louder, until the words of the song were drowned in the uproar. It was then that the singer began to sense that something more than the song was causing the amusement. He became aware of flakes of flour on his shoulder; he put his hand to his head and it came away white. Amid howls of joy, the song ended abruptly not halfway through, never to be given to the light again.

So, the washing-up finished, we again settle down to our usual evening, and another twenty-four hours of the winter are completed.

CHAPTER 7

THE PASSING OF WINTER

The dark and dreary night of winter goes,
Each day the sun its glowing disc uplifts
A little higher over hinter snows,
And gleams more brightly through the lessening drifts.

All who sojourn in the Antarctic anxiously await 22 June. With it comes the feeling that at least half of the winter has been successfully weathered. It is a day of universal rejoicing. From now on the sun will lengthen its brief stay at noon, and day by day creep a little higher above the northern horizon. Day by day, also, we can look forward to the approach of better conditions, when, leaving the hut behind us, we will push out into the unknown regions that surround us, and add our discoveries to the little that is known about this strange continent. Day by day, also, we come nearer to the time when, our labours satisfactorily concluded, the ship will arrive to take us back to regions where blizzards are unknown.

We often discussed at this time the question of what constituted an ideal climate. If a plebiscite had been taken among our company, the verdict would have been unanimous. It is a climate of perpetual sunshine, where not even the faintest breeze blows from one year's end to another.

Midwinter's day came in with happy augury, and we had a few hours' calm. A spirit of optimism was in the air; the super-optimists even expressed the belief that with the lengthening days the blizzards would abate, and we would have good conditions again. In our hearts we knew this was not so, but for a few hours at least the future could be ignored. By universal consent a general holiday was declared, and in twos and threes we scattered over our small domain, exploring it afresh, though by this time the detail of every rock, every ice-filled gully, was known by heart.

The Passing of Winter

Some of us, geologically inclined, roamed among the glacial moraines, which on the landward side were piled at the edge of the ice. Here we turned over the rocks in search of new specimens that would add something to our knowledge of the structure of the country.

Moraines, incidentally, are deposits of the rocky detritus that has been scraped from the surface by the ice-sheet that ever advances overhead. Borne along by the moving flood of ice, the fragments are ground together, chiselled and polished, to be deposited at last where the edge of the ice-sheet comes to rest. Sometimes huge boulders are borne by ice floating far to sea. From the ship, hundreds of miles from land, we often saw masses of rock and mud embedded in the bottom portion of icebergs that had overturned. As the icebergs melt, their burdens sink and add to the deposits forming on the bottom of the neighbouring ocean. With them are the bones of fish, shells and the hard parts of other marine organisms. At some future age, when these deposits are consolidated into formations of rock, the ice-borne boulders will be found in shales containing the fossil remains of the animals that now live in these seas. Such boulders or erratics are found in many parts of the world where ice does not now exist. Even in New South Wales, in the Maitland district and elsewhere, large ice-worn masses of granite occur embedded in shale, in which are shells, starfish and other organisms that lived hundreds of millions of years ago, in a period when glaciers poured down from the neighbouring mountains into the sea.

Near our hut there was evidence that the ice-sheet had receded slightly. At one time it must have passed completely over this rocky peninsula. The rock itself was scored and grooved, gouged out in hollows, and sometimes highly polished as if a giant lapidary had been at work.

The moraines themselves gave an epitome of the geological formations for probably hundreds of miles to the south. All the rocks belonged, evidently, to a very ancient period or periods, right at the dawn of the world's geological history. They were similar to many found in South Australia, the Monaro Tableland and some other localities, and quite probably were of Cambrian or Pre-Cambrian age.

Laid down in the waters of seas that existed countless ages ago, at this time life had just dawned on the surface of the world. Fossils have been found in various places in these very old rocks, corals and sponges for the most part, but here no trace of life remains. The stresses and changes to which they have been subjected have long since destroyed the traces of any organisms that were embedded. The rocks have been buried vast distances beneath the earth's surface, exposed to enormous heat and pressure, thrown into great folds or shattered completely, elevated into mountains, and worn down again by wind, rain, frost and ice. They have been penetrated by huge intrusions of molten rock, partially fused and recrystallised, and altered almost beyond recognition.

Here are sandstones converted to solid quartz, limestones that have been crystallised into marble, and soft mud that has changed to slate and schist. Among them is a great variety of minerals, also traces of the ores of copper, lead, zinc, antimony and other metals. It is quite possible that mineral deposits of great richness exist, buried deeply under the ice-sheet that covers all the land, but removed far from any possibility of human exploitation until, perhaps, in some remote future age, when the ice will have melted, and the Antarctic continent emerges from its long sleep.

But to return to midwinter's day. It might truly be said, for reasons that will be presently shown, that this was Dad McLean's day. Out of sheer affection it is probable that Dad received more chaff than any other member of the expedition. He had taken his medical degree just prior to leaving Sydney, and the first flush of enthusiasm for his work had not been dulled by the exacting routine of general practice. He was extraordinarily keen about all he did, and his enthusiasm led him not only to attempt everything, but at times to rush things without considering minor details. He was game to the core, and a badly broken nose, incurred before the inception of the expedition, testified to this. Hunter, who was a contemporary of his at the Sydney University, told me the tale. This tendency to try everything once led Dad to enter for the lightweight championship of the University, in which he was up against a clever, strong fighter, trained to the hair. Before the second round was over, and when the referee mercifully stopped the contest, Dad was out on his feet, his nose broken, both eyes closed, but instinctively still full of fight.

In the hut he had a happy knack of making absurd little mistakes, which were a source of continual delight. He would make bread without baking powder, mix self-raising flour for glaxo. On one occasion he had made some barley broth and called me over to express an opinion. It looked very well, but I asked him if he had washed the barley. He looked astonished and asked if it was necessary. In reply I put a little uncooked barley into a basin and poured some water upon it, when quite a number of nice fat weevils and grubs floated to the surface. However, I kept his secret for the time, and everybody enjoyed the broth very much. This was but one of his many 'championships', none serious, but invariably of the sort to create amusement.

We were all so fond of Dad that opportunities to laugh at him were seized on with double avidity. Yet in all the things that mattered he was one of the best, always to be depended on, kindly, generous, brave, and white all through.

When the Great War came, Dad was in England, and lost no time in offering his services to the Empire. As a medico he was attached to a Scottish Regiment, and I met him in London after we had both come out of hospital. His health had broken down after very strenuous service in France, and he was invalided to Australia, only to rejoin an Australian unit before he was properly fit. In France again, he did splendid work and was awarded the Military Cross for continually attending wounded under heavy fire. It is easy to picture Dad carrying on day after day, long after his physical powers had called a halt. Again, from those who were with him come tales of his unfailing cheerfulness, unselfishness and devotion to duty. Like Dr Wilson, of the Scott expedition, he had that power of winning the affection of others, and of passing on some of his own cheery personality and courage to those weaker than himself. When he ultimately returned to Australia he brought a weakened constitution in which already the deadly germs of TB had obtained a footing.

Even when he realised the end was near, he never lost his cheerfulness, and to those of us who visited him in hospital, his bright

'Hello, Dad', the invariable greeting which got him his nickname, never suggested that he knew his days were few. He spent this last period of his life in endless experiments, some painful, on himself, hoping thereby to throw some light on his ailment that might help others similarly stricken to recover.

Here's to your memory, Dad. To have known you is enough to have made life worthwhile, and your influence is still an all-sufficient denial to the pessimist who insists on the inevitable selfishness of mankind.

Our dinner that night was a special one, with an elaborate menu, followed by all sorts of extras, including wine and cigars. After the usual loyal and other toasts, the Doctor rose to his feet. His speech, as nearly as I can reproduce it, was as follows:

'Gentlemen, scientists and near-scientists of the Australasian Antarctic Expedition.

'It is not often that when so many distinguished people are gathered together one can, by universal consent, be chosen to receive the homage of the others. Yet in this case there is one amongst us whose feats transcend anything that has ever been done before. His achievements are such as to evoke not only astonishment, but to enrol him for ever amongst the great. For this reason, a very pleasing duty has been imposed upon me, and all his comrades have asked me, on their behalf, to present him with a medal and an illuminated address, to express their admiration of his deeds. I trust that when in future he wears this medal on great occasions he will remember the days he spent in Adélie Land, and also the appreciation in which he was held. I will now call on Dr Archibald McLean to come forward.'

Throughout the speech Dad had listened with great interest, wondering what it was all about. He was the only one not in the secret, and his face was a picture when he heard his name pronounced. Amid loud cries of 'Come on, Dad,' he was at length persuaded to rise and receive his decoration. This was a work of art in itself. Needless to say, Hurley was the originator of the scheme, but Bage and others had helped in the fashioning of the medal. It was made of aluminium in the form of a penguin, and was attached to the ribbon upside down, or, as stated in the heraldic language on the illuminated address, 'Penguin invertant'. The reason for this position was due to the fact that Dad kept careful records of such things as the blood pressure of the fellows, as well as the temperatures of birds and seals. When he wished to take the temperature of a penguin it was always held upside down for the purpose. Attached to the medal was a ribbon about 18 inches long, on which were numerous bars of aluminium, each recording one of his 'championships'.

As soon as the first shock was over, Dad appreciated the joke as much as anybody, and made quite a good response. He afterwards treasured the medal greatly as a souvenir, but it was, I believe, unfortunately lost on the journey home. The presentation over, we had a hilarious evening, and with Stillwell at the organ, sang choruses of everything we knew – and some things we didn't.

Everyone in turn provided amusement for the rest, often without intention. One of my own best exploits happened on a day when I was cook. It had been somebody's birthday, and the occasion warranted, as always, a special feast, with wine and cigars to follow. In those days, beyond an occasional cigarette, I was practically a non-smoker but, carried away by the festive occasion, I sampled one of the cigars, and, to make matters worse, attempted to emulate Hurley and others in blowing smoke-rings. When halfway through, I began to have doubts about the wisdom of such a proceeding. Unobserved, I thought, I slipped out to the outer veranda to relieve my troubled feelings. The cold air, however, acted as a deterrent, so after a few minutes I returned to the hut, only to again experience the same symptoms. Again I surreptitiously slipped out, with the same result; in fact it took four such journeys before success and some relief came. Returning for the last time, but feeling as if the world had come to an end, I prepared to face the agonising prospect of a long wash-up. It was then good old Badget came to my rescue.

'Go on, Joe,' he said, 'you get off to bed. We'll do the washing-up.'

Heedless of good-natured but tactless remarks I crept off, for the moment, at least, beyond the reach of any chaff, but it was a long time before I lived down this incident, and longer still before I was game enough to experiment with a cigar again.

These incidents, told in after years, seem trivial, but at the time they loomed big in our annals. In the journalistic sense they were 'news', and news became very valuable as the winter wore on. With outdoor activities so circumscribed, more and more of our time was spent within the hut, yet at the same time scope for scientific work became more limited. Our activities were now chiefly in the direction of preparing for sledging in the summer. This was a very big job, which will be dealt with in due course. But any break in the routine was welcomed as a gift from the gods. Thus, the birth of a pup to Ginger was hailed as an event. Incidentally, this pup, named Blizzard, thrived wonderfully, and became a great pet. For the latter part of the winter the story of the expedition is made up of such items.

For instance, the wind average was always a source of conversation and speculation. At the end of each month a Calcutta sweep was held on the result, and the drawing of the numbers and the auction took place on the morning before the final day's reading, so that no one would have an unfair advantage. Madigan, as the man on the inside, presided and acted as auctioneer. Currency was in squares of chocolate, thirty squares to a cake, and each cake a week's ration. Bidding was fast and furious, and several, whose financial resources were strained, combined to buy in favourite numbers. The first sweep was disastrous to Dad, who in his excitement bid several times against himself, and speculated far above his means, but all to no purpose, for he lost the lot. Unable to pay his debts, he was declared bankrupt, and a further auction held of some of his effects, including candles (precious to those who wished to read in their bunks), matches and tobacco. It is pleasant to record that he paid thirty squares in the cake, and even showed a surplus.

We often read aloud after dinner, various members taking it in turns. Anything that appealed to one would be submitted to the general opinion, but a few books were read right through. *The Trail of '98* was one, and provoked lengthy discussions on the actions of the main characters. W.W. Jacobs was a strong favourite, and was generally entrusted to Herbert Murphy, to whose style the doings and sayings of the nightwatchman were eminently suitable. We had quite a good library. C.D. Mackellar, one of the London sponsors of the expedition, and after whom the islands off our base were named, had presented some hundreds of volumes which were divided among the bases.

These included histories of many other expeditions, north and south, and it was very interesting reading them under comparable conditions.

We did not neglect the lighter side. Hurley, our comedian, always had some stunt going, and went to extraordinary trouble in the preparation of his jokes. For these, Hunter and I acted as his chief assistants, and quite early the three of us had been designated 'The Sydney Its'. One night Hurley and I dressed up as an Aboriginal man and woman, and came out of the limited space of the darkroom just as the others sat down for dinner. We had a number of gags prepared for the occasion, and Hurley made quite a hit, while I did my not-very-good-best to act as his foil. This made us more ambitious, and we formed the 'Its Society for the Prevention of the Blues', the ultimate achievement of which was no less than the production of a grand opera. Though this did not take place until the main winter months had passed, it was the culminating point of our activities and well deserves a mention in this chapter. It necessitated also an increase in our cast, and Dad, Correll and the pup, Blizzard, were roped in. Frank Stillwell became the orchestra, and Bickerton acted as chief dresser, with a self-appointed roving character as the Village Idiot. The opera chosen for the star performance was a new one, which as yet had never been given in any of the world's great centres. This was *The Washerwoman's Secret* (Laseron), a tragedy in five acts, with a complicated and highly dramatic plot. The songs were written by the various members of the cast and memorised. Of course, there could be no rehearsals, so all conversations had, perforce, to be impromptu. For weeks we prepared for the great event, gathering in little knots to discuss details. These mysterious conferences, of course, caused much curiosity on the part of those not in the know, and to allay this we openly prepared and gave a small performance on the eve of the great event. It was not until *der Tag* itself that a poster, now duly censored, was exhibited, announcing the opera and the following characters:

> Dr Stakanhoiser ... Hoyle
>
> Chevalier de Tintail ... Johnnie
>
> Baron de Bent ... Joe
>
> Count Spithoopenkoff ... Little Willie Smith

ANTARCTIC EYEWITNESS: South With Mawson

Madam Fuclose ... also Joe

Dr Stakanhoiser's dog ... Blizzard

Village Idiot ... Bick

Orchestra ... Stillwater Willie

and

JEMIMA FUCLOSE ... Dad

There was much ribald comment by the public, but when doors were open early there were no absentees. The audience, not much larger than the company, took up positions of advantage and prepared to jeer. The stage was the kitchen, and the question of scenery was solved by various notices – 'This is a Door', 'This is a Drawing-room', and so on – the notices being taken down and replaced as the scene demanded. Everything went like clockwork. Bick had rigged Dad up as the heroine, with towels and other gadgets, and, with his face shaved and a plentiful supply of red watercolour from Alfie's paintbox, the leading lady looked not only beautiful but bad. Hurley provided the comic relief, and his flow of impromptu patter had a touch of genius. One scene, however, nearly ruined the production, yet it was one of the hits of the evening. Dr Stakanhoiser operated on Madam Fuclose, who in dying disclosed the secret of her daughter's birth. The doctor, with hammers, saws and other surgical instruments, got to work while his victim, for safety's sake, had placed an iron plate over her vitals, hidden, of course, from the audience. All went well until an extra hard blow of the hammer missed the plate, causing the patient to sit up and use language entirely unfitted to a dying woman. It was some minutes before the scene could be continued, much to the delight of the audience. However, from then on there was no hitch, and from eight till nearly eleven o'clock we all kept going until, both villains dead after the duet 'Mort de Botheo', the hero and heroine happily reunited and, Dr Stakanhoiser giving his blessing, the curtain descended or at least an announcement was made that it was all over. The general opinion was, moreover, that it was a great success.

Individual birthdays were outstanding events, and were seized upon as occasions for celebration, special dinners and presentations. When birthdays failed to materialise within adequate periods, other

80

anniversaries were sought and once, for want of better, we kept up the anniversary of the lighting of London by gas.

On birthdays the cook's song, if possible, generally referred to the guest of the day. For instance, on the occasion of Mertz's birthday, the first verse of the poet's effort might be considered typical. Here it is – the tune was 'Old Farmer John':

DER MAN FROM SVITZERLAND

From Svitzerland a man dere came
Und Xavier his name vos.
Avay down south to go he has
Der reason is becos
He's far too fond of all ze gals.
Und zey luf him, you know,
For ven he say may I come mit,
Zey smile und say, 'Vat Ho!'
Oh donnerwetter, strike me pink, his pot is on ze fire,
He say, 'Vill you?' She say, 'Please do,'
Und smile at him so nice,
He lose his head, say, 'Ve vill ved,'
She fall upon his necks,
Now who dats run avay like dis?
Sapristi! Sapristi! vy 'tis our old friend X.

Even Mertz himself became infected with the popular craze of songwriting. His opportunity came on 1 August, which was Swiss Confederation Day. This, of course, made a day of celebration, with Mertz as cook and the man of the hour. From a mysterious box, which he had saved for the occasion, he produced all sorts of wonderful luxuries, tins of strange preserves and dishes we had never heard of, but which added welcome novelty to our diet. His song, in a way, was a masterpiece, in spite of the fact that his English was still rather limited. He had picked up a great deal since we had first known him, including much Australian idiom, which often came out in unexpected places. I give four verses from the original eight:

BASILISK
(Tune: Zwebery-Om-Pom-Pom)

1

I'm Basilisk, the king of the dogs,
Zwebery-Om-Pom-Pom.
With plenty of swank through life I jogs,
Zwebery-Om-Pom-Pom.
Ginger Bitch is my lawful treasure,
But with all the others I have big pleasure.
Zwebery-Om-Pom-Pom-Pom-Pom, Zwebery-Om-Pom-Pom.

2

Last night I watched old Close come out,
Zwebery-Om-Pom-Pom.
He didn't know what he was about,
Zwebery-Om-Pom-Pom.
He was fifty minutes at the screen,
The funniest thing I ever was seen.
Zwebery-Om-Pom-Pom-Pom-Pom, Zwebery-Om-Pom-Pom.

3

Now Ninnis thinks he's just the thing,
Zwebery-Om-Pom-Pom.
At cracking whips, but no such thing,
Zwebery-Om-Pom-Pom.
For every time he makes a shot,
He gets himself tied in a knot.
Zwebery-Om-Pom-Pom-Pom-Pom, Zwebery-Om-Pom-Pom.

4

The eighteen mens I don't trouble about,
Zwebery-Om-Pom-Pom.
For the stores I'm easily in and out.
Zwebery-Om-Pom-Pom.
I pumped ship against the bacon today,
These little things make life quite gay.
Zwebery-Om-Pom-Pom-Pom-Pom, Zwebery-Om-Pom-Pom.

The Passing of Winter

Thus June, July, and August 1912 passed. As the first rounding of the Horn is to the sailor, so a winter in the ice is to the polar explorer. It puts the hallmark on his experience. Having successfully emerged from the embryonic stage, he is now fully fledged and can take his place in the select fraternity.

CHAPTER 8

PREPARATIONS FOR SLEDGING

Me thought I hung a-dangling
Upon a slender rope,
The azure depths beneath me,
Above my only hope.
'Twas then that I remembered,
Through moments ages long,
When I had sewed my canvas belt,
I had made the stitches strong.

It was obvious from the very beginning that Adélie Land was not going to yield its geographical secrets without a bitter struggle. Naturally we were all keenly curious as to what lay beyond our immediate surroundings. To the east and west our initial exploration was limited to the small area of rock on which our hut was built. Beyond this the ice presented an impassable barrier. Bordering the sea, the ice above the cliffs was too dangerous to traverse. The slopes were very steep and the surface, moreover, shattered into a maze of crevasses. The only way into the interior was immediately to the south of the hut. This was steep, but uncrevassed in its lower part, with a grade becoming easier as one ascended. The limit of our view from the hut was a skyline of ice, about half a mile to the south and some hundreds of feet above sea-level.

The nature of the surface beyond was very important to the success of the expedition, and steps were taken soon after landing to investigate the problem. The first attempt was on 29 February 1912, when Dr Mawson, taking with him Bage and Madigan, hauled a sledge 3 miles up the slope. The wind was so severe, however, that after anchoring the sledge they returned to the hut. On the following day they set out again, and reached a point 5.5 miles from the hut, where they camped the night. This locality, as a depot, was destined to be very important in all later sledging journeys. The following morning, having anchored the sledge, they returned to the hut in a blizzard, and it was not until five months later that this point was again attained and the sledge recovered.

Even this short experience was invaluable, and as the nature of the climate became more and more apparent it was evident that if sledging was to be done at all, it would probably be done under exceptionally severe conditions. This necessitated that all preparations should be made with the utmost care, for not only the comfort but the lives of the sledgers might well depend on some small detail of equipment that foresight had provided.

A sledging outfit for a party can be classified into several sections: clothing; transport, that is, the sledge itself; housing, which includes the tent and sleeping-bags; food, under which heading would come cooking equipment; scientific equipment, such as sledge-meter, theodolite, navigating instruments and others, depending on the particular objects of the journey; and sundries, such as spade, alpine rope and ice-axe. Weight was of vital importance. Every ounce of gear that lessened the amount of food that could be dragged, lessened the scope of the party. Except for those who could reach the points on the coast where penguins or seals might be found, there could be no living on the country, and there was no timber for fuel or repairs. In short, the parties would be dependent for their lives on what they carried with them.

Consequently every detail was exhaustively examined, and any suggestion that would lessen weight or make for efficiency was keenly tested and, if suitable, adopted. For instance, in the matter of clothes, toggles were used instead of buttons, for they were not only more secure, but much easier to fasten in a very cold temperature. For this latter reason also, all sorts of ingenious methods were adopted to economise in the way of fastenings. In a high wind, with a temperature below zero, the buckling of a single strap became an arduous and lengthy process, likely to result in frostbitten fingers, and nothing is more painful.

A very important item was the tents, and these were carefully overhauled. They were conical, mostly of stout japara, with a flap that spread outwards on the ground, and on which ice, food bags and other pieces of gear were piled to keep the whole secure. The pitch was low so that wind pressure was down rather than up, preventing the tent being blown away. Entrance was by a short tunnel-like arrangement, which could be gathered and securely tied on the inside. The supports consisted of five stout bamboo poles, hinged into a top metal centrepiece. It was intended that these should be erected first and the tent lifted over the top, but this was found impracticable in any wind, so strips of canvas were sewn in position in the inside of the tent and the poles securely sewn into these, so that the whole tent was in one piece. Even then, considerable practice was necessary, and the united efforts of three men were required to erect the tent in a stiff gale. To this end, we all, at one time or another, made the attempt outside the hut, and thus acquired the necessary technique. This was as follows: first, enough large blocks of ice or hard snow were cut and placed handy; then the tent was laid down with the apex upwind and the entrance on top, so that it would be in the lee when the tent was raised; next, one man crawled inside and, with the other two hanging on, the tent was lifted and the man inside spread the three windward legs, one directly upwind, the others far enough apart to keep the material taut and at the same time give sufficient room for the leeward legs to fall into position. This required a considerable knack as the whole time the wind would be tearing at the structure, and it took the united strength of all hands to prevent it being blown away. If the legs were too close, not only did the material flap annoyingly, but it was likely to be torn and the space inside would become uncomfortably restricted. Once up it was found difficult to readjust the position of the legs, and if this was unsatisfactory the only thing was to do the whole job over again. The ballast was now piled on the outside flaps, and a canvas tent floor, which could alternatively be used as a sail for the sledge, was laid down, and all was ready for occupancy.

The sleeping-bags were those that we had used in the early days before the hut was built. There were a couple of three-man bags, designed for warmth, but the single-man bags were generally preferred as giving some measure of privacy. They were made of reindeer skin with the hair on the inside. A slit allowed the insertion of the body and once in, the entire body including the head was completely enclosed, the opening being fastened from the inside. If the sleeper required air, he parted the opening near his face, but generally speaking, if it was very cold, more than sufficient seemed to sneak in for such minor things as breathing.

Food was the next consideration, and here the object was to get the maximum nutriment with the minimum of weight. The details of the rations had been worked out before the expedition left London, and such things as proteins, fats, sugars and calories duly considered – sufficient to say that 34 ounces constituted the allowance of food for one man for a day. The various items were sorted out and weighed into bags, and these in turn placed in a larger bag, which contained rations for three men for either seven or fourteen days. This simplified things greatly; any party setting out would take as many bags as required, knowing that they had sufficient food for a given period.

The main item on the menu was hoosh – hot, thick, and satisfying. The chief ingredient of this was pemmican, specially dried best beef, with the addition of 50 per cent of pure fat. Ground plasmon biscuit was added to this, and the whole, when water was added, made a sort of thick, porridge-like soup. This was cooked over a primus in a Nansen cooker made of aluminium. The cooker would be filled with ice, and when the central compartment boiled, the ice in the outer space would be thawed, thus saving fuel. The hoosh would then be made and served in mugs, and eaten while the cooker reboiled. Then came the next course, cocoa – *real* cocoa. One part of cocoa, two of sugar, four of glaxo made the mixture, and of this one mug made three mugs of beverage that sent the blood tingling into the fingers and toes. Thus were the morning and evening meals; for lunch the ration was butter, chocolate, tea and plasmon biscuit, the latter so hard that it had to be broken with an ice-axe. Still it was very satisfying, and if the weather was good it was pleasant to nibble alternately at a piece of frozen butter, chocolate and biscuit, and sip between whiles from a hot mug of tea.

The sledges themselves were made of best American ash, in addition to some made in Sydney from spotted gum and Australian mountain ash. The last-named were rather inclined to split, while those of spotted gum were very strong, but rather heavy. At the front of the sledge was the instrument box made of three-ply, and at the rear another to house the primus and cooker, which were carefully fitted so that a capsize would not damage them. Kerosene for the primus was strapped to the back of the cooker box in small tins, each sufficient for a week's cooking. All the other gear – tent, sleeping-bags, food bags and spare clothing – was packed on the sledge and strapped into place, and care had to be taken to see that the load was properly adjusted and secure.

On all the sledging journeys except one, the sledges were man-hauled. The two teams of dogs were taken by Mawson himself on his far-eastern journey, and with them it was possible to travel much faster, that is, provided conditions were good. On the other hand, in bad weather and on very rough surfaces, dogs are not an unmixed blessing, as their care imposes quite a lot of labour on the men. For the purpose of man-hauling, each man made his own harness of stout canvas, fitting it comfortably, and made sure that all the fastenings were strong. His life might well depend on this, for in the heavy crevassed areas adjoining the coast, any moment might see him dangling in his harness in a bottomless abyss, his fate depending on the security of his sewing and the rope attached to the sledge above.

All these preparations took time and throughout the whole winter everyone was engaged, between his other duties, in making ready. Food had to be ground, chopped, mixed and weighed, tents strengthened, endless small bags sewn, sledge harnesses made, sledges fitted, and so on. Nevertheless, everything was ready long before the weather allowed us to make a start.

Yet some attempts were made to break away, at least partly, from our winter confinement. As early as 29 July, Mertz and Ninnis took advantage of a temporary lull in the wind to get several loads of foodstuff up the first steep slope of the plateau.

Then on 9 August 1912, Mawson, Madigan and Ninnis set off with both dog-teams, only to find that at a height of about 1000 feet even the temporary calms we sometimes had at the hut ceased to exist, and that the wind never stopped at all, but blew with an intensity that seemed impossible. Nevertheless they camped 3.5 miles from the hut, and the following day reached the sledge that had been abandoned 5.5 miles inland five months before. They found it secure, but much worn and weathered by the continual bombardment of drift snow. Here they found it impossible to go on, so spent two days in excavating an underground cave in the ice in which they were quite comfortable and protected from the wind. This they called 'Aladdin's Cave', and later it became the starting point for all the sledging parties that left the hut.

A shelter was also dug for the dogs who snuggled down and seemed quite comfortable in the low temperatures. The party spent two more days in the cave and then, the weather moderating slightly, pushed a further 2.5 miles to the south; but weather conditions were again so appalling that they returned to the cave, where they spent a further two days, going out each day to feed the dogs. On the 15th, in a heavy wind, they set out for the hut, freeing the dogs, who followed for a while, then disappeared. When they arrived at the hut the dogs had not put in an appearance, and it was concluded that they had returned to Aladdin's Cave. Several attempts were made during the following days to rescue them, but it was not until the 21st, six days later, that Bage, Hurley and Mertz managed to ascend in the teeth of the wind and reach the cave. Sure enough here were all the dogs, huddled together for warmth and, with the exception of Basilisk and Pavlova, all frozen to the ice. They were very weak – too weak to bring back immediately – so perforce were taken into the cave with the three men, where they were given hot food.

In these cramped quarters the whole party stayed for four days, dogs and all, a most uncomfortable time; but at last another slight lull allowed their return to the hut. All of the dogs recovered except one, Grandmother, who was so weak that she had to be brought back on the sledge. But in spite of all efforts she died four hours later.

So we came to the beginning of September, when our knowledge of Adélie Land extended to 8 miles to the south. This was little enough, it is true, but the results were highly important, inasmuch as it was proved that here was a highway, with a good surface and free of crevasses, up which all future sledging parties could find a way.

All preparations were now complete and, given even moderate weather, exploration farther afield could begin in earnest.

CHAPTER 9

FOUR CALM DAYS

There comes an interlude. Forgotten then
The long grey months which lie behind.
It is enough, though grey days come again,
Contentment in the hour to find.

At the beginning of September 1912 a miracle happened and we had four calm days – really calm days, with the sun shining brightly, and the temperature steadily rising until it attained no less than 18°F. Not a soul remained in the hut except the unfortunate cook and messman, and these two, at every available opportunity, stole outside to bask in the warm sunshine. It was almost an inconceivable joy, after six months of continual hurricane and blizzard, to wander about in comfort. Burberries were dispensed with, mittens were no longer necessary, and balaclavas were rolled up to leave the ears bare. Where were the hardships of the polar regions? Given weather like this an expedition would be little more than a picnic on a large scale.

At first it seemed too good to last, and for the first day the eye continually searched the south for the rolling clouds of drift snow that would herald the return of the blizzard. Yet all that day the calm, warm sunshine continued, and when the sun had disappeared in the evening there was a new atmosphere in the hut. No longer was it a question of trying to make the best of a bad job. Everyone bubbled over with good spirits, jokes and chaff were bandied about with double freedom, and the Doctor wandered about beaming benevolently on all.

Almost with the cessation of the wind, the sea began to freeze. Beautiful crystals or ice flowers formed on the surface, then round pancakes of ice, growing and growing until their edges met, and a continuous white sheet stretched to the far horizon.

Four Calm Days

This day Mertz, Ninnis, Whetter and I took a team of dogs and a large load of foodstuffs up to Aladdin's Cave. Though the dogs did most of the hauling, the 5 miles' climb seemed a long way after the enforced lack of exercise for many months. It was my first glimpse of the real plateau, though on occasions I had been over the first steep slope. The surface was of hard glacier ice, and always upwards, though the grade became easier as we progressed, with patches of hard snow carved by the wind into knife-edge ridges called 'sastrugi'. Small cracks or crevasses began to appear, but only a few inches to a foot across, and presenting neither difficulty nor danger.

As we ascended the hut soon disappeared, then the outlying points of our little province, and finally the Mackellar Islands. We were now on the plateau proper. To the north, beyond the even horizon, the distant sea appeared, a few white dots marking the presence of far-off icebergs. In every other direction was a desolate, unbroken plain of white, rising almost imperceptibly to the south. There were no hills, no rocks, nothing to break the endless monotony and utter lifelessness, and in the absence of wind no sound save the grating of the sledge runners and the panting of the dogs. Presently, far ahead, a few black objects appeared, then a flagpole emerging above a mound of snow. Even in this short distance it was a welcome relief to the eyes, a veritable oasis in a desert of ice. The black objects resolved themselves into bags of food, to which presently we added our own load. Then we examined Aladdin's Cave. In excavating this a trench had first been dug sloping downwards into the ice, then a square chamber, about 6 feet long by 6 wide and 5 high, had been opened out. The entrance had become choked by fresh snow, but this was soon shovelled out, and we spent an hour underground enlarging the cave somewhat. Then, after a meal, we prepared to descend.

At first the dogs were allowed to run loose, but by some curious perversion of reasoning, instead of following they at once returned to the cave, so they had all to be tethered and led back to the hut. This habit was very annoying, and soon after our return two were again missing. On the next trip to Aladdin's Cave one was seen, but returned of his own volition to the hut. The other was never found, and probably fell down a crevasse somewhere on the plateau.

The belated freezing of the sea now awakened long-abandoned hopes of dredging. Even on this first day of calm an attempt was made, and a party ventured onto newly formed floe. It was very thin and dangerous, and they had not proceeded far when Dr Mawson went through, and got a very unpleasant wetting. At the same time Hurley, obtaining photographs by himself, had a similar experience, which might have been very serious as without aid he had great difficulty in extricating himself and his camera from the water.

During the second day the ice was still too dangerous; but on the third, in spite of the hot sun, it had thickened to about 4 inches and was strong enough to bear the weight of a man. This was the opportunity we had long awaited. With all our gear loaded on a sledge, Hunter and I set out, only to find that the sticky surface made it almost impossible to drag the sledge. It was then that a small collapsible metal cart, carried almost as an afterthought, came in handy, and soon we were proceeding at a good pace over the surface of the ice. It was tricky work nevertheless, as occasional lanes of water and thin patches of ice were apt to let not only the cart through, but ourselves also. Often we were forced to take the bad parts at a run, and had some anxious moments as the ice bent underfoot, or even a wheel or a foot went through.

About a mile off land we stopped and made our first haul. To do this we took advantage of any thin lanes of water, and, after lowering the dredge, cleared a way for the rope, to the distance of about 300 yards. We now hauled the dredge in, and great was our excitement as it came to the surface. Alas! This first haul in some 25 fathoms of water was fruitless, for the dredge had become entangled with the rope, and had dragged along the bottom mouth up. However, all the day was ours, so down it went again. This time our labour was rewarded, and by the weight as we hauled it up we knew we had got something. And something we had got, for as the dredge cleared the surface, we saw it full and overflowing with every form of sea life it is possible to imagine.

Our joy, as we emptied the contents into our tub, was extreme, and worth all the weary months of waiting and hope deferred. In this one haul alone we had procured a veritable zoological collection.

Here were sponges, sea-urchins and starfish galore. Strange shells were tangled with the seaweed, and beautiful little lace corals encrusted its strands. Curiously shaped worms wriggled in and out of the mass, while red and green shrimps and other crustacea crawled over everything. And most conspicuous of all were the giant sea-spiders, red in colour, and from 6 to 7 inches across the legs. These curious sea animals deserve a word to themselves. Actually they belong to a special order of their own, termed the Pycnogonids, quite removed from the usual crustacea such as crabs and shrimps, but more akin to the true land spiders. They are found all over the world, several small species occurring in Australian waters, but the size and colour of the Adélie Land specimens were exceptional. This haul was but the first of many and soon, our tub full, we were on our way back to the hut. From now on, dredging was the order of the day; and leaving Johnnie to start the sorting, another party of us set out to procure further specimens, with equal success. That night was a busy one, for we had innumerable specimens to sort, bottle and preserve. Right through the night we worked, concentrating on the more fragile and delicate forms, which required immediate treatment to prevent their disintegration.

Morning came and found us again out on the sea-ice, now becoming rather rotten in the hot sun. This was the fourth day of the calm, and it seemed as if the weather had broken at last and that summer had come. Meals did not matter under the circumstances, and it was after 2 p.m. when, our tub full again, we returned to the hut. At three o'clock that afternoon, Bickerton, Madigan, and Correll set out again on what was destined to be the last attempt at dredging during our stay, and what, in fact, proved very nearly to be the last act in their lives.

We could see them as three tiny specks a long way from the shore, too far to see any details of what they were doing. Suddenly somebody called attention to the far-western slopes of Common-wealth Bay, down which rolled ominous clouds of white. High above us, also, fleecy white wisps scurried to the north. A breath of icy air brushed us as it passed.

No time was to be lost, and three shots from the rifle echoed a warning note to those on the ice. But they had seen the danger and already, as fast as they could, were making for the land. It was literally a race with death. Already a breeze was blowing, and an odd gust of greater violence caused the frozen sea to stir ominously. Nearer and nearer they came, and harder and harder blew the wind. In a group we all stood on the solid ice of the boat harbour, and anxiously watched their progress. Slight cracks were already beginning to open in the floe, and it seemed as if they would never make that last 100 yards. Now they were 50 yards away, now 20, then willing hands reached out to pull the cart across the fast-opening gap between the sea-ice and the shore.

It was a narrow escape – so narrow that at the time we hardly realised it. As the party reached safety, the wind was at gale force and rising every minute. Within a few minutes a lane of open water many yards wide fringed the shore; within twenty, what had been a smooth expanse of white was a storm-racked inferno of driving spray. Not a vestige of ice was in sight.

That night and through the days that followed, the blizzard howled with renewed vigour, as if to make up for the brief respite it had given us from its fury.

CHAPTER 10

THE COMING OF THE PENGUINS

We have travelled afar for nearly a year
  By the bergs and the drifting pack;
But a message is born on a gale from the land,
  And the mating call hurries us back.

Back from the cool green depths of the seas,
  Back from the edge of the floe,
Where we rested awhile with never a thought
  Of the killer-whale waiting below.

We have gambolled and flashed through the curling waves,
  Through the drift and the driving spray,
To the ice-bound rock we call our home
  In the land of the nightless day.

If I have not yet spoken much of these quaint denizens of the Antarctic, it is because our acquaintance with their habits was started at the wrong end. That is to say, when we first arrived in Adélie Land it was at the end of the nesting season. All the young were not only hatched but nearly mature, and almost ready to embark on their voyaging to the ice-pack and the waters of the north, where they would spend the winter, only to return to their rookeries on the coast when the breeding season came again in the following spring.

This is the habit of the Adélie penguin; the emperor, on the other hand, chooses the depths of winter in the coldest parts attainable to rear its young. We saw few of the latter, however, beyond some stray visitors that apparently came ashore on a visit of curiosity. Very few rookeries of the emperor are recorded; one is at Cape Crozier in the Ross Sea area and another was found by our second base far to the west. What little is known of their nesting habits was discovered by Dr Wilson of the Scott expedition, who made a most hazardous sledging journey to the Cape Crozier rookery in the depth of a midwinter night.

Our dealings were mostly with the Adélie penguin, many of whose rookeries were in the vicinity of the hut. He is the commonest of all Antarctic penguins, a quaint little chap about 18 inches high, with a jet-black, glossy coat and snow-white waistcoat. As he stands bolt upright his feet just show below the lower feathers and, with his strong little flippers held rigidly to his side, he looks a trim, plump, little gentleman, very conscious of his dignity and social position. Generally speaking, he showed neither curiosity nor fear, and ignored our presence altogether, taking us, no doubt, for emperors or some larger penguins. A mitten thrown into a group would, however, attract momentary attention, and the birds would gather round it and, bending their heads, peer at it closely, maybe to peck it gently with their beaks, then, satisfied that it had no particular interest, take no further notice. It seems that they are somewhat short-sighted on land. When moving about they walked slowly, but when they desired to hurry leaped from rock to rock with surprising agility, or attained real speed by falling forwards and using their bodies as toboggans, propelling themselves with their legs. In this way they could progress just about as fast as a man could run.

Our first penguin hopped out of the water on 12 October, in spite of the fact that the wind was blowing at 70 miles an hour. Dad found him and brought him in triumph to the hut. We hailed him, like the swallow, as the harbinger of spring. The following day was one of the worst of the year, an average wind of 70 miles an hour, irregular, with terrific gusts that attained upwards of 250 miles an hour. In spite of this, more birds arrived, and continued to come ashore in a steady stream. One bird that Frank Stillwell brought in was an albino, a little smaller than the others, with a pale grey coat instead of the usual black. This variety was at once turned into a 'specimen'.

At every opportunity we went out to watch them, and it was fascinating to note the unerring judgment with which they made their final leap. At this time of the year the sea was bordered by an ice-foot, formed of the consolidated snows of the winter, overhanging the rocks beneath, and often presenting a vertical face 5 or 6 feet above sea-level. As a group of penguins approached the shore they would pause some 20 yards off, raise their heads and estimate the distance. Then they would dive and swim under the water with incredible speed, a moment later shooting into the air with their flippers spread out to balance, to land neatly on their feet. Occasionally they erred in their choice of a landing-place; for instance, when, in the early days, stores were being unloaded from the whaleboat, one landed on the tail of Dad, who was stooping to lift a case. This sort of thing always happened to Dad. It was hard to say who was the most astonished but, with a squawk of dismay, the bird scrambled to the side and went overboard again. The wireless masts that were being towed ashore were also a source of deception and several times penguins attempted to land upon them, only to splash into the water on the opposite side.

All these first arrivals seemed to be males. The females did not arrive until their hubbies had set up house. The wealth of a householder lay in the number of stones he possessed, and nearly every bird that landed carried in his beak one that he had procured from the bottom of the sea. Having chosen his site in the rookeries, he carefully arranged his stone or stones about him, and sat down to await the arrival of his mate. Whether the same pair mated for more than one year we could not find out; certainly there seemed some competition to acquire the females as they arrived, and these would often inspect several nests before they made their choice. In any case there would be many bachelors and maidens who had not yet embarked on the sea of matrimony, besides widows and widowers whose spouses had met untimely ends at the jaws of sea-leopards and killer-whales.

The female having chosen her mate, the pair showed their affection by falling into ecstatic attitudes. With their breasts almost touching, they would stand facing each other for hours, their beaks elevated vertically into the air, the whole body perfectly rigid. It looked very uncomfortable and ludicrous, and beyond meditation and communion of souls, seemed to have no particular object. Often when so standing, they did Sandow exercises with their flippers.

In the rookeries the nests were often only a foot or two apart, and continual squabbles seemed to take place between neighbours, mostly on the grounds of trespassing. These quarrels were complicated by the passage of birds to and from their nests, a passage often vigorously disputed by those whose territory was encroached upon. Argument was incessant on these points. No longer, when it was calm, did the ears throb with the silence; the raucous cries of the penguins filled the air to the exclusion of everything else. I am sorry to say also that the birds were inveterate thieves, and the invariable objects of their thefts were … stones. Happy the pair who had a well-lined nest, the mansions of the well-to-do consisting of nice circles of evenly matched stones. But, as with all wealth, its safeguard necessitated double vigilance, for neighbours on four sides watched incessantly for the unguarded moment. When this came one would rush across, seize a stone and return triumphantly with his ill-gotten gains to his own nest. Penguins cannot count, so the satisfaction caused by this successful raid was not dimmed by the fact that the temporary absence had allowed another bird on the far side to steal one of the raider's stones. So it went on in an endless cycle, by which none was better off, yet all were evidently convinced that their wealth steadily grew.

Early in November the birds began to lay and soon nearly every nest contained one or two greenish eggs, somewhat larger than a duck egg. These made a welcome addition to our menu, and fried eggs and omelettes were the order of the day. In making omelettes, X was in his element, and in the few days left to us before we began sledging he was in continual demand, whether it was his turn to cook or not. We found the eggs very palatable, with no fishy taste whatever, but they were very rich and one egg made quite a substantial meal.

While incubating the eggs, both the male and female bird took turns in sitting, or rather squatting, for the eggs are covered by the soft downy feathers between the legs. While one bird sat, the other generally went to sea for food and would join a steady procession of birds on the way to the ice-foot. Here on the brink of the water they would pause. The procedure was always the same. Each seemed to be reluctant to be the first to make the plunge, and as one advanced to the edge and peered over, there would be a concerted effort by the others to jostle it. At last, one, losing its balance, would be forced to go, and steadying itself a moment, make the neatest dive imaginable, taking the water head first with hardly a splash. At once all the others would line the brink and crane their necks to see what happened. With the signal 'all clear', there would be no further hesitation and, one by one, they would dive in, to reappear a few moments later porpoising out to sea.

This to us comical procedure nevertheless had a very good reason. The natural enemy of the penguin is the sea-leopard, as savage and voracious as his namesake on the land, and with the very nasty habit of lurking under the ice-foot for the first unhappy bird to come over. Then there is a sudden swirl in the water and the penguin disappears. Instinct has therefore created a great reluctance to be the first; but once it is shown that there is no danger, all trepidation disappears and the birds take to the water with confidence.

During most of the period of incubation, the majority of us were absent sledging, but during the few days between sledging trips at the beginning of December 1912 I was able to renew my acquaintance with these interesting birds. Also a few weeks later, while sledging on the east coast, we found the eggs just beginning to hatch. The newly born chicks are pretty little chaps, balls of grey fluff about twice the size of a young chicken. The prettiness soon disappears however, as day by day they grow at an inordinate rate. At this stage they can best be likened to shapeless grey bags, above which are ever-open beaks with a limitless capacity. The unfortunate adult birds now have to work overtime. One always, and sometimes both, will be at sea, finding food to meet the youngsters' demands. When this happens, the rookeries are nearly deserted of adults, with the half-grown birds shepherded into groups and guarded by a few sentries to protect them from their natural enemy, the skua gull. In the vicinity of every rookery there are always skuas nesting, and these forever hover about, waiting to snap up an egg or an unguarded chicken.

Whether parents recognise their own offspring when so indiscriminately mixed it is impossible to say; quite probably at this stage the feeding is on the communal system. Certainly, every bird returning from the sea is greeted by loud squawks from a row of chickens, each with a beak wide open to the sky. Selecting one, it thrusts its head into the youngster's throat and deposits therein its load of shrimps in the incipient stages of digestion. For the moment appeased, the young one subsides, but its appetite is insatiable, and when the next adult arrives, it resumes its squawking and attitude of expectancy with the rest. The adult, its task accomplished, rests awhile, joining the others on the ice away from the rookery, has a sleep, a chat with its neighbours, perhaps has a little walk, and then prepares to go to sea again.

The birds grow rapidly, and by the end of January are practically mature. They are now left to fend for themselves, and during February the old ones begin, one by one, to leave for the open sea and the pack-ice to the north. The others follow in good time, but first they have to moult. Until the down is replaced by the hard, scale-like and waterproof feathers, they cannot swim, and wander round forlorn and miserable. Every blizzard sees a diminution of the birds on shore, and at last only a few tardy ones are left. After a snowstorm they look indescribably ludicrous and miserable, the remnants of their down matted into lumps with ice and clinging to the surface of the new feathers beneath. Then one morning, after a heavy blow, we go out to find the rookeries deserted, and for another eight months have the place to ourselves.

The emperor penguins are no less interesting than the Adélies, but we saw very few of them. In fact, their habit of breeding in midwinter in a few restricted localities has rendered difficult any attempt to study their habits. In the summer they are great travellers, and are found thousands of miles from the nearest known rookery. The first we saw was on 21 October when Hunter and I discovered one that had just landed on the ice of the boat harbour. Unfortunately for him, we wanted a specimen badly, so tackled him at once. Emperor penguins are very powerful and care must be taken to avoid a blow from their flippers, which could easily break an arm. The best way is to startle them so that they turn to flee, and then to make a football tackle and fall on them, keeping a firm grip while they are dispatched. This one stood over 4 feet high and weighed 70 pounds. To give an idea of the great power that lies behind the flippers, the two breast muscles when removed gave us 36 pounds of solid meat.

In order not to damage birds that were required for specimens, the method of killing them was to pith them, that is to insert a needle into the brain through the cavity at the base of the neck. With the emperor this had to be done very carefully, otherwise an infusion of blood distorted the eyes and stretched the eyelids, quite spoiling the shape of the skin. It was a job I loathed doing but, acquiring some skill, I became executioner-in-chief, which was preferable to seeing the matter perhaps bungled by inexpert hands.

A few days later we acquired two more specimens, then did not see any more until we picked up the second base at the end of February 1913, when a number greeted us on the ice-floe adjoining the hut.

Apart from the penguins we had other bird company during the summer months. There were, of course, the skua gulls, the pirates and scavengers of the south. The Adélie Land skua is a slightly different species from that of Macquarie Island, but very similar in appearance, a large grey bird about the size of a hawk. When we first landed there were a few about the penguin rookeries, but the killing of a seal brought them in great numbers, and they fought continuously over any pieces they could reach. They were very bold and hopped round almost underfoot, even disputing titbits with those doing the cutting up. When the carcass was abandoned they swarmed all over it, and over long pieces of entrail indulged in a regular tug-of-war.

Associated with the skua as a scavenger was the giant petrel, or 'nellie', a big clumsy bird on land, but like all these sea-birds, very powerful and graceful in flight. They were not so common as some of the others, but we obtained a number of specimens. It was the giant petrel that first introduced us to the spitting habit of the petrel family, a habit we found later, to our discomfort, more pronounced in some of the other species. When alarmed, these birds have the power of regurgitating their partly digested food, sometimes to some distance. The giant petrel, owing to its clumsiness on land, generally had great difficulty in taking off and would half run, half flutter, for a considerable distance before rising into the air. If chased on these occasions, it would always part with its previous meal or meals.

During February and March 1912 numerous flights of Antarctic petrels and Cape pigeons passed over the extreme northern point of the peninsula, always flying from east to west. They came with incredible speed across the wind, hardly a flutter in their long wings as they passed close overhead. Procuring specimens was a difficult matter, but Dr Mawson and Bickerton proved quite good shots with a gun and provided me with many an hour's work during the winter months. The Antarctic petrel is a beautiful bird, with rich brown head, back and wings, and white front; the Cape pigeon is smaller and mottled brown and white. Neither of these nested at Cape Denison, but a year later the *Aurora* found rookeries of Antarctic petrels on a high rocky outcrop about 10 miles to the west, and our own sledging party found abundant nests of the Cape pigeon and other birds 20 miles to the east. Apart from these, a number of the most beautiful of all, the snow petrel, inhabited the rocks in the vicinity of the hut, as did the smallest, the Wilson petrel, a tiny bird not unlike a swallow.

All the petrel family indulged in the habit of spitting, and some were past masters at the game. The snow petrel, for instance, greatly surprised those who first disturbed them in the rocky clefts that formed their homes. A blob of orange-red oily matter, consisting of digested shrimps, would be hurled unerringly to a distance of several feet and would leave a stain hard to remove. It is difficult to give a reason for this habit, unless it be to drive away skuas, which are the only possible enemies they have on land. They certainly use it against their own species when annoyed. One day several of us watched two snow petrels, one of which was forcing its attentions on the other. For a while they fluttered about, then the one bird, which could not shake off the unwelcomed intruder, turned at last and let drive, catching the other just under the eye. This had the desired effect, for while the spitter flew triumphantly away, its disconsolate, would-be seducer rubbed its head vigorously in the snow in a vain attempt to remove the ugly red stain on its pure white feathers.

Bad though the snow petrel was in this way, the Cape pigeon far excelled it, both in range, calibre and marksmanship. We had an experience of this later when sledging, which will be dealt with in due course. Even the little Wilson spat in its small way and, taken all in all, it puts a plebeian blemish on these aristocrats of the sky. The only other petrel to be mentioned is the silver-grey, of which we saw very few, but again while sledging we found a couple of nests and were able to procure both birds and eggs.

No other birds of any kind inhabit this area but, before concluding the chapter, I must mention the seal pup, the only one we saw throughout the whole of our stay. On 18 October, a Weddell seal landed on the ice of the boat harbour and gave birth to a pup. He was a beautiful little chap, with silk-like hair, a smooth round head and big soft eyes. Unfortunately the place chosen by the mother was a bad one. The ice had long since been squeezed into big folds, and at high tide the water was apt to seep into the bottom of the folds and make them quite slushy. It was in one of these hollows that the pup was born. For a few days we watched it, then the warmth of its body caused it to sink in and it became firmly frozen, unable either to free itself or feed. The mother was frantic and whenever we came near, desperately tried to reach us. Again and again attempts were made to lasso her, but without success. At last, in sheer mercy and to prevent the pup suffering a lingering death, the mother was shot. We dug the pup out and carried it to the hut, where for a few days it seemed quite contented. It was fed during this time with its own mother's milk given from a bottle, but obviously it could not be saved, so it was chloroformed and painlessly dispatched, to the great regret of all.

CHAPTER 11

SLEDGING ON THE PLATEAU

Pull with a will
For the way's uphill,
In our teeth the wind and the drift.
It is ten below,
And we stick in the snow,
So our journey is not swift.
But every foot which goes to a yard,
And every yard to a mile
Is distance run
And a bit that's won,
Which allows us to rest awhile;
To rest awhile in the lee of the sledge
'Ere the cold drives us on again,
With the going hard,
We must fight each yard,
To conquer a new terrain.

It is with some diffidence that I write in detail of my own two sledging experiences. They were neither very lengthy – one slightly under three weeks, the other just over four – nor comparable in importance with the longer and more arduous journeys made by other parties. At no time did we run short of food; the hardships, if any, were of the everyday type common to all sledging, and the risks run were not particularly great. In fact, on the one occasion when the whole of our party was very near disaster, the cause was one entirely dissociated with polar conditions. Similar accidents to this do indeed occur almost every day in civilised communities.

Nevertheless it is much easier to write of things that have been personally experienced, even if the setting is neither heroic nor of outstanding interest. Moreover, these two journeys, though following closely on each other, are in striking contrast and in a way epitomise all sledging. They represent the two extremes – the first a bitter struggle against the elements, in which there was plenty of hard work and discomfort, and little to be seen; the second under much easier conditions, with constantly changing scenery and something fresh to be discovered day by day. Through them, perhaps, if the picture be adequately drawn, may be appreciated the far greater feats performed by our other parties, culminating in the epic story of Dr Mawson himself, which will be told in a later chapter.

Following the four days of calm at the beginning of September 1912, hopes beat high that at last the blizzard was moderating, and three reconnoitring parties made ready to set out, east, west and south. On the 7th the first party left; on the 23rd all were back. Each had a tale to tell. To the south, Webb, McLean and Stillwell struggled for 12 miles, and here dug a shelter similar to Aladdin's Cave, which they called 'The Grotto'. Attempts to go in the teeth of the wind proved abortive, and after three days in the cave and magnetic observations by Webb, they were literally rushed back to the hut by a 75-mile wind.

Ninnis, Mertz and Murphy managed to reach 18 miles to the south-east after four days of battling in which their tent was severely damaged, making it imperative for them to return. On the way back in the usual hurricane, the sledge was often blown sideways onto wide crevasses, which fortunately at this time were well bridged with strong ice.

The third party, Madigan, Whetter and Close, did the best of all, for in eleven days they pushed 50 miles to the west and back, in an average wind of 58 miles an hour, and with the temperature down to 35°F, below zero. They had a terrible time and on the return journey had the uncomfortable experience of having their tent collapse and split from top to bottom. Fortunately they had taken the precaution of sleeping in their burberries and, moreover, were only 13 miles from Aladdin's Cave. They reached it after a trying forced march and the next day arrived back at the hut, exhausted and badly frostbitten. It was obvious from these experiences that sledging must still be deferred.

Another month passed and it was decided that, come what may, all parties should set out at the beginning of November. Actually it was the 7th of this month before the longer journeys began.

Prior to this, however, the personnel of the sledging parties was announced and general instructions laid down. The eastern party consisted of Madigan, McLean and Correll, and their object was to explore the coast as far as possible to the east of the great ice-barrier or glacial tongue that formed the eastern boundary of the open sea off Adélie Land. Stillwell, Hodgeman and Close would accompany them part of the way as a support party, and then commence a detailed map of the coast immediately to the east of winter quarters, returning to the hut for further supplies by the end of November. Bage, Hurley and Webb would go due south to the region of the magnetic pole, the object of this expedition being mainly to obtain magnetic observations in this area. Murphy, Hunter and myself would act as their support party, go with them as far as possible and return to the hut by the end of November. On our return the parties would split, and Bickerton, Whetter and Hodgeman would go to the west with the aeroplane sledge towing an ordinary sledge as far as their supply of petrol allowed, then abandon the engine and man-haul their way home. Stillwell, Close and I would again set out to the east, to complete the map of the adjacent coast. Dr Mawson, Mertz and Ninnis, with the two dog-teams, constituted the far-eastern party; their object was to travel fast and far, beyond the limits of the others, and extend the geographical knowledge of the continent to the farthest point possible. It was decided that all sledging parties should return by 31 December, with 15 January as the utmost limit.

Bick's aeroplane sledge was, by the way, doing yeomanly service at this period. Early in October it had been dug out of its hangar, and on a trial trip roared its way up the first steep slope in great style. The aeroplane engine had been fitted to a large sledge, high enough for the propellers to clear the ground, and was capable of drawing quite a considerable load. Its advent lightened the labour of all, for on every available occasion it took a load to Aladdin's Cave, not only of petrol for its own consumption, but of stores for all the other sledging parties.

November came and all were ready for the great adventure. Day after day, however, hurricane winds and thick drift made a start impossible. At last, on the 7th, the weather lightened somewhat, and in the afternoon Murphy, Hunter and I decided to make a break and try to get to Aladdin's Cave the same evening. Thus we were the first away, and the others turned out to give us a cheer. Our sledge was comparatively light, as we would pick up our food and extra bags for the main magnetic party when we reached the cave. From the start it was hard work and, moreover, we were not yet in the best of condition, for the long incarceration in the hut had impaired our energies somewhat. In the teeth of a 40-mile-an-hour blow it was sometimes as much as we could do to move the sledge at all up the steep slope, and we had to rest frequently to get our breath back. After about three hours, when still only 3 miles from the hut, we were met by clouds of drift snow which restricted visibility to a few yards. Rather than camp, it seemed easier to return to the hut, so, anchoring the sledge securely, we set off down the hill, arriving in time for dinner and a comfortable bunk for the night.

Thus ended the day rather ingloriously, but on the following morning the drift had ceased and though the wind, as usual, was strong, we set out again, followed shortly by all the others. We found our sledge without trouble and made good progress to Aladdin's Cave, where we were soon joined by Madigan's and Stillwell's parties. Again thick drift prevented us moving farther, so we spent the rest of the day enlarging the cave, until it was large enough for five of us to sleep in comfort. The other four camped in one of the tents outside.

It was an eerie experience, this first night in the cave. Before very long the narrow entrance became entirely filled with snow, and then we were completely cut off from the outer world. Everything was perfectly quiet and there was no sign of the blizzard raging outside. We could see, for light filtered through the roof, a peculiar blue light which made faces look ghastly and unfamiliar. With the tent floor down, however, we were quite comfortable, and after our first sledging meal of hoosh and cocoa, unstinted, for as yet we had not touched our rations, we settled down into our warm sleeping-bags and dropped off to sleep after a yarn. The temperature that evening was −2°F.

The morning of the 9th found us still completely snowed in, and it was necessary to dig our way out to ascertain conditions outside. We were up at 6 a.m., only to find a 70-mile wind blowing, with heavy drift. There was nothing for it but to spend the day in the cave and wait for better things. There were five of us, Madigan, Murphy, Hunter, Correll and myself, and quarters seemed a little smaller than before. We took it in turns to read *The Virginians* most of the day, but in the afternoon nearly got stifled, owing to the snowing-up of small crevasses that had supplied us with air. The first intimation of this came when Madigan tried to light a cigarette and the match would not burn, so we opened up the entrance for a breath of fresh air. Our clothes, too, were becoming damp, for apart from snow that had filtered in, moisture from the body did not evaporate, but condensed in the woollen fabric. The temperature this day was −11°F.

The following morning was much finer, with a wind of about 40 miles an hour, very little drift, and a temperature of −7°F, so we were up early and got a start at 9.45 a.m. This breaking camp is quite an undertaking, and we appreciated to the full the foresight that had minimised the number of fastenings. When emerging from our sleeping-bags the first proceeding was to change socks. During the day we wore two or three pairs of heavy woollen socks, and at night soft fleecy ones, which when not in use were stowed near the body to keep them dry. Then the cooker was brought in from outside and we partook of breakfast. This done, we donned burberries and commenced to load the sledge, the tent being left until the last. All in all, even in good weather it took us about two-and-a-half hours before the last strap was fastened and we were ready to move on. For the midday meal it was generally necessary to erect the tent, except on those rare calm days when the primus could be lit in the open.

We now said goodbye to the others and soon all were on their respective ways. The pulling was now very heavy, still uphill, with the wind in our teeth, and over soft snow and sastrugi. Our load weighed about 650 pounds, and we were a very light team, only averaging about 10 stone per man. By 1 p.m. we had made 3 miles and 100 yards, and stopped for lunch. In the afternoon we pushed on, but presently had an upset, which necessitated the unloading of the sledge, as it was jammed between the sastrugi. We now crossed many small crevasses and some large ones up to 10 and 12 feet across. Frequently a foot would go through one of the small ones, but the large ones seemed quite safe. The day was now much better and the wind had dropped considerably. By 6 p.m. we reached the Grotto, the cave dug by Webb's party nearly two months before, and the farthest point south yet reached by the expedition, making 6 miles for the day. By 9.45 p.m. the tent was fixed and we were ready to turn in. To the north we could see, about 2 miles distant, some tiny black dots that were the main party. This was our rendezvous, and we felt they had done wonderfully well to come so far in the day. The wind had now died down, and though the temperature was –8°F we felt quite warm. Our little tent in the great waste looked quite homely. We were now out of sight of the sea, and about us was nothing but a great white plain as far as the eye could see.

Bage, Hurley and Webb arrived about midnight, pretty well done up, for they had come from the hut in one day. They were a very powerful team, all over 12 stone, and strong in proportion. On the 11th a start was not made until midday, and now both teams travelled in company. As we pushed forward into the unknown the weather looked very bad, but every yard was valuable and we kept going while we could. This was one of those days we called 'snow-blind days', on which an overcast sky and drift overhead did away with all shadows. The light was quite bright, yet we moved in a white void in which nothing was distinguishable; it was impossible to tell where the surface ended and air began. We fell over ridges we could not see, and blundered into sastrugi 4 and 5 feet high. These were the days when snow goggles of amber-coloured glass were essential, but very soon they became frosted with ice and the tendency was then to take them off and strain the eyes in an effort to see what lay ahead. All of us were to suffer for this later.

The surface was heavy and soft, and soon the wind began to rise, accompanied by drift snow, so that visibility was restricted to 20 yards. For a while now Hurley changed places with Murphy, to give our team a little more weight, as we found it difficult to keep up with the others. By 4 p.m. we had won another 2 miles, and were again compelled to pitch camp, 13.5 miles south of the hut. The drift had got thicker and thicker until it was like pea soup, but the temperature was comparatively warm, 4°F, at 4.30 p.m. That night was very uncomfortable; our clothes were very damp from the snow, and the moisture permeated the insides of our sleeping-bags, so that we shivered inside them and found it difficult to sleep.

We spent 12 November within the tent, heavy wind and drift again making a start impossible. We were comfortably warm but abominably damp, with a temperature of 10°F. Even to get the cooker in was an effort, and we had only one meal, a big one of hoosh and cocoa at midday. For the rest of the time we read aloud, finishing *The Virginians* and starting on *The Pickwick Papers.* Later in the day it stopped snowing, making our chances better, but with prospects of a very heavy surface on the morrow. My chin was very sore, the result of frostbite two days before.

The next day, the 13th, was a very heavy one. We were all up at 8 a.m., and got a start at 11.30, in a wind of about 40 miles an hour, still with fairly thick drift. The temperature had risen to 16°F, and the heavy, soft snow of the day before lay inches deep. This day we only stopped twenty minutes for lunch, which we ate cold, huddled in the lee of the sledge. Though the wind dropped later to about 25 miles, progress was very slow, and it took us ten hours to do 5 miles and 700 yards, making 18 miles 1520 yards from the hut. We had indeed got to the stage when 20 yards were 20 yards. This night we were damper than ever, for the drift had forced its way into everything. The hair on the inside of our sleeping-bags was matted with ice, which was thawed out by the warmth of our bodies, so that, though we turned in warm enough, as the wet crept through we woke shivering and slept little in spite of fatigue.

Another day of blizzard. During the whole of the 14th it blew a hurricane and we could not move from the tent. We got wetter and wetter, and our sleeping-bags were soggy with the damp. Johnnie had to go out in the morning and came in a minute later with his clothes full of snow. Then Herbert went out for the cooker, and brought more in with him. The tent got smaller and smaller as the piling snow bulged it in, and we became cramped for room, finding it impossible to stretch at full length. However, a warm meal comforted us somewhat. The noise of the tent flapping prevented us reading aloud, so most of the time we just lay, with what patience we could muster. So passed another day and night.

The 15th was another day of hurricane, but with lessening drift. Most of this day we lay in our bags, sadly cramped for room, and trying to think of new profanity. Several tears had now developed in our tent, and these at least gave us something to do. To mend them we took it in turns to go outside, one trip, one stitch. The man inside passed the sail needle through the fabric, and the man outside passed it back again on the other side of the tear. Then he came inside, and while the feeling came back into his numbed hands, the second man went outside and did his stitch in turn. In this way the job was finished, though it was some hours before the last stitch was put in.

It was still blowing hard on the 16th, but drift had ceased and it was quite clear. We were out early, glad to move from our cramped quarters, but it took us a long time to get started, and we were not away until midday. All our burberries, helmets and mittens were frozen stiff as boards, and it took time and patience before we eventually got them on. The day improved very rapidly as it went on, and by 6 p.m. was nearly dead calm, with a temperature of –4°F, a wonderful relief after our previous experience. By 8 p.m. we had made 5 miles and 880 yards, when, owing to snow beginning to fall, we decided to camp.

Our things were now slightly drier, as during the day we had spread our bags inside-out on top of the sledge, but I found that my fur mitts, which had been tied to the mast, had gone, the lamp-wick that held them being broken. From now on I would have to depend on my woollen mitts, which was awkward, as they froze so stiff.

With the clearer weather our horizon had widened, and we could see something of the country over which we travelled. Not that there was much to see. Before us the land still rose in an endless stretch of white snow, carved into millions of waves and sastrugi by the wind. There was nothing else but unbroken plateau. Our distance from the hut was now 24 miles and 800 yards.

This night was a bad one for all of us as, in spite of our attempts to dry them, our sleeping-bags were wetter than ever, and we slept very little. We got up at 7 a.m. on the 17th to find snow drifting outside, but we got away at 10 a.m. By 2 p.m. we had done 4 miles, put up the tent and had a brew of tea. In the afternoon we had only done a mile when we found that two tins of kerosene were missing from the back of our sledge. This was a serious loss, so Murphy and I walked back 2.5 miles along our tracks to search for them. Luckily we found them both, three-quarters of a mile apart. Walking without dragging a heavy sledge was quite a pleasure, particularly as there was very little wind now blowing. On our return we found that the others had relayed the sledges on a little and pitched camp. Our total mileage was now 30 miles and 230 yards, and the temperature was –4°F. We managed to get our sleeping-bags a little drier that night by brushing out the moisture which had crystallised like powder inside. We were very tired, as the pulling had been very heavy in soft snow, yet I slept little, being cold from the damp.

At last we had a perfect day. It was nearly dead calm when we rose on the 18th, and we were on our way at 9 a.m. By noon we had done 4 miles and 700 yards, our fastest progress to date. It got hotter and hotter as the day wore on, and the bright sun shone down from a cloudless sky. Gradually we began to discard clothing – burberries, helmets, sweaters and mitts – and unbuttoned what we could of the remainder. The shade temperature rose from –8 to 10°F, and we suffered greatly from thirst. It is a curious thing, this thirst which develops as the sledge is dragged along, a thirst unslaked by the sucking of ice or snow, which leaves the mouth and throat drier than ever. We stopped at noon, and the weather was so calm that we boiled the primus in the open. How we enjoyed that meal, a mug of tea before us, a piece of chocolate in one bare hand, a piece of butter in the other, nibbling alternately at each. If only all sledging was like this it would be a comparative picnic. On again in the afternoon, making the most of the conditions. We halted for tea at 6 p.m., then went until 8.15 p.m., by which time we had covered 11 miles and 1300 yards for the day. The last 4 miles had been much flatter, but in spite of this, pulling had not been much easier on account of the very soft snow. The sastrugi were, however, much lower, and it looked as if we had passed through the coastal wind-belt into somewhat calmer regions.

Rising betimes, on the morning of the 19th I felt very tired as, in spite of a dry bag, I had slept very badly. This was another perfect day, and though the morning temperature was zero, the absence of wind made it quite warm. Speaking of morning does not mean that the sun had just risen; at this time of the year we had nearly continuous daylight. At midnight the sun dipped below the southern horizon for about an hour, then swung in a great arc round the horizon, rising to a maximum elevation of about 45° at noon. Starting at 9.30 a.m., we went until 8 p.m., and covered exactly the same distance as the previous day, 11 miles and 1300 yards. Again we doffed various articles of clothing, and found the heat during the afternoon quite oppressive, the thermometer reading 14.5°F. The glare of the sun was also painful, and though we all wore goggles, Murphy and Bage both suffered from snow-blindness. By night Murphy's eyes were very bad, and Johnnie put in some zinc and cocaine capsules. It had been a hard day over soft snow all the way. Our distance from the hut was now 53 miles and 1075 yards. There had been no change in the scenery, except away to the left, where we glimpsed what appeared to be a cliff of ice or snow on the eastern horizon. The absence of perspective made it difficult to guess what it was. It might have been a mountain 50 miles distant, but it was a break, and any break in the plateau was more than welcome.

We woke on the morning of the 20th to find Herbert's eyes worse, and he was unable to bear the light at all, so had to have them bandaged. It made things hard for us all. The weather was again perfect, and we made an early start. Johnnie and I had now to do all the pulling. Herbert did his best, walking blindfold and continually stumbling over the uneven ground, but he could put very little weight on his rope. Johnnie was ahead, and between us we could just keep the sledge going. Every now and then it would stick in a softer patch and stop. Then I had to lift the front, run backwards a few yards and, while Johnnie strained to keep it the right way up, hurl myself forward into my harness to help keep it going. This happened about every 20 yards, and try as we did we could not keep up with the other team with their even heavier sledge. Every now and again they waited for us, and occasionally gave us a hand, but it was cruel going. By the evening Johnnie was very tired and I was completely done. We camped a little earlier, having done 9 miles and 1300 yards, 5 miles of which were completed by lunch. The temperature in the morning was 4°F, at noon 14°, and in the evening 1°.

The 21st was the last day on our outward journey. I had a better night and felt much fresher in the morning. The plateau here seemed to consist of long, low undulations running east and west, and during the previous day for a while we had come slightly downhill. Ahead of us the country rose to another of these ridges, and we reached its summit after travelling only 4 miles. From here there was a wide view of the plateau, and it seemed a good spot to establish a depot. The distance from the hut was 67 miles and 700 yards. Consequently it was decided that here we would say farewell to our comrades, who would then proceed by themselves to the limit of their time and rations. The rest of the day was spent in building a snow mound 10-feet high, its summit surmounted by a black, wooden flag, which would be visible for many miles. At its base was stored the surplus food, which would carry the magnetic party on their return journey to the hut. That night at midnight the sunset was beautiful, the whole of the plateau diffused with rosy pink.

The following day, 22 November, was our fifteenth day out. We put in an easy day, and while Webb carried out a series of magnetic observations, we built two more snow mounds, about a mile east and west of the main one. These would form additional landmarks for the location of the depot. Then we sorted stores, retaining one week's rations to see us back to the hut, and giving the southern party choice of any of our gear they required. A last meal together, we then flew the Australian flag and the Union Jack side by side, as some sign of our occupancy of the plateau, Hurley took photos and we shook hands all round. It was a solemn moment, this parting in the wilderness. We were on our way back to the hut and comfort; the others still had a long and arduous journey before them, which would test their endurance to the utmost. At 7 p.m. we turned our sledge, our last memory a glimpse of Hurley's cheerful grin, then we were on our way homewards.

A very different matter this from our hard struggle outwards.

Our sledge was lightened and the slight wind was at our backs. Herbert's eyes had improved and, though out of focus from the effects of the zinc and cocaine tablets, he could see sufficiently to do his share. By 9.45 p.m. we had done 6.5 miles, but as it came on to blow, with some drift, we pitched camp and were in our bags by 11.45 p.m. It was quite warm, the temperature 5.5°F.

The next day saw a hurricane blowing with thick drift, and during the night we wondered if our tent would stand the strain. We had hoosh at 3 p.m. and as the weather was moderating somewhat, prepared to set off at any time. It was not until five o'clock the following morning, however, that we arose and, with the weather still bad, made a start at 7.40 a.m. Now, with the wind behind us, we made splendid progress and by 6 p.m. had done between 16 and 17 miles. We could not tell exactly as our sledge-meter had broken down. We were all now very fit and Herbert's eyes were improving all the time, though my lip was very sore, having split in the hot sun some days previously.

The following two days were similar to the last, though the snow was very soft, which made pulling hard in spite of the wind at our backs. We averaged about 17 to 18 miles on each day, in spite of numerous upsets in high sastrugi, which we could not see on account of the absence of shadows. On the evening of the 26th we saw the sea above the horizon, and now we knew we were nearing home. The day got better as we went on, and in the afternoon it was beautifully warm and sunny. Apparently, however, we were off our course somewhat, for we got in among a number of large crevasses and had to make many detours, but some we crossed, with one man well ahead on the alpine rope. We estimated that we were too far to the westward, and that the hut was about 10 to 12 miles to the north-east. We felt that this should be our last camp before making it. The 27th was indeed our last day out. This day Johnnie's eyes were rather bad from snow-blindness, and mine were feeling the strain. A little incident now occurred that showed how hard it was to estimate size and distance on the plateau. We had not gone a mile when, looking out for landmarks, a black object loomed up on the northern horizon. We discussed what it was. It looked like a new mountain in the distance, but no mountain was in this direction, so after a discussion I left the others and walked towards it to see if I could not get a better view. A very few yards decided it; it was a bag of food left by Mawson in the autumn, at a spot 8 miles south-west of the hut.

The surface was now good, the weather fine and it did not take us long to reach Aladdin's Cave. The last 5.5 miles were a mere detail, our sledge running of its own volition, two men behind it as a brake, the other ahead to steer. By 3 p.m. the hut was in view, and a few minutes later we were sitting in comfort telling our adventures to Hannam, Whetter and Bickerton, who had remained.

Hannam was the cook that night, and the luxury of that dinner is something to be remembered. I volunteered as nightwatchman, in order to have a bath, but we all sat up late, and washed and luxuriated to our hearts' content.

A picturesque formation of frozen sea spray frames the *Aurora* in Commonwealth Bay.

The *Aurora* covered in snow and ice. The weight of this build-up upset the balance of the ship, hence it was vital to remove the ice.

Adélie penguins listening to the gramophone which Mawson brought to the rookery.

A large penguin rookery. The birds showed no fear of the explorers.

Frank Hurley

At the foot of the ice-cliffs. A member of the Mawson expedition negotiates dangerous stretches of ice along the coastal downfalls near winter quarters.

National Library of Australia

The arduous work of unloading stores. Note the sheer legs for swinging boxes off the boats.

The *Aurora* off the Great Ice Barrier.

Hoadley looking through a theodolite. Surveying the area was a constant task whenever conditions would permit.

The hut in winter, shrouded by snow swept up by a blizzard.

Even under shelter, conditions could be less than hospitable.

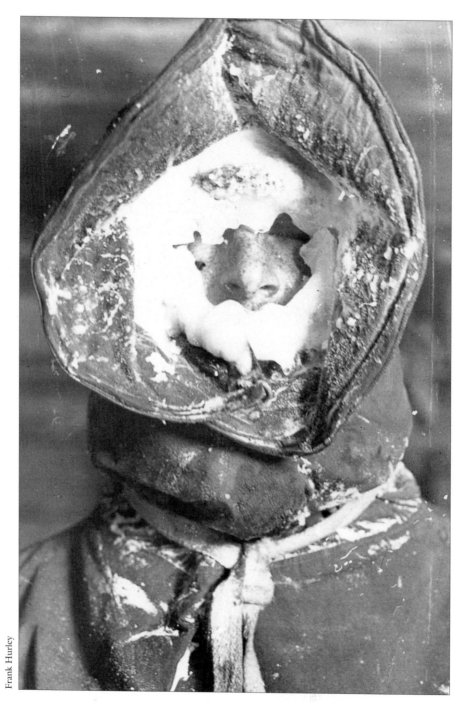

The ice-encrusted face of one member of the party returning to the hut during a blizzard.

A mushroom cloud made of ice. The sea shaped icebergs into extraordinary and beautiful forms.

Walking into a gale in Adélie Land.

Inside the hut, oblivious to the shriek of the ever-present wind outside, the men ate, slept, researched and entertained themselves as best they could through the long, dark hours of winter.

Frank Hurley

The south magnetic pole was reached by Bage, Webb and Hurley. Flags were speared into the ice to commemorate the achievement.

A sledging party at Madigan Nunatak. The two men in the photograph are Close and Stillwell.

Bage preparing the sledging ration in Aladdin's grotto.

Frank Hurley

Adélie penguins – three lonely strays find a lost brother after a blizzard.

Frank Hurley

A cavern eaten out by waves.

Ice coastline.

Frank Hurley

Lt. B.E.S. Ninnis, R.F. In the course of the expedition, Ninnis and Mertz, who were close friends, both died. Mawson survived after great hardship to tell their stories.

CHAPTER 12

TO THE MAGNETIC POLE

Ours is a tale
Of an endless gale,
And a sledge that drags behind.
We are passing through
A country new,
To see what we can find.
To see what we can find, my lads,
On a plateau bare and vast,
While the meter shows
How each long mile goes,
Till three hundred miles are past.
Three hundred miles and back, my lads,
To the end it's a tale of strife,
Of a depot missed
In the blinding mist,
And a bitter race for life.

To return to Bage, Webb and Hurley: after our departure they faced another eight weeks on the plateau, under conditions more arduous than ours. If I have quoted from my own diary in the previous pages, it is with no intention of exaggerating our own part in the undertaking, but rather to give some idea of what the magnetic-pole party underwent throughout their 600-mile journey.

Most of their story is a repetition of the first two weeks, a story of daily blizzards, bad surfaces, temperatures mostly below zero, long arduous days, snow-blindness, frostbitten fingers, magnetic observations made under acute physical discomfort, and, finally, a missed depot and a bitter race for life against the spectre of starvation.

For comparison, it must be remembered that up to the time we left them there was no need to economise in food; afterwards it had to be carefully guarded, and every ounce saved to extend the range of their journey and ensure their safe return. Our tent was heavy and windproof, theirs smaller, lighter and draughty. We carried extra clothing; at the depot they scrapped everything that was not absolutely necessary. Their risks were also much greater. At the worst we were within a few forced marches of the hut, but they had to depend on picking up this tiny depot in a wilderness with no landmarks, and other similar depots to be established farther south. To miss one of these depots in thick drift, with visibility limited to a few yards, would be very easy, with disastrous results.

Bage has written the story of this journey in the history of the expedition, but he has not done justice to his own part in it. Only those who knew him can realise how far his quiet determination, resolution and foresight carried them through. I can picture Badget still, with his stocky figure, thinning hair and an old pipe. His pipe was part of him, and he had it in his mouth even when not smoking. There was one he treasured greatly; even when it broke he mended it with adhesive tape. He was always cheerful, ready with a hand to anybody who needed it, yet he was one of the quietest members of the expedition. When he undertook a job he set about it with a quiet thoroughness that was characteristic, and the job when done needed no improvement. He was a born leader of men. The death of Bage was characteristic of his life. In the early days of Gallipoli, a salient known as 'The Pimple' had been pushed out from the Australian lines, in the vicinity of Lone Pine. To straighten out the angles of this it became necessary to build a new trench in advance of that already held, and Bage was ordered to mark this out in broad daylight and in full sight of the Turks some 250 yards away. It was practically certain death, yet the job was completed before a burst of machine-gun fire killed him and wounded most of the small party that had been detailed to give him covering fire. I had it from one who was with him when the fatal order was given that he went to his death quietly and without fuss. That was Bage.

Hurley would joke in the face of death. The rougher things were, the more cheerful he became and the more he poked fun at anything and everything. Powerful physically, he was an ideal mate for such a trip. His fertile brain and imagination made a comedy of the most desperate situation, and he had the knack of imparting a touch of romance to such things as a Christmas pudding made of pemmican fat, ground plasmon biscuit, raisins, glaxo and sugar, and boiled over the primus in an old pudding cloth. Under his influence that day, a little pure alcohol with added boiled raisins became the nectar of the gods, and he composed fantastic and absurd poems on this and all other occasions. One could never be downhearted with Frank, even when things were at their worst.

Webb was of an entirely different nature. Naturally rather austere, he was conscientious to a degree and remarkably efficient. No matter what the conditions, he allowed nothing to prevent him doing his job. He was a man in whom respect engendered affection; he made friends slowly, but was of the staunch type who would never let anyone down. In France he had the reputation of being something of a martinet, but his men had the utmost faith in his efficiency, and he never asked of anybody what he was not prepared to do himself. The three made a wonderful team.

Bage says in his diary that they watched us out of sight with mixed feelings, and the plateau seemed curiously lonely when we had gone. This was on 22 November 1912, and on the 23rd the hurricane that held us up for a few miles to the north caused them to lie up also. This was Webb's birthday, and they celebrated by having some extra lumps of sugar in their tea.

On the 24th they moved off in a 50-mile-an-hour wind and bad light. They made 8.75 miles that day and were thoroughly exhausted. From then until the 28th it was the same story, fighting southwards in the teeth of winds from 40 to 60 miles an hour, with one day on which they could not move at all. One day the distance was 12 miles; on another 4.75 miles saw them thoroughly exhausted. They were now 100 miles from the hut, in a climate becoming colder as they went south. In this camp the temperature was −16°F. Here a series of magnetic observations was taken, and the declination was 88°54', a promising increase over that at the hut, which was 87°27'. In explanation of this, it has been stated before that a free-swinging magnetic needle in this area points downwards to some spot within the earth's crust, and when above this spot should be exactly vertical, that is at an angle of 90° with a perfectly level surface. Every rise in the angle, therefore, indicated an approach to the magnetic pole and was eagerly watched by the sledgers. Actually they were doomed to disappointment, for after this the declination of the needle played queer pranks and, after rising rapidly within a short distance, receded again, and then for some 65 miles remained practically stationary before it began again to rise steadily. These observations seemingly pointed to a subsidiary pole adjacent to the main one.

During the next fourteen days they made another 100 miles, and established a depot 199.75 miles from the hut. During this time they had three good days, of which two were those rare, windless, sunny days that make sledging a pleasure. With a temperature of –2°F rising to 14° they found it unpleasantly hot, actually within the tent there was a thaw. When camping in the wind they had long since found some relief by erecting a breakwind of snow, thus saving the tent from possible damage and providing useful landmarks for the homeward journey.

All this time there was no break in the monotonous scenery of the plateau, until on 3 December they ascended a valley in a peculiar ridge, with a steep escarpment to the north. Here were three large mounds 200 feet high, covered with huge crevasses up to 40 feet across, many of which they had to cross. This place they called 'The Nodules', and a similar ridge could be seen about 20 miles to the south-west. It was a peculiar thing to find such a crevassed area so far from the coast. A possible explanation is that in this locality the ice-sheet is moving over the tops of mountains beneath, and as it is lifted into ridges splits into huge vertical fissures.

The second depot was established on 12 December at a height above sea-level of 4850 feet. Here they lightened the sledge of everything that could be dispensed with and, taking food sufficient for seventeen days, set out on the last stage of their outward journey. During the next seven days they covered 83 miles, most of the time in good weather and bright sunshine, though all were suffering from snow-blindness. Here the dip was 89°35', and it was evident that the actual area of vertical dip or the magnetic pole itself could not quite be attained. However, they went on until 21 December, when, pitching camp, they went a further 2.5 miles until the sledge-meter read 300 miles.

This was the farthest point reached on the journey. The height of the plateau at this spot was 5900 feet above sea-level, and the temperature this day was –25°F, though it was the height of midsummer. The dip was 89°43.5' and consequently they were about 50 miles from the magnetic pole, and by continuing on the same course for another 175 miles would have reached the spot attained by Mawson on the Shackleton expedition three years before.

Now began the homeward journey. They had with them eight days' food; there were ten days' rations at the 200-mile depot, and another one at the 67.5 mile. Provided the weather was moderately kind and they picked up the depots successfully, they should have no difficulty in reaching the hut; but there was always the danger of being held up unduly by heavy blizzards, or of missing the depots altogether in the thick drift.

With the lightened sledge and the wind behind they made splendid progress, from 14 to 20 miles a day in all sorts of weather, varying from fine, sunny days to those in which the wind blew at hurricane force and drift snow affected the visibility. Snow-blindness at this time was the worst enemy and it was seldom that it did not affect one or two of them, so the zinc and cocaine tablets were in great demand.

They made the 200-mile depot on the day after Christmas, and had their deferred Christmas dinner, the main item of which was Hurley's Christmas pudding, made of odds and ends of their rations and boiled in the cooker over the primus. They toasted the King and smoked cigars saved for the occasion.

On 28 December they made their record run, with the sail hoisted and a strong following wind, no less than 41 miles being covered in twenty-two hours. This put them so far ahead of schedule that they had four-and-a-half days' surplus food, a fact that ultimately saved their lives. They decided to increase their rations for a week, and to save three days' worth for emergency.

So the journey went on. On the 31st Hurley suffered badly from snowblindness and when, on the following day, he had recovered somewhat, Bage was so bad that at the end of a 20-mile run he had to ride on the sledge for 3.5 miles. The pain gave him a sleepless night. Fortunately the going was downhill at the time. On the following day he again had to ride on the sledge for a mile, but his eyes improving somewhat, he was able to pull. By 3 January they were within 11 miles of the depot, and reduced their rations by one-half in case of missing it.

This was the most trying part of the whole trip, as on the next day the wind rose with every mile and drift snow became thicker and thicker. The sledge-meter had long since gone to pieces and the only method of estimating the distance was by checking up on the snow mounds at outward camps, and by correcting the latitude by measuring the altitude of the sun. They knew they were in the vicinity of the depot, and could probably see it if the weather was clear, so there was nothing for it but to camp and wait.

The next day was 5 January, and all day it snowed; but at 9 p.m. it cleared sufficiently to make an observation, which showed them to be only 4 miles south of the depot. On the 6th they moved on, and a glimpse of the sun at noon showed them to be on the exact latitude of the depot. But there was no visibility and the white wall that encircled them effectively hid the mound and flag that marked the position of the much-needed food. All that day they explored systematically east and west, moving the sledge and walking away from it in every direction, but not daring to go far lest they lost touch in the thick drift.

It was a tantalising position. Almost in touch was abundant food; above them occasional glimpses of the sun showed that the drift was not far above the surface, yet in it they were as effectively blinded as on the darkest night. The situation, too, was fast becoming serious. On half rations in that climate, strength is apt to diminish rapidly and, unless they could locate the depot within reasonable time, might well fail them in a dash for the hut, nearly 70 miles away.

Another twenty-four hours passed, and still there was no break in the drift. Given five minutes, or even just a moment, of unrestricted vision and they would be safe, but that moment would not come. So 7 January came and went with the same maddening conditions.

It was 3 a.m. when they finally decided to make a run for the hut. Taking stock of their provisions, they now had one full day's ration, in addition to enough pemmican for half a hoosh, nine raisins, six lumps of sugar, enough kerosene for two days and a pint of pure alcohol. This was portioned into five parts to last five days. All inessentials were stripped off the sledge in order to lighten it; the spade, ice-axe, spare clothing, even the camera and scientific instruments were abandoned, and at 7 a.m. they set off.

Twenty miles plus a day was the schedule – not a great deal with a following wind, but the days of waiting on a reduced ration had sapped much of their strength. There was also the uncertainty of being able to keep the most direct route to their goal. Moreover, blizzards of exceptional strength might force them at any time to lie up, with disastrous consequences. Ordinary blizzards did not count. Already, throughout the whole trip, travelling had been done in weather that normally would have been considered too bad for sledging, and it was only something really exceptional that caused a halt.

It took all their endurance to keep going. They would march an hour, halt five minutes, then on for another hour, five minutes' spell again, and so on, until everyone had agreed that 10 miles had been covered, then they would call a halt for lunch. Lunch consisted of one-third of a biscuit and one-third of an ounce of butter, washed down by a mug of warm water in which was a spoonful of sugar and one of alcohol. An hour's spell and they were off again, going until the day's run was estimated at 20 miles, and then they camped. Evening found them much exhausted and barely able to erect the tent. The watery hoosh and warm water with alcohol did little to appease hunger or supply warmth to systems weakened by long exposure and lack of food, yet Hurley, with his usual grin and facetious remarks, invested it with the atmosphere of a dinner at the Ritz, and the others smiled at his efforts. There was no warmth in the sleeping-bags that night. It needs hot food and plenty of it to keep the blood coursing through the veins, and they slept but little, shivering as they lay waiting for the morning and the day that would decide their fate.

The day came, a 60 miles-an-hour wind and thick drift – such a day as is the curse of sledging. Yet they went on. It was bitter work getting into frozen burberries, into finnesko from which all the hair had been worn, and which were hard as boards. Bitter work, too, to hang onto the tent as it came down in that howling wind; bitter work to fasten those straps on the sledge, to rig up the sail and to take a reef in it lest they go too fast and capsize; bitter work to drag the front sideways, lest it make too much leeway. The course was kept by the sastrugi, those wind-cut ridges whose constant direction is a great boon in these featureless regions. The wind was cruel, but not like the outward journey, when it drove into the face and pushed the sledge backwards against the puny efforts of the pullers. Now it seemed to say: 'If I cannot destroy, I will at least sweep these insignificant mortals from my realm.' The sail filled and the sledge drove along, and ahead and to the sides its attendants trudged, stumbling over sastrugi they could not see, picking themselves up and wearily plugging onwards, hour after hour and mile after mile, an unending drudgery, until weary limbs would go no further and a halt must perforce be made for lunch. Lunch this day was at 6 p.m., and after this they pushed on until midnight. Twenty miles surely, when suddenly underfoot appeared hard blue ice instead of the snow surfaces which had so long prevailed. By now they estimated they were 27 miles from the hut, but this ice on the outward journey had disappeared only 13 miles away. Probably they were too far to the east, but, on the other hand, might have done a greater distance than estimated.

As they camped that night hopes beat high, and when the morning came with a clear sky and light wind they felt that this should be the last day of their trials. The sea was in sight as they set off to the north-west, but presently they got into a badly crevassed hollow and had a long, laborious pull uphill before they reached a good surface again. By this time they were in rather a bad way, and could make but slow progress. Hurley was snowblind and had one eye tightly bandaged. Bage, also, could hardly see, and Webb moved mechanically as a man in a dream. They topped the ridge and Bage, in the lead, recognised in the distance the Mackellar Islands. He shouted to the others, and even as he shouted went straight down through the lid of a crevasse.

This was the last adventure. His sledge harness held, and from his precarious position he was soon hauled by the others. All was straight sailing now. With their remaining strength they plugged along to the west, and by midnight Aladdin's Cave came in sight, a veritable oasis in a desert.

A few dog biscuits were lying on the surface, and these made a preliminary stop-gap while they dug out a food bag and prepared for a real, hot meal.

This was virtually the end of their journey. Refreshed from a good sleep and after numerous meals, they made their way down to the hut and arrived at 5 p.m. on 11 January 1913, after one of the most arduous trips undertaken by any sledging party. It is a tribute to their endurance and determination that they pulled through at all. Moreover, the sum total of the expedition's scientific work was added to greatly as a result of their journey. Not only did it prove the nature of the country for 300 miles inland, but the magnetic observations carried out by Webb and the others were of outstanding value. The results of these, combined with other records made at the main base and also at the second base, 1500 miles to the west, have since been included in a full monograph by Webb himself, and their ultimate value in the great field of terrestrial magnetism cannot as yet be estimated.

CHAPTER 13

SLEDGING ON THE COAST

Adown the hills, the glacier's icy mass
For ever grinds its slow resistless way,
The riven slopes, where hides the deep crevasse,
Plunge down at last into the rock-strewn bay.

The first days in the hut after sledging are days of endless luxury. It is wonderful to sit down at a table and enjoy a real meal. It is wonderful to be able to doff burberries and mitts, and write or read in comfort. It is wonderful to be able to take one's clothes off, and don a pair of comfortable pyjamas, and to snuggle down between warm blankets that are perfectly dry. It is wonderful to feel secure, no fear of crevasses, frostbite or of running short of food.

Immediately after our return I suffered severely from the effects of snow-blindness, which up to this time had left me less affected than the others. It is a very painful affliction and at its worst feels just as if the eyes were full of gravel. Zinc and cocaine were our standard remedy, and this has the curious after-effect of distorting the lens of the eye so that it is out of focus. It made me long-sighted, and for a few days everything nearer than a few feet was quite blurred. This gradually wore off, however.

With the return of Stillwell, Hodgeman and Close from the east, the time came for us to set out again. Hodgeman was going to the west with Bickerton and Whetter, and I was to accompany Stillwell and Close to the east, to explore and map a portion of the coastline. On their previous journey Stillwell had mapped in the coast adjacent to its junction with the great glacier tongue that flowed from a valley in the plateau. Now we were to cover the section between his previous work and the eastern end of Commonwealth Bay. This was only about 20 miles in a direct line from the hut, but to reach it we had to make a considerable detour inland in order to avoid the very dangerous crevassed area that bordered the sea. Our start was delayed somewhat by the fact that Stillwell's sledge had become badly damaged by rough ice, and we had to refit one of mountain ash. The one we had used on the southern journey was being taken by the western party. We saw them off on 3 December 1912, and they made an imposing sight, the large aeroplane sledge towing the other up the steep slope in a way that filled us all with envy.

The weather had become beautifully warm, temperatures up nearly to freezing point, with the hot sun melting the snow on the rocks, and turning the hollows into real lakes. Yet when we were ready to move off, the usual blizzard arrived, and thick drifting snow deferred our departure to 9 December. It was my birthday and Frank Stillwell gave me a little copy of Tennyson, which accompanied me on the trip. We left after lunch, and Hunter, Hannam and Murphy came out to see us off.

Once again we pulled our sledge up the slope, only to meet drift snow a short distance from the hut. It became worse and worse as we got higher, so that we missed the 2-mile and 3-mile flags altogether, and by the time the sledge-meter recorded 5.5 miles, we were hopelessly at sea. To find Aladdin's Cave was the problem. Numerous crevasses were in the vicinity, so we concluded we were to the east. Working slowly to the west for over two hours, we halted our sledge every 100 yards, then set out on foot in different directions, counting paces so as not to lose touch with the sledge. At last to our relief, the flagpole of the depot loomed up faintly through the driving snow. It was not long before we were snug in the cave, and after a good hot meal were in our bags by 1 a.m. After the good weather we had experienced at the hut, it seemed as if all sledging parties were doomed to strike bad conditions on their first days out – almost as if the plateau resented their presence and did its utmost to discourage them.

We woke on the morning of the 10th warm and comfortable, and with little thought of danger. Snowed in completely, the cave seemed curiously remote from the outer world, only the blue light that filtered through the ice showing that the sun shone through a foot or so overhead. There was no inkling as to the weather outside, but as we had brought the primus and cooker in with us, we deferred investigation until after breakfast. Frank officiated at the cooker while Close and I sat on our sleeping-bags and watched. We had our hoosh, and while the cocoa came to the boil, I started to change my sleeping socks for those worn through the day. It was at this moment that Frank complained of feeling giddy and asked Close to open up the entrance. Close rose and leisurely pushed an ice-axe through, making a small hole that was probably our salvation. But before he could do more there was a thud and we looked round to see Frank collapsed in a heap on the floor. Wondering what had happened, we rushed over to him and then Close, too, pitched forward across him, just as if he had been struck by a pole-axe. I suddenly felt weak and faint, and the few feet to the entrance seemed a long, long way. The thought was uppermost in my mind that if I did not reach it we were all doomed, so I set off on a long, long crawl, inches at a time. At last, levering myself into the entrance, I managed to push the ice-axe up and enlarge the hole that had already been made. Then came Stillwell, crawling likewise, to use my body to gain a little height and complete the work. Close was reviving, and as the cold air came rushing in we gradually recovered and were able to take stock of what had happened. The primus was out, and a thick skin of ice was already forming on the cocoa, which at the moment of the catastrophe was just about to boil. My foot felt very cold, and I found it bare. Then I remembered I was changing my socks at the time. Fortunately it must have been resting on one of the sleeping-bags, otherwise it would have been frostbitten. It had all been so sudden, with no warning of any kind. Even during those anxious moments when I thought I was becoming unconscious, I was actually coming to. Frank alone had felt a preliminary giddiness. We found by our watches that we had all been unconscious over two hours, and had undoubtedly been saved by the small hole made by Close.

In discussion afterwards we came to the conclusion that this near-disaster had been caused by poisoning from that deadly gas, carbon monoxide, which has no smell, produces no feeling of suffocation, and gives no preliminary warning of its presence. Other parties had slept and cooked meals in the cave without ill-effects, but no doubt since then drift snow had choked the small cracks and crevasses that supplied air. All had gone well until the primus, burning in an atmosphere deficient in oxygen, had commenced to generate the carbon monoxide. Stillwell, bending over it, was the first to succumb, while I, who was the farthest away, was the last. The influx of fresh air had dispersed the deadly gas, and allowed the primus to burn normally until, the supply of kerosene failing, it had gone out. It had, indeed, been touch and go, and it is a curious thing that this, the greatest danger we faced on the whole of the expedition, should have been from a cause entirely unforeseen and not in any way associated with the usual perils of polar exploration.

For a long time we felt too weak to move, but crawled back into our bags for some hours. Then Close revived sufficiently to go outside and reappear presently with the medicine chest. We carried a small supply of brandy for an emergency and this bucked us up a bit, after which some caffeine tablets also did good work to quicken our pulses, which were very weak and slow. Later still we all emerged and erected our tent, determined to spend no more nights in the cave; but first we wrote a warning to prevent any other sledging parties from having the same experience.

After a day-and-a-night's rest, we moved off on 11 December and, after sorting stores, started at 10.40 a.m., in a strong wind of about 40 miles-an-hour and intermittent drift, and with a temperature of 20°F. We were all very tired, still feeling the effects of the previous morning, and found it hard work pulling the sledge over the soft snow with the wind partly against us. Still, we made 8 miles and 810 yards by 6.30 p.m., and turned in, dead tired. The following day was a repetition of the last, the wind somewhat easier with very little drift, and ourselves feeling better hour by hour. We did 10.25 miles, still on a heavy surface, with the sea just visible to the north. In the afternoon we were cheered by a visit from a Wilson petrel, which hovered over us for a few minutes and then made off. It was good to see some other live thing in this dead region. We were disturbed this day to find our sledge badly damaged, a long piece 4 feet in length having split off one of the runners, and our sledge-meter, too, was badly out of shape, with two spokes missing. This was a serious mishap, as the whole of our surveying was dependent on it. We hammered it into shape somewhat, but it was still very rickety.

The next day, 13 December, was a day of 'pea soup' drift, in which we were forced to lie up; but the next day was beautiful and by the afternoon was dead calm. With a temperature of 13°F, rising to 24°, it was very hot dragging the sledge over a heavy surface, but it was a pleasure to discard burberries, mitts, jerseys and crampons. We now kept a lookout for Madigan Nunatak, which had been discovered by Stillwell's party on their first journey, some weeks before. A nunatak is literally a mountain peak emerging from the ice-sheet that covers the land. We first saw it as a speck of black in the distance and by 6 p.m. camped under its lee.

It was only a small weathered patch of rock, some 160 yards long and 30 wide, rising 60 feet above the level of the ice, but a welcome relief in the endless expanse of white. Even after only a few days on the plateau, it was good to feel solid rock underfoot, to have again some sense of solidity and substance at hand, and a feeling of finity. The world of ice at times seemed not only infinite but unreal, and so lonely that it felt as if no other living thing existed in the universe.

We spent the evening taking photographs and exploring the nunatak. We found it to consist of gneiss, similar to the rocks at Cape Denison. The most important point geologically was that the rocks showed no sign of glaciation, proving that the ice-sheet had not flowed over it for a long period, if ever. Instead, the action of frost had weathered it into bizarre shapes; its surface was cracked and shattered, and the cracks were filled with decomposed material. A few lichens scantily clothed some of the rocks, and we collected specimens of these, the only vegetation in this part of the world. A Wilson petrel flew overhead, also two large grey birds that we had not previously seen.

The following day was perfect and we spent a profitable morning collecting geological specimens. Then, after Frank had taken a latitude shot and I had taken more photographs, we moved off north-wards towards the sea. The surface was heavy, but a slight following breeze encouraged us to put up our sail, and we made good progress, covering 10 miles by 8.30 p.m. After previous experiences, this was sledging *de luxe*. The sea was now in sight again and white dots on the horizon showed the presence of far-distant bergs. We now looked forward to the next day, with its prospects of new sights and discoveries.

We revelled in the sunshine on 16 December, which was another beautiful day. On a good surface we made rapid progress, and in three hours had done 6.5 miles, when we stopped for lunch – lunch in the open with no need to cover our fingers, and the primus burning freely in the still air. It was real picnic weather. The sea was now much clearer, and almost at our feet we could see great bergs and masses of floe against the blue background. That afternoon, as we advanced and got lower and lower, numerous small islands came into sight, some ice-capped, others of bare rock. The ice-capped islets looked not unlike great mushrooms, the top portion a mass of the frozen spray of winter, now undercut by the waves until it overhung right round.

We came right down to within half a mile of the coast, over an easily graded snow-covered surface. Before us the slope then dipped rapidly and was badly crevassed, terminating seawards in the usual cliffs of ice. A little to the west a small outcrop of rock seemed connected with the land by a causeway of ice, and this, apparently, was the only rock here possible of access. We turned our sledge and travelled parallel to the coastline for a measured mile, to serve as a base for our survey; then, while Frank took angles with his theodolite, Close and I erected the tent and prepared hoosh.

After our evening meal, Frank and I walked down to the coast and succeeded in gaining the outcrop of rock previously mentioned. We found it composed of a garnetiferous gneiss, traversed by dykes of basalt, and covered with a large rookery of Adélie penguins, who made a great fuss as we passed between their nests. On a small ice-foot a dozen giant petrels were resting, one of them an albino. Here, also, we saw an Antarctic petrel and Wilson petrels, besides two skua gulls' nests, each of which contained two eggs. We robbed one, and were viciously attacked in so doing. As one bird swooped at me, Frank hit it with an ice-axe and we thought it killed, but it soon recovered and flew away. On our return journey to the tent, Frank carried the eggs in his pyjama coat, and on arrival found one broken. It made a terrible mess, and as the poor chap was a non-swearer he had no relief.

We did not move camp the next day, but spent it in surveying, mapping, geologising and photographing. It was very warm, 29°F at midday, and in the sun everything was thawing. On the morrow we planned to move westwards and continue the survey of the coast, then cut inland, cross our previous route and strike the coast again to the east. A very bad area of heavily crevassed country lay just to the east of the camp, and it would be necessary to make this detour to avoid it.

The morning of the 18th was too windy for accurate theodolite work, so, while Frank walked east and fixed a couple of snow mounds for surveying, I stayed in the tent and changed plates for the camera. We had an early lunch and then moved east. Our method of procedure was to move the sledge some distance, then I would go ahead to some prominent point, such as the summit of a ridge, and here erect the ice-axe or our bamboo mast as a mark. While Close walked back to pick up the previous mark, Frank would take bearings with the theodolite. Then we would all take the sledge on and begin anew. In this way the survey became complete in every detail, but it was slow work and up to midnight we only covered 3.5 miles. But the weather was delightful and the ever-changing scenery was very beautiful. To our right lay the sea, vividly blue, and studded as far as the eye could see with thousands of bergs and pieces of floe-ice of every conceivable size and shape. Every ridge brought a new vista, new bergs or new islands nestling at the foot of the barrier.

Sometimes we had to alter our course on account of crevasses, and these we generally avoided by making a detour inland. Crevasses are dead-vertical cracks in the ice-sheet, caused by its moving over irregularities in the rocks beneath, and they vary in width from an inch or so to over 30 yards. Their depth depends on the thickness of the ice, and in places they must be hundreds, if not thousands, of feet deep. They are very seldom open, but generally covered with a lid of ice, which may be quite solid or only an inch or so thick, and so rotten that it breaks with the slightest weight. Looking into them, all that one can see are two vertical walls going down into azure nothingness. Sometimes the walls consist of bare ice; sometimes they are coated with ice crystals or stalactites, with an occasional cornice or ledge of snow. They are the nightmare of sledging, not so much on the hard glacial ice where they can be clearly discerned, but where new snow-fields lie, as they are then often quite concealed and are very dangerous. Roped together on the sledge we did not fear them greatly, but when travelling singly we had to take every care. Near the edge of the barrier they were very bad, and in making offsets to the coast we could rarely approach nearer than 100 yards.

Once again we had a calm, hot day – wonderful after the eternal wind. With a 24-hour day we worked at all sorts of hours and, having gone to bed at 2 a.m., we slept until 10 a.m. then carried on until 9.30 in the evening. That day we surveyed a little over 2 miles to a point from which we could see the rocks of our base and the Mackellar Islands 20 miles away to the west. From offsets to the coast we saw it, as usual, terminating in steep ice-cliffs, very dangerous near the edge, and with no rocky outcrops to which we could descend. The quantity of floe-ice off the coast was very great here – large, flat pieces up to 400 yards across, consisting of stratified snow and standing from 10 to 15 feet out of the water. We concluded that these were the remains of the sea-ice of winter, frozen among the islands and built upon by snow blown down from the plateau.

This point was the western limit of our survey, and on the 20th we turned inland and then to the east again. After a hard pull uphill, we again approached the coast, crossing our route of a few days before, and camping ultimately some 400 yards from the barrier's edge, after a day's run of 9 miles. In one place we passed a ridge covered with enormous crevasses that ran round in a series of terraces, the top lips being several feet higher than the lower. Frank and I walked across to them and found some 30 yards across and quite open. We did not like the look of them, for though they narrowed to the sides, some seemed to pass right under the snow-field on which we had been travelling. This was very bad country and our camp was already pitched when we found it was half on the lid of a 12-foot crevasse, which, fortunately, seemed to be an old one filled with snow. Nevertheless, we moved onto better ground. There seemed to be crevasses all round us here, and from then on we rarely moved about unless roped together. The day had been very hot, the temperature rising at midday to 20°F, and we were all sunburnt.

We did not move camp until lunch on the 21st, as Frank spent the morning mapping a group of islands immediately beneath us. Close and I went ahead and built snow-mounds for our traverse for about a mile and a half. After lunch we pulled our sledge about 4 miles to the east, again building snow-mounds. Unfortunately, wind and surface drift restricted visibility, necessitating our covering this area again. It was a very difficult stage, as we got mixed up with a number of bad crevasses. Some forced us to make continual detours; others we crossed where hard snow had formed a suitable bridge. In these cases one man always went well ahead on the alpine rope, then if he found it secure the other two, followed by the sledge, took it at a run. Occasionally a foot went through, but we had no mishap. On one occasion the crevasse was so wide that the three of us and the sledge were on it at the one time – a very dangerous proceeding. Ahead of us the coast was bending southwards in a large bay, the eastern shore of which Stillwell had already mapped. The head of this bay would form the limit of our present work. All day radiants of cirrus cloud overhead and banks of nimbus in the north showed that our spell of fine weather was at an end, and we made our tent doubly secure as we turned in.

Sure enough, the following morning brought the inevitable blizzard, with a wind of 50 miles-an-hour and thick drift snow. We lay in the tent all day, reading a little, yarning or listening to the flapping of the tent and the beating of the drift, which sounded like a sandblast. The morning of the 23rd was a little better, but the sky was heavily overcast, and wind and surface drift made it too bad for theodolite work. After hoosh, the three of us walked down as near as we could get to the edge of the barrier and built a couple of ice-mounds on prominent points, then made east and built another on a ridge about a mile away. The shore was still the same, with rocky islets even more numerous, but we could find no accessible rocks. Crevasses were very bad, and foolishly we had not roped together at the start. Then Close went up to his waist in one we could not see, which was partly filled with snow, and after this we took no chances. Stillwell put his foot through another that was not visible, and then I did the same. We broke the lids of several and looked down. One was particularly beautiful, the walls lined with perfectly formed tabular ice crystals, some of which were several inches across. When we reached the tent again the weather was getting worse, and in the afternoon it was too bad to go out.

Christmas Eve was another bad day and we could not move until 5 p.m., when the wind suddenly dropped and the sky cleared to the east. We worked until 1 a.m., really Christmas morning, and measured the distance between the various snow-mounds while Frank took angles with the theodolite. We turned in with the prospect of a fine day to come.

Christmas Day came in with a sky as black as ink, and heavy snow and drift in a moderate wind. Christmas Day – and our minds turned homewards, also to those other little parties scattered hundreds of miles apart, each, no doubt, thinking similar thoughts. We wondered if they were all safe, and drank their healths in *café au lait*, which we had kept for the occasion. We did not move until late, but, the weather improving, Frank and I went out with the theodolite and walked back 3 miles to complete this portion of the survey. In the afternoon the sky cleared like magic, but a nasty wind made theodolite work very cold. This Christmas very nearly proved my last, and my escape was narrow. For safety, we had roped together, but at the last moment, and to save time, I left Frank to locate a snow-mound about half a mile away, which had fallen down. I had gone about half the distance when quite suddenly I felt myself going through into nothingness. Luckily I fell forward and my arm caught the far edge of a crevasse some 5 feet across, while one toe lodged on a piece of ice sticking out from the wall, which, nevertheless, kept crumbling beneath my weight. The other foot groped in space. Here I hung for a few seconds, my head level with the surface. I cooeed, but Frank was out of earshot, though actually he had seen me disappear and was even then running towards me. But before he reached me I had managed to wriggle carefully onto solid ice again. It was fortunate that I had fallen directly across instead of at an angle, as another few inches would have caused me to miss the side altogether. We looked down through the hole to the blue depths beneath, and by throwing pieces of ice down tried to estimate the depth. They would tinkle as they struck the wall far down, then again, fainter and fainter, until we could hear them no longer.

Christmas dinner that evening was a function I will never forget, vested, as it was, with an atmosphere of adventure and good comradeship. The hoosh tasted better than any roast turkey and the coffee was as stimulating as champagne. Then there was Frank's cake. Before leaving the hut I had made one for the occasion, but it was too big, so we ate it; then Frank tried his hand at another. It was certainly good but we argued long as to whose was the best. Then we had some figs, almonds and raisins, and a tin of fancy biscuits. We toasted the King, our families and friends, our comrades and ourselves, and finally turned into our bags at peace with the world.

The morning of the 26th was still bad, with a heavy gale and surface drift, so we spent it mending our sledge-meter, which had quite broken down. A large piece had broken out of the rim, and this we bound in with splints of bamboo taken from the boom of our mast, held in place by copper wire. Copper wire also was used to replace some of the missing spokes, and, all in all, it made a fairly respectable job. Taking stock of our provisions, we found that we had made the last week's rations do for nine days, and still had a little pemmican and biscuit left, in addition to a full week's untouched – enough to allow for a further nine days: five to complete our survey and four back to the hut. With the repair of the sledge-meter we were able to take it out in the afternoon and complete the work commenced the day before; but in the evening the weather was again very bad.

Once again on the 27th we were delayed by the weather, and did not start until midday; then, working until 1.30 a.m., we completed another 3 miles of the survey, including two offsets to the coast. We were fortunate, however, to find another group of accessible rocks. These we reached by picking our way over a mass of crevasses, then down a 45° slope of ice for over 100 feet. Here, roped together, we cut steps for most of the way. Further examination of this area was deferred until the following day.

In the morning Frank and I again descended and spent several hours collecting geological specimens. This group of rocks was the largest we had yet visited – about 260 yards in length and 60 feet high. The rock consisted of a very coarse gneiss containing large garnet crystals, some of them 2 inches across. A large penguin rookery covered most of the area, and most of the nests had one or two chickens in, some newly hatched, others from nine to ten days old. Wilson, Antarctic and snow petrels hovered about, but we could find no chicks. Some distance to the east we could see another still larger group of rocks which looked possible of access. In the afternoon we resumed our traverse, completing another 3 miles without incident. This evening we had penguin steaks for our dinner, fried in the lid of the cooker, with a piece of copper wire for handle. It was a welcome change in our diet, and we all voted it excellent. We worked late, and by the time I had finished changing plates it was 2 a.m.

It was at this moment that we were fortunate enough to witness the birth of an iceberg. Just as we were about to turn in, a sudden, prolonged roaring made us jump to our feet and rush outside. Away to our right beyond the bend of the bay, the coast was in sight, and a mile or so away sheets of spray flew high in the air. A great mass of ice, broken off from the barrier, rose high above the waves, then plunged downwards until it was almost submerged. Then up again, first one side and then the other, while all the time a noise as of concentrated artillery fire filled the air. We watched it for half an hour, by which time its movements had become less violent; but for a long time after we had turned in the gradually diminishing roar continued, until at last it ceased altogether. It was not a big berg as bergs go, but we felt pleased that we had not missed the sight, though it was too far away to obtain photographs.

The next two days gave us the most important discoveries of our trip. Making to the coast in perfect weather we found an easy access to the large rock masses we had previously seen, and found them a most interesting place. There were two main outcrops, each some 300 yards across, and connected on the land side by a snow causeway, which numerous penguins used as a path. On the seaward side the rocks terminated in cliffs up to 100 feet high, and here we found more birds than we had previously seen. Our first discovery was two nests of the large silver-grey petrel on a ledge high above the sea, each of which contained eggs. It was a stiff climb, but at last I took a photograph (with legs dangling from a narrow ledge), and also captured one of the birds, taking two of the eggs for specimens. This was on the western side; on the eastern rock we found a large rookery of Cape pigeons. Of these we procured seven specimens and about forty eggs. Both these finds were important, for up to this time the silver-grey petrel had never been found nesting, and the Cape pigeons only in latitudes much farther north. Nests of snow petrels were also abundant; but though we searched for a long time, we could find nests of neither the Antarctic nor the Wilson petrel.

Photographing and robbing the nests was no joke. I have spoken of the spitting habits of the petrels and it was now we saw, or rather felt, them at their worst. On the narrow ledges, often with feet dangling over a sheer drop, there was no getting away from it, and Frank and I were soon in a horrible mess. The Cape pigeon was easily the worst, both in range and aim, but the snow petrel ran it a close second. Six feet was nothing to the former, and one little chap just to my right got me on the side of the head every time I moved. I was photographing a group of nests in front of me at the time and had to finish the job.

The spit of these two species presents a striking contrast in colour, that of the snow pigeon being red, while the Cape pigeon favours a bright yellow. Their combined effort made of us complete pictures of the modern schoolyard.

Geologically these rocks were of much the same type as those we had already seen, and belonged evidently to the same formation of gneiss as at the winter quarters. In the centre, however, a huge intrusive sill of basalt, parting the gneiss at an angle of 45°, made a striking contrast, while from it numerous small dykes penetrated the surrounding rock in every direction. Laden with specimens of rocks, birds, eggs and photographs, we returned to the tent, our job now practically finished.

At 3 p.m. on the 30th we were ready to move off on our home-ward journey, but first Stillwell wished to complete the traverse as far as Madigan Nunatak, so we still built snow-mounds on our way uphill. The following morning saw the sky overcast, and after 2 miles heavy snow was falling and we pitched camp. There is little more to be told. This blizzard held us up for three days, in which there was little wind, but the snow was so thick that the visibility was restricted to a couple of yards. The temperature was warm – too warm in fact; about 24°F outside, but inside the tent it rose above freezing point, and caused a thaw. Everything became wet and our discomfort was added to by the weight of accumulating snow, bending the tent wall inwards and restricting our room, so that at last it was impossible to stretch at full length. All sledging parties were to be back at the end of December, so on 3 January we decided to abandon the traverse back to the nunatak, and make a break for home at the first sign of moderate weather. The following day saw an improvement in conditions, with no snow and only a light wind, and it was a pleasure to be again on the move. We made 11.75 miles this day, over a very heavy surface, and were very tired when we camped, as three days cramped in a sleeping-bag does not improve one's condition. We still had plenty of food: the last week's ration had lasted eight days, and we had in hand enough, if necessary, for four or five days more; the only thing of which we were short was cocoa. The nunatak we had left on our left, and were now only 24 miles from the hut.

The next day, 5 January 1913, was our last day. Setting out at 6 a.m., we moved forward into a white wall of snow, which hid the sastrugi and made it hard to keep a direction. Still we pushed on, and both the weather and surface improved so that we made good progress. There and then we decided to make the hut without erecting the tent again. Late in the afternoon we sighted the Mackellar Islands, but, keeping too far to the north, ran into a great amphitheatre of badly crevassed country, all broken into steep and jagged terraces. Our sledge-meter had long since petered out and we had no means of judging distances. We had a stiff pull uphill out of this area for about 2 miles, finally coming out onto the ridge a little below the Aladdin's Cave depot.

We were all quite fresh, though Close's feet were sore from the rough ice and all our lips were cracked and sore from exposure to the sun and wind. The last stage was an easy one, and as we came down the slope to the hut we looked hopefully out to sea for some sign of smoke from the *Aurora*, which was now due. Thus ended our sledging at 11 p.m., after a final day's run of about 25 miles in seventeen hours.

CHAPTER 14

LAST DAYS IN ADÉLIE LAND

From off a land where peaceful rivers flow,
  Where hills are green, and bright-hued flowers grow,
The scent of gum-trees came afar to me,
  Borne by a ship from out the northern sea.

Our work was now practically finished, and there remained but the return of the other sledging parties and the coming of the *Aurora*. With the arrival of the magnetic-pole party there were nine of us in the hut. Every day now we scanned the northern horizon for the wisp of smoke which would herald the approach of the *Aurora* and letters from home. There was a general feeling of relaxation in the air, and a sudden realisation that there was a world outside the Antarctic. For over a year we had been so self-contained that it had seemed as if we had always lived under the same conditions. Memories of another life had faded into the subconscious, only now to be revived with the prospect of returning home.

We revelled in the warm sunshine and easy conditions, though there was still much to be done. Photographs had to be developed, and I was delighted to find I had some seventy negatives of our last sledging trip. Johnnie Hunter and I also had much packing to do, and were busy in assembling the zoological collections ready for shipping.

As the days wore on some anxiety began to make itself felt at the non-appearance of the other sledging parties; also that the *Aurora* had not yet arrived. When she did come she took us all by surprise. Walter Hannam went outside for a moment during lunch one day and rushed in immediately to say that the launch was entering the boat harbour. It appeared that at two o'clock on the same morning she had made the coast and come to anchor under the shelter of the barrier to the west. Here she was hidden from sight of the hut by a ridge of rocks, and while many times during the morning eyes had searched the sea to the north, none had thought of walking the short distance that would have revealed her to our view.

Lunch for the moment was forgotten, and as the launch drew up to the landing-place she was vociferously cheered. To quote Captain 'Gloomy' Davis: 'We were greeted most warmly by nine wild-looking men, some with beards bleached by the weather. They all looked healthy and in fair condition after the severe winter, as they danced about in joyous excitement.'

After the captain, the next to step ashore was Eitel, the secretary of the expedition; and after we had shaken hands all round, he produced great piles of letters, parcels and newspapers. These we deferred for the moment, while, with an air of proprietorship, we showed our visitors round; then, when the launch had gone off to the ship with a load of specimens, we settled down to our mail. Letters, of course, are personal matters, of interest only to the individual; but when it came to the newspapers it was surprising how little we could find to read. So much of the news of the moment is of passing interest that, unless it is followed day by day, it has no retrospective value. Australia had lost the cricket Tests; the *Titanic* had been sunk with great loss of life; the Balkan War had been waged; Scott was spending another year in the Antarctic – these events seemed to be all that had happened while we were away, though after our return the gap in our knowledge of worldly affairs was sometimes revealed in conversation with other people.

That evening we entertained a party from the ship to a real dinner, such as our experience had rendered possible and, after the usual ship's fare, our visitors were inclined to scoff at tales of hardships on shore. Among them, I was greeted by an old schoolmate, Fletcher, now first mate of the *Aurora*, whom I had not seen for many years.

After the first excitement was over there was nothing to do until the arrival of the other sledgers, apart from sending off to the ship loads of specimens and other gear. Day after day went by and anxiety deepened. Captain Davis wished to leave not later than 30 January, in order to pick up the second base, some 1500 miles to the west.

We learned for the first time of the rather precarious position in which they had been landed. When the *Aurora* left Adélie Land a year before it was hoped to establish this base 400 or 500 miles along the coast, and indeed it was felt quite possible that sledging parties from both bases would link up with each other. Actually, however, the shores westwards of Commonwealth Bay proved just as inaccessible as they had to the east. A great belt of heavy pack-ice lay off the coast and, after many attempts to penetrate, the *Aurora* was forced always to the west, and even to the north. Just when it seemed that any idea of landing would have to be abandoned and the party returned to Australia, an ice-shelf similar to that off Adélie Land was found, with open water on its western side. Unlike Commonwealth Bay, however, the open water did not extend to the land, and the progress of the ship was stopped by solid floe-ice, remaining from the previous winter, and not yet broken out.

It was a time for desperate measures: either the establishment of a second base must be abandoned or the party landed far from the shore. At the junction of the sea-ice with the cliffs of the barrier, ramps of snow gave access to the top. It was rather a dangerous experiment, as no previous expedition had ever considered wintering on the unstable surface of an ice-barrier. These are invariably fissured by numerous crevasses, and large portions continually break away to form new icebergs. Moreover, the distance to land was over 15 miles, and all sledging parties would have to traverse this dangerous area before beginning real exploration. The eight members were, however, unanimous in favour of taking the chance and, with all their gear, had been landed on the floe-ice adjacent to the barrier. By means of sheer-legs and tackle, it had all been hauled to the top, and some distance back from the edge where it was proposed to erect the hut. In this position they had been left and Captain Davis was naturally concerned as to their possible fate. Only a few miles farther west the German expedition under Drygalski had been frozen in quite early in the year, and it was necessary, if the second base was to be rescued, that the attempt should not be made too late in the brief summer season.

This was the position during these days of anxious waiting. The weather was intermittently good. From the point of view of those on shore, the occasional blows were now so much accepted as the normal climate that there is no mention of them in my diary. But on

142

the ship it was another matter, and constant vigilance was necessary to prevent her from being swept either on shore or onto the rock islets and reefs that lay off the winter quarters.

On 16 January 1913 three figures appeared coming down the slope at the back of the hut, and a few minutes later Madigan, Dad McLean and Correll were being welcomed, after an absence of nearly ten weeks.

Theirs was an interesting story of a most successful journey some 270 miles to the east. As this book is mainly a personal narrative I do not propose to do more than to sketch their adventures, though perhaps the detailed account of our own journey to the east will convey a general impression of the conditions they experienced. As with the magnetic-pole party compared with their supporting party, they had to travel farther and faster, to conserve food and face a much wider range of difficult country. To understand their journey it is necessary to study the map of this part of Antarctica, this map, of course, being largely the results of their own discoveries.

The nature of the ice-covered plateau for some hundreds of miles to the south of the winter quarters has already been shown, and it is evident that this plateau extended not only to the west, but to the east, where it finally abutted on the high range of mountains forming the western shore of the Ross Sea some 600 miles away. Generally speaking, this plateau sloped steadily to the sea, but 40 miles east of the hut the first of two broad valleys intersected it in a south and north direction. Down these valleys the ice moved with accelerated pace in two huge glaciers, which pushed out to sea in great floating glacier tongues. The first of these glaciers was later designated the 'Mertz Glacier', the second the 'Ninnis Glacier', after our two comrades who sleep for ever on their slopes. The effect of the glacier tongues was to hold back the pack-ice accumulating in the sea to the east, and this in turn prevented the frozen floes of winter breaking away from the land, so that the coast was quite ice-bound and unapproachable by shipping. It was the western margin of the Mertz Glacier that formed the limit of the open sea through which the *Aurora* came to our winter quarters. The whole of the surfaces of both glaciers was traversed by a labyrinth of pressure ridges and crevasses, and their transit was a matter of great difficulty and danger.

It was through this terrain that Madigan's party had pushed. South-east of Madigan Nunatak they established their first depot on Mount Murchison, an eminence on the side of the first of the great glaciers. From here they descended a side valley until they came to the surface of the glacier. This was very dangerous country, and first Correll fell through a crevasse, and then Madigan, to the full length of his sledging rope. Madigan's was a trying experience as they were going downhill at the time with Madigan ahead and the other two checking the speed of the sledge behind. His fall was about 14 feet, and here he dangled at the end of the rope, supported by his harness, and feeling the sledge slowly slipping above. The other two managed to anchor the sledge with the ice-axe, then hauled him up uninjured but breathless from the sudden shock. Correll's adventure was somewhat similar, and it was characteristic of McLean that to the end of the journey he felt it almost as a personal grievance that he was the only one not to have a crevasse experience.

In the valley right on the margin of the glacier, a high mountain peak, which they called 'Mount Aurora', was the first of many interesting discoveries. The face of the mountain was studded with rock, and any outcrops of rock in this world of ice were invaluable for the light they shed on the geology of the continent. Leaving the tent some 2 miles away, they reached the summit by cutting steps in the ice, only to be overtaken by bad light and falling snow. The descent was accomplished with great difficulty, and in the rising drift the tent was only located by the accident of happening on their own tracks, which were then followed back. It is a risky thing under any circumstances to wander too far from camp in this treacherous climate.

The crossing of the Mertz Glacier was a very difficult proceeding, and a way had to be picked along narrow ledges between the chasms which yawned on every side. This part of the glacier was afloat, and when they emerged upon the eastern margin they came onto solid floe-ice, which provided a good surface for several days. On the right the coast appeared, with here and there large rocky outcrops of granite, which were visited on the way back. Crossing the Ninnis Glacier tongue, they again came onto frozen sea, some 40 miles from the land, to which they sledged, after making a depot on a prominent point.

Here the most interesting discovery of their whole journey was made, in the form of a gigantic bluff of rock over 1000 feet high and 4 miles long, surmounted by sheer cliffs of columnar dolerite, 600 feet high. The columns, perfectly formed, looked like huge organ pipes closely packed together, and made an awe-inspiring sight. Through the sloping talus at the cliff base were outcrops of horizontally banded sandstones of unknown geological age, and in these traces of fossil plants pointed to a remote time, when the climate was less severe, and shrubs and possibly trees flourished in the neighbourhood. In other parts of the Antarctic there is further evidence that the continent was not always ice-covered, and on the shores of the Ross Sea there are even beds of coral interstratified with other sedimentary rocks.

This was the farthest point attained by Madigan's party, and here, 270 miles from the hut, they turned back.

Near the shore the sea-ice was very thin, and numerous lanes of open water accounted for great numbers of Adélie penguins, which had their rookeries in the surrounding rocks. Farther back they found rookeries of Cape pigeons similar to those we had found on our own sledging journey, and also several nests of the silver-grey petrel, and small mite-like insects that crawled in the damp moss on the underside of stones. These constituted the only real land animal life found during the whole of the expedition.

The remaining story of their return journey is the common one of all sledging. Good days and bad days; days when 12 to 15 miles were reeled off over a good surface; days when every yard had to be fought for, and when the sledge-meter at the end of many hours of toil showed a miserable record of miles won. There were the usual periods when thick drifting snow made it impossible to proceed at all, and other times when the pale uncertain light of overcast skies brought attacks of snow-blindness.

They crossed the Mertz Glacier and arrived at the foot of the valley leading to Mount Murchison, at the summit of which was the final depot, with ample provisions to take them to the hut. Their food was practically finished, though they had with them about 1½ pounds of penguin meat secured before they left the coast. It was only 8 miles to go – a comparatively easy day's march. Then their troubles began. Where before there had been hard sastrugi was now nothing but soft snow. They sank to their thighs, and even then did not find a hard surface beneath them. By lifting the front of the sledge they made a yard or two at a time, and when after many hours they were forced by exhaustion to camp, 2 miles was the result of the day's toil. The following day it was even worse, so, by leaving most of the heavy gear, they attempted to get the sledge forward, with the idea of returning for what was left. In this way they did a little over a mile before arriving at the limit of their strength. During this time they lived on a broth made of the shredded penguin meat, but this was now exhausted and starvation stared them in the face, though food was only a little more than 4 miles away.

It was necessary that one should go, so Madigan, leaving the others in their sleeping-bags, decided to make the attempt. It was a long, arduous journey. Hour after hour he toiled in soft snow up to his waist, and when he eventually arrived at the summit he was thoroughly exhausted. He found the depot literally at his feet. What had been a mound of ice 8 feet high now emerged a bare 2 feet above the snow, with the flag still bravely waving from its summit. Six feet of snow had fallen in the few weeks of their absence, and had covered even this windswept spot to that depth. Fortunately he had taken the spade with him, and at once set to work to excavate the bag of food which was so badly needed. Having partaken of some, he at once set off on his return journey and, by following his own track, made better progress. Yet, so slowly did he travel that while yet only a short distance from the tent, he was able to shout directions to the others to fill the cooker with snow and light the primus; and when he arrived the water was ready for the preparation of their much-needed meal. He found McLean and Correll cold and miserable, and they had been quite unable to sleep. His journey of 8 miles had taken eleven-and-a half hours.

Fortified by food, and after a rest, they resumed their journey, and with the sledge lightened of everything that could be dispensed with, they eventually worked it to the top. From here all was plain sailing, and with two long marches of 20 miles they reached Aladdin's Cave, to find a pile of oranges and a note saying the ship was in.

With the arrival of Madigan's party only two were now still out, and at 1 a.m. on the 18th, Bickerton, Whetter and Hodgeman came in from the west, where they had reached a point 160 miles distant. The whole of their journey had been on the plateau, with the sea nearly always in sight on their right, and they found no salient features of geographical interest. In this direction the plateau continued unbroken by either mountain or prominent valley, while beyond the limits of Commonwealth Bay solid pack-ice bordered the land as far as the eye could see. Most of their journey had been man-hauled. Only 18 miles from the hut the aeroplane sledge had broken down beyond repair and they had abandoned it, thence proceeding in the same way as the other parties. Theirs was the same story of varying surfaces, of drift snow and blizzard, crevasses and bad light, with odd days of calm sunshine in which it was a pleasure to pull the sledge. Nevertheless, by mapping the salient features of the coast they had added another sector to the known contour of the Antarctic continent.

All in all, our expedition had now completed a very fair amount of geographical work. Over 400 miles of coast had been explored and mapped, and the nature of the interior proved to a distance of 300 miles, and there yet remained to be added the results of the second base, which were sure to be considerable. One interesting find made by Bickerton's party was a curious piece of black rock lying on the surface of the ice. It was some 5 inches long and 3 inches in the other two dimensions, and has since been proved to be of meteoric origin – actually the first meteorite to be found in the Antarctic.

Bickerton's arrival was a great relief, and now there only remained Dr Mawson's party to be accounted for. The last day by which all sledging parties should return was 15 January. As day by day went by the sense deepened that something tragic had occurred. The feeling of joyous release imparted by the arrival of the ship was gradually replaced by one of intense anxiety.

Dr Mawson had left instructions that if anything happened to him captain Davis was to take charge, and when he was a week overdue the captain called Bage and Madigan into conference. It was now decided that all preparations should be made for a party to spend a further winter in Adélie Land and, as conditions warranted, to search in the south-east for some trace of the missing men. The choice of those who were to stay was a serious matter. The prospect of another such winter as we had already experienced was not a pleasant one, particularly as it would be devoid of those hopes and aspirations which had before done so much to keep up our spirits. Moreover, there would be the absence of so many good comrades, and, in addition, with the ship had come the call of home.

To Captain Davis came the unenviable task of choosing who was to stay. Madigan was to be in charge, and with him were Bage, Bickerton, Hodgeman and McLean, while Jeffries, who had accompanied the ship, volunteered to take charge of the wireless. The ship, if Mawson did not arrive by the 30th, was to leave and pick up the second base. With hands from the ship helping, the wireless topmast, which had blown down in September, was re-erected, fresh stores and coal were landed, penguins and seals killed, and everything done to make the exiles secure for another year. We went about our tasks with heavy hearts at this time, and those of us who were to depart had almost a guilty feeling at thus leaving our comrades behind.

When 30 January came there was still no sign of Dr Mawson and his two companions. To the last moment we clung to the slender hope that some minor accident had thus delayed them, but reluctantly this hope departed. Their rations were limited, and even now there was evidence that the short summer season was near its end. Day after day the wind blew with varying intensity; but even when clear at the hut, clouds of whirling snow on the plateau showed that the respite was short-lived. Search parties had gone nearly as far as Madigan Nunatak, and had seen nothing, but had built several snow-mounds with food on top, just in case some starving wanderer should happen across them. Nothing more was to be done except to make our farewells. Even then the weather was determined to make this as difficult as possible. For seven days the blizzard howled, and for seven days the *Aurora* beat into it to hold her position off the coast. Every anchor carried away, and with her engines at full she steamed into the wind. Sometimes we could just see her, amid the spray, battling in the comparative lee of the ice-barrier; at other times she would be driven to sea, only to fight her way back again. It was not until 7 February that a few hours' lull came, and the launch put out for the shore.

It was a matter of minutes before we boarded her. The relief party came out with us for a last view of the ship. There was no time for prolonged farewells. Few words were spoken, but the last handshake said what the tongue could not utter.

My last impression is of Dad, who for the moment looked as if he had the impulse to climb on board; then he turned his back, only to turn again and wave for as long as the launch was in sight. When next she returned to the ship none but her crew was on board.

Within an hour the misty outline of the plateau was fading in the south.

CHAPTER 15

HOMEWARD BOUND

In the passing years it is good to know
The ties of a friendship won,
To have lived in full for an hour or so,
To have shared in a task well done.

The ship, as we stepped on board, was a mass of ice. Spray had driven aboard and frozen, until she looked like a model ship in a confectioner's window. The rigging to the masthead was covered with white; the fo'c'sle head was filled with solid sea-ice to the depth of over a foot. On the bridge the officers had had a very bad time, as they wore no burberries, and their clothing was not designed for such conditions. Watches were reduced to two hours – as much as a man could stand.

As the ship steamed northwards, all hands set to work to chip as much of the ice away as possible, and as we passed into calmer regions it was necessary to keep a sharp lookout aloft, for the ice as it thawed fell in large pieces to the deck, to the danger of those below.

On board was a small receiving set, and at 8.30 that evening Hannam, by chance, was listening in. It was then that the message came in morse over the air. Its curtness was tragic: 'Mawson arrived. Mertz and Ninnis dead. Return at once and pick up all hands.'

The shock stunned us all. When all hope had gone, the relief of the Doctor's safety was great, but that the Cherub and X were really dead seemed beyond belief. There were no details, just the bald statement; nothing to be discussed, yet we gathered in knots and discussed the possibilities.

The ship was heading south again, and by morning we were once more off Cape Denison. A hundred miles to the north, we had been steaming under a warm sun on a smooth sea; here the wind swept down from the barrier with its usual force. All that day it increased until the evening, when at hurricane power, it covered the ship again with spray, which froze as it fell. The barometer was even lower than usual in this place, where it never rises to the level of other latitudes. We could just see the land through the driving spray.

It was then that Captain Davis came to the wardroom and called all the land party together. He laboured under repressed emotion, the only time we had seen him so affected. He spoke curtly in low tones. He said that a grave responsibility rested upon him and, before deciding, he wished to take us into his confidence and would welcome any suggestions or criticism of his action. He pointed out that while more than anxious to stand by and pick up those who were now on shore, he was very concerned as to the possible fate of the members of the second base. They had been landed in a very precarious situation, to this time unprecedented in the Antarctic, and might even at this moment be in desperate need. Moreover, the season was late, and the Drygalski expedition had found the sea frozen at this time of the year. On the other hand, those left in Adélie Land were safe for at least another year, with a secure hut and ample provisions. We knew better than he did what the weather was like, and it might be possible to pick them up within twenty-four hours, or we might have to wait for weeks. There was not overmuch coal on board – barely enough to see us to the second base and back to Hobart. The decision had to be made now, whether to stand by for a certain period or proceed at once to the relief of Wild's party leaving Dr Mawson and his companions to be rescued in the following summer.

There was silence for a while, and the wind howling in the rigging seemed to supply an answer. Then somebody, I forget who, spoke. His remarks were unanimously endorsed by all. We had the greatest confidence in Captain Davis and whatever he decided we would accept to the full, and stand by him when it came to his accepting responsibility for his actions.

He sighed with relief, and then said simply: 'Well, gentlemen, I think we should go at once to the relief of Wild's party.'

Almost at this moment a wireless message was being sent from Dr Mawson, which was not received. In it he instructed Captain Davis to use his discretion in this very matter, and if he thought it necessary, to proceed at once to the west. Its receipt would have taken a great load of responsibility from the captain's mind.

Once again the *Aurora*'s bow was turned northwards, soon to pass out of the region of blizzards into far calmer waters that lay ahead. The journey to the west was similar in many ways to our approach to Adélie Land a year before. For the most part we steamed over blue seas between icebergs and floe; sometimes pushing through long lines of loose pack, on which Weddell seals, crab-eaters, sea-leopards and numerous penguins rested. Flocks of sea-birds fluttered about us, whales sometimes dived beneath our bows or spouted in the distance; and once we secured with a hand-net a small dead fish of an unknown species which floated on the surface, and which was bottled as a specimen to add to the collections.

On the first day after leaving Adélie Land we sailed for hours past a gigantic iceberg, fully 40 miles in length, situated where open water had been a year before. This was evidently the mass that we had previously taken for solid barrier, and round which the *Aurora* had found a way to the south. Broken from the Mertz Glacier tongue, it had now, in the course of twelve months, drifted some 100 miles to the west.

Then there came a day when we sailed southwards along the margin of another barrier, similar to that we had left 1500 miles to the east. As we passed cape after cape and bay after bay, all hands were on deck waiting for the first glimpse of Wild and his men, whom we had not seen for so long. The third mate, De La Motte, was in the crow's nest, and the skipper called to him:

'Can you see the hut, Mr De La Motte?'

'No sir, but I can nearly see it.'

The roar that came from Gloomy gave us the first real laugh that we had had for some time.

At the foot of the barrier was a narrow shelf of sea-ice some hundreds of yards wide. At its edge stood a number of figures, some of whom we could see waving their arms. We rubbed our eyes, and counted again. There should have been eight, but here were twenty or more. Then, as the distance lessened, the figures separated into two groups. Eight of them were men, the others emperor penguins.

All, then, were safe. Our relief was more than great. The tragedy at the main base was so recent that subconsciously we had almost dreaded this moment, lest we learn that further calamity had overtaken us.

The ship moored right alongside the floe, and as the mooring lines were taken ashore the eight swarmed on board, and everybody was shaking hands and talking at once. For a while there was some confusion, for, with a year's growth of hair and beard, and with the effect of a year's exposure, we found it hard to recognise them, and they us.

We landed and climbed a snow ramp onto the ice-shelf. Well back from the edge was the hut, still half-buried by the snows of winter. Here they had lived the lives of troglodytes. Tunnels extended into the drifts on every side – tunnels that had been used to store the food cases in order to save the ceaseless exertion of digging them out of the snow above. We returned to the sea-ice and interviewed the emperors, who stood in groups discussing the great monster that lay nearby, and also the curious activities of those other penguins who came out of its vitals. They waddled slowly towards us and stood in rows solemnly bowing a greeting. They were very stately and dignified, and lacked the bustling self-importance of the Adélie penguin.

I would like to tell the story of the second base in full. In some ways their experiences had been similar to our own, in other ways very different. But only one of themselves could do justice to the tale, and so I do not propose to give more than an outline of their adventures.

The thing that struck me most at the time was the obvious affection the other seven had for Frank Wild, the leader. It was more than affection, it was almost worship. I never had the privilege of becoming closely associated with Wild, but from what others told us his leadership was inspired. Not a conspicuous figure at any time, yet there was something in his presence that inspired confidence. Like Kipling's sailor, he was a 'man of infinite resource and sagacity', to which might be added the word 'experience'. This was his third trip to the Antarctic, and he had fully absorbed the lessons learned on previous expeditions. Moreover, his quiet cheerfulness, forethought and kindly consideration for those with him never slackened for a moment. He was, in truth, an ideal man for his job.

Generally speaking, if Adélie Land is the worst climate in the world, that in the vicinity of Davis Sea is the second worst. It is true that blizzards were neither so continuous nor so severe; on the other hand, the more frequent spells of fine weather tempted the party to sledge both in the late autumn and early spring. On all these occasions severe blizzards at very low temperatures, when they inevitably did come, gave the sledgers some very unenviable experiences.

On one occasion Jones, Dovers, Harrison, Moyes and Hoadley were confined to their tents for no less than seventeen days by wind and thick snow. This was towards the end of September, when they had proceeded south-west over the sea-ice for the purpose of laying a depot on the coast for the western sledging party in the summer.

Another trying experience befell an eastern depot party consisting of Wild, Jones, Moyes, Harrison, Dovers and Watson at the end of August. Sledging over the Shackleton Ice-Shelf to the south-west, they discovered various islands and nunataks, and finally camped about a quarter of a mile from a high escarpment of ice-capped rock. During the night a tremendous avalanche came down, reaching to within 100 yards of the tents, to be followed by others, which gave the whole of the party an anxious and sleepless night. In the darkness it was impossible to shift, and when in the morning they were about to make a move, a sudden terrific squall of wind split Wild's tent and rendered it useless.

They had not hit on our expedient of sewing the tent legs to the tent itself, and on many occasions had considerable trouble from the collapse or splitting of the tents. Incidentally, in this, as well as other matters, they were greatly handicapped by the lack of a sewing-machine, the one intended for their use having been inadvertently landed at the main base.

On this occasion a blizzard raged for five days, during which they were forced to dig a shelter in the ice and listen throughout to the continual avalanches that thundered down from above. The temperature fell during this period to −30°F.

The main summer sledging journeys added another 300 miles of coastline to the geographical results of the expedition. Between the wars, two summer cruising expeditions, led by Sir Douglas Mawson, have largely defined and mapped the gap between the two bases, so that, all in all, his explorations have increased the knowledge of the shore of Antarctica by over 2000 miles.

The eastern party consisted of Wild, Watson and Kennedy, and they left at the end of October. With them was Harrison, who volunteered to act as supporting party as far as a sledge that had been left at a nunatak some 60 miles to the east. Harrison had the remaining dogs with him, those that had not succumbed to various accidents through the winter, and anticipated no difficulty in making his lonely return journey. As it happened, this sledge had been carried away by a blizzard, so, as the party needed two sledges, Harrison accompanied them throughout. As Jones, Dovers and Hoadley had left in the meantime for the west, Moyes had a long and lonely wait at the hut, under the belief all the time that Harrison had perished.

Wild's party was not able to make a great distance to the east. The great ice-sheet of the Shackleton Ice-Shelf stretched in front of them and adjoined the coast for as far as the eye could reach, but was intercepted by a huge glacier that flowed down a valley in the plateau and tore a way through the ice-sheet that covered the sea. For weeks the party tried to find a way across, but without success. Where the rapidly moving glacier, with the weight of billions of tons of ice behind it, met the fixed barrier ice was a scene of unutterable chaos. Like a colossal plough it had shattered and heaved the ice on either side into great furrows and chasms, absolutely impassable by sledges. On its margin was one great chasm over 1000 feet across and hundreds of feet deep, the bottom and sides mangled and torn into jagged fragments, between which lay bottomless gulfs. It was a scene of terrific and awe-inspiring grandeur, but presented an impassable barrier to the explorer. Some miles to the north of this the party tried to cross but, after pushing for many days in a tangled maze of crevasses and *séracs*, were compelled, with difficulty, to retrace their steps. From here they moved to the south and climbed the plateau in an endeavour to cross the glacier, only to find conditions very little better. From a mountain (Mount Barr Smith) over 4000 feet high, they obtained a view of the coast beyond, with another great glacier flowing down the slopes, which they called 'Scott Glacier'. The limit of their time reached, they turned back and, after the usual sledging adventures, reached the hut. It was a most successful journey, even though they were all disappointed in not penetrating farther to the east.

In the meantime Jones, Hoadley and Dovers were sledging along the margins of the plateau to the west. Numerous ice-falls bounding the borders of intersecting valleys forced them to keep inland at an average distance of 10 miles from the coast, and, in common with all other parties, crevasses and blizzards were an ever-present source of danger and discomfort. Their most interesting discovery lay in an island off the coast, which they were able to reach over the frozen sea surface. This they named 'Masson Island', and on it found a large rookery of emperor penguins, as well as rookeries of the Antarctic petrel and silver-grey petrel. The Antarctic petrel extended the range of the colour scheme of petrel spits by the addition of a bright green tint to the yellow and red we had experienced in Adélie Land.

The journey reached its extreme western point at the Gaussberg, an extinct volcano discovered by the German expedition under Drygalski in 1902. This peak, rising some 1400 feet above sea-level, is in the form of a peninsula connected to the mainland by an ice causeway, 600 feet high. On reaching the summit they found cairns and other evidence of the visit of the German scientists.

A word must be added of the lonely vigil of nine weeks spent by Moyes at the hut. When Harrison did not return he concluded that he had perished, and at one stage took a fortnight's provisions and set out alone to make some search. With the vast expanse of the Shackleton Ice-Shelf before him, the futility of such a proceeding was soon evident and he returned to the hut to await the return of the other sledging parties, at the same time maintaining single-handedly all the necessary scientific records. It was a dreary wait, accentuated by the depression at what he thought was Harrison's fate. When Wild's party returned and he knew Harrison was safe, his joy was beyond all bounds.

The ship was due at the second base on 30 January 1913, and when this date had come and gone, anxiety began to make itself evident. At the time of her arrival, 23 February, all hands were laying in a stock of seal and penguin meat, and were preparing to spend a second winter in the ice. Something above the northern barrier, which looked like a penguin, but which presently resolved into the mainmast of the *Aurora*, was the first intimation of her arrival, and long before she arrived gear and specimens were being sledged to the water's edge.

There was now no reason for delay. With the united efforts of both parties, a few hours sufficed to see everything on board, the mooring ropes were cast off and the *Aurora* edged out from the floe. Here, there were no farewells. Over the stern, at the end of the bubbling wake, a little group of emperors faded quickly to black dots, then vanished altogether. We were homeward bound.

There is little to be recorded of the return voyage. For some hundreds of miles our course lay through a sea covered with myriads of bergs and pieces of broken floe. The rapidly lengthening nights made navigation difficult, and at times dangerous, but the anxieties of the captain and his officers were not reflected in the wardroom, where the land parties found plenty to discuss in the experiences of the previous year. Then came the open sea, with westerly gales and huge following seas, mountains of water half a mile from crest to crest, which raced onwards and looked as if they must engulf us beneath their weight. Then the stern of the *Aurora* would rise up and up, and, poised beneath the crest, with all sails set and the engine at full speed, she would race onwards with them, to sink again into the trough behind. The gales died down, and when almost home, headwinds delayed us for days, only to die down again.

There came a time when, on a calm sea, the outline of distant land rose straight ahead. As we steamed into Port Esperance, hills covered with green came into sight. There was a curious odour in the air, at which tree-hungry men sniffed eagerly. It was the scent of the gum-trees wafted from the land. Houses began to show among the trees; then a wave of excitement spread through the figures that lined the rail. The few field-glasses on board were focused on a figure that stood in a garden fronting a cottage, and eager hands borrowed them in turn until all had gazed their fill. Yes – there could be no doubt about it – it was a girl!

CHAPTER 16

THE TOLL OF THE PLATEAU

When the brooding spectre of the snows
Sends a death blast from the Pole
To jealously cloak its mysteries,
Then the plateau takes its toll.

Would that the story of the expedition could end with the happy return of all our members to Hobart. In many ways this was a sad homecoming, and amid the enthusiastic welcomes and our own pleasure at the unaccustomed sights and ease of civilisation, there was an ever-present heartache which took the edge off all our joy. Not only were seven of our comrades even now facing again the rigours of an Adélie Land winter, but two others we knew we would never see again. With the establishment of the wireless the story of their loss and of Mawson's terrible journey came over the air. But only those who were there at the time, and who know the conditions he endured, can fully read between the lines of the bare narrative and appreciate to the full the fortitude and indomitable resolution which at last brought him through.

His story is one of the great epics of polar exploration. His account of it has already been published in the official history of the expedition, but no apology is needed for the retelling of the tale. In the years to come it will be told and told again whenever great and heroic deeds are recalled.

The fateful journey began on 10 November 1912. I did not see it start, as the members of our party had shaken hands with him two days before and were at that moment laboriously hauling our sledge a few miles to the south. With him were Cherub Ninnis and dear old X, both of whom we were destined never to see again. Their objective was far afield, beyond the limit of all the other eastern parties, and in order to travel fast they took both teams of dogs, eight in each, two sledges, and food for nine weeks.

I have already described the nature of the country to the eastwards, the plateau sloping to the sea, intersected by the great Mertz and Ninnis Glaciers, and of their outward journey there is little to recall beyond the usual tale of narrow escape from crevasses, or the discomfort of snow-blind days and blizzard. Their way lay parallel to the coast, over both glaciers, then as far eastwards as time permitted. With two powerful dog-teams they made rapid progress, often covering from 18 to 20 miles in a day, and on 12 December had reached a point 300 miles east of the winter quarters.

One little incident recorded by Mawson on this day lingers in the memory. For some days Ninnis had been suffering from a whitlow on his finger, which had kept him awake at night. At length Mawson lanced it, and both he and Mertz were delighted that he had slept better than on the night before. It is easy to picture the concern Mertz, in particular, would feel for Ninnis in any such trouble. The two had joined the expedition together in London, and had been associated longer and in a more intimate manner than any other members of the expedition. During the winter months we had all been drawn together, but between Mertz and Ninnis there existed a very deep bond. Mertz, in his warm-hearted, impulsive way, had practically adopted Ninnis, and his affection was almost maternal. Ninnis, less demonstrative, reciprocated this to the full, and indeed it was hard to dissociate them in our thoughts. It was always 'Mertz and Ninnis' or 'Ninnis and Mertz', a composite entity, each the complement of the other. Over such a thing as a painful whitlow one can imagine the solicitude of Mertz, his own rest broken by thoughts of his friend's pain.

On 12 December, 300 miles from the base, all was well with the party. The surface was good, with only an occasional old snow-filled crevasse to suggest possible danger. The dogs were pulling well, and Mertz, ahead on his skis, led the way. Behind him came Mawson, with one sledge and team of dogs, and some distance in the rear Ninnis with the other sledge. Presently Mertz looked back and waved his ice-axe, the signal for any unusual feature. Mawson, riding on the sledge, came to the indistinct margins of a crevasse, similar to thousands which they had already crossed. It seemed quite old and probably filled, so he hardly noticed it, except instinctively to wave the usual warning to Ninnis behind. Ninnis noted the warning and swung his sledge to cross it at right angles. Suddenly Mertz, waving frantically, brought Mawson to a standstill. He looked behind, but nothing was visible save the unbroken horizon of ice to the west. No sign of Ninnis, the sledge or the dogs. Unable for a moment to realise what had happened, both raced back to where a hole yawned in the lid of the crevasse they had just crossed.

The hole was some 12 feet across, a profound chasm that went down to limitless depths. Sledge tracks on one side led to the edge, but did not reappear on the opposite brink. Some 150 feet down was a small ledge, and on it lay a bag of food and two dogs, one inert, the other with a broken back. It whined feebly for a moment or two and then was silent. Apart from the ledge, the blue changed slowly to blackness, and no sound came from the awful depth.

They called and called for hours, but no answer came. The whole of their rope did not reach as far as the ledge, and there was nothing that could be done. Mertz was almost frantic in his grief, and Mawson had to dissuade him from the mad attempt to descend on such rope as they had. All that night they stayed on the spot, calling at intervals into the abyss, reluctant to leave lest by some unforeseen miracle Ninnis might yet be alive.

In the morning two figures stood with bowed heads in lonely solitude. A few hours before they had been three, all in the best of spirits and confident in the success of their undertaking. In one tragic moment overwhelming disaster had come with relentless swiftness, and the plateau had taken its toll. Dr Mawson read the burial service by the side of the crevasse, while Mertz stood uncovered, heedless of the frigid breath of the wind. The last words were spoken, and they stood awhile in silence, then Mertz uttered a broken 'Thank you', and they both turned away.

They now took stock of their situation. With Ninnis had gone the best team of dogs and most of the provisions. The tent, spade and many other valuable items, including pannikins and spoons, had also gone. There remained six dogs, food for one-and-a-half weeks, the cooker and primus, and fortunately ample kerosene. There was no food for the dogs. The tent presented a greater problem, but was improvised by utilising the tent floor which remained, and making a framework from Mertz's skis. Then, with heavy hearts they turned their faces towards the distant goal. That they would ever reach it seemed the barest of forlorn hopes, but action was imperative to ease the shock of the recent tragedy.

For a few days progress was rapid – 12, 18, 20 miles – then the strain began to tell. None of the dogs was in good condition, and first Scott and then Johnson were killed. It was a heart-breaking task, for the poor brutes pulled until they dropped. Their flesh was tough and stringy, and even when mixed with a little of the precious pemmican and boiled for a long time had very little nutriment. Mary went on the 18th and Haldane, after being barely rescued from a crevasse on the 19th, failed on the 21st and was killed also. Pavlova lasted until the 23rd, and Ginger, one of the favourites, survived until the 27th.

It was a tale of gradually reduced day's runs. The toil of sledging on the cold plateau requires much good food to retain the heat of the body, and under reduced rations strength ebbs much more quickly than in milder climates. With hunger comes a difficulty to sleep, and lack of sleep further weakens already impaired powers. On some days they did from 9 to 11 miles; at other times 4 miles represented the maximum effort. It became increasingly difficult to erect the makeshift tent, and inside there was barely room for the two sleeping-bags, and no comfort.

Another week passed and the Ninnis Glacier was at last crossed. On 30 December after a great effort they covered 15 miles, but Mawson noticed that Mertz seemed unduly depressed. Up to this time he had assumed a cheerfulness that implied a determination to win through; now he became weaker and rather listless. Again on the following day he seemed ill, but struggled on for a few miles until he could go no farther. He made no complaint, and it was only when Mawson questioned him that he admitted to violent pains in his abdomen.

The next five days were terrible ones, during which the remaining vestige of hope disappeared. Mertz was rapidly becoming weaker, while Mawson was still comparatively strong. In Mawson's diary, on the 6th, appears the following note:

'A long and wearisome night. If only I could get on; but I must stop with Xavier. He does not appear to be improving, and both our chances are going now.'

To few men, fortunately, comes in life that crisis which is the extreme test of loyalty and cold-blooded courage. Deep down in the hearts of most of us there is that lurking doubt as to how we would respond when the test came. Knowing Mawson as we did, there could never have been any doubt as to his actions at this stage. By himself there was still a slender chance that he might reach the base, but with a weak and ill comrade to care for besides himself, it was only a question of time before both must perish. If such a thought entered his mind, it would not for a moment be considered; instead his only concern at the time was for his friend and companion. There is a curious parallel in an event that was simultaneously happening a few hundred miles away, where Scott and his companions were struggling back from the Pole with a sick comrade, whom, in spite of his protests, they would not leave, an event culminating in the heroic self-sacrifice of Oates and the death of all.

Physically Mawson and Mertz were in striking contrast. Mertz was stockily built, a man of immense strength and restless activity. As a high-powered machine needs ample fuel, so he needed sufficient proper food to maintain his strength. Mawson, on the other hand, was tall and wiry, and even at the hut ate very sparingly. His type, under the strain of insufficient and indigestible food, was likely to last much longer.

A summary of those few days shows the tragedy of it all. On the 2nd they could not move owing to bad weather. On the 3rd they did 4 miles, but Mertz's foot became frostbitten and compelled them to camp. The 4th was a good day, but Mertz was too weak to move. The 5th was bad again, with Mertz much worse. On the 6th Mertz made another effort and, as the surface was downhill, Mawson dragged him on the sledge for 2.5 miles when he became so cold that they had to stop. At this stage the skin was peeling from both their bodies, and the spots thus left were raw and sore.

The 7th was the last day. Mertz was so weak that he had to be helped in and out of his sleeping-bag. At 10 a.m. he fell into a kind of fit, and when he came to, seemed dazed and unaware of his surroundings. He could not eat and during the day fell into further fits. Mawson, worn out by watching, dozed for a while in his own bag, and when he awoke and stretched out an arm, he found his companion stiff.

Thus died Xavier Mertz – X as he will always remain in our memory – whose big heart and unfailing cheerfulness had endeared him to us all. Though of another nationality, he had dove-tailed perfectly into our life at the hut, borne our jokes and reciprocated them with the utmost good humour. Always ready to adapt his moods to those about him, he was the perfect comrade on such an adventure. He sleeps on the eastern slopes of the great glacier that bears his name, just 100 miles from the hut at Commonwealth Bay.

Now Mawson was alone – alone in a land where loneliness weighs like a giant pall. Even with three men together, well equipped and with abundant food, there is an ever-present feeling of a hostile presence, hovering and waiting for a chance to strike. But alone under such circumstances, with his comrades already gone, very little food, and in his heart no hope, he faced the greatest test of all. It was so easy to give up, to save the heartbreaking strain of winning a few more miles before the inevitable happened, to lie in the sleeping-bag, have perhaps one or two good meals to ease the eternal ache of hunger, and then await the painless lethargy that heralded the end. To answer this crisis as he did shows well the indomitable nature of his character.

Though he had abandoned hope, he yet thought that by making an extreme effort he might reach some accessible point, where a search party would, at some future date, recover the records of his journey, and learn the details of their fate. First he took the body of Mertz and piled blocks of snow about it. Cutting the sledge in two, he fashioned a cross from two half runners and erected it above the grave; then once again he read the burial service. Then he turned and went on the long, hard way, alone.

Before him lay the nightmare-like surface of the Mertz Glacier, full of the danger of hidden crevasses. Dragging his half sledge behind him, he struggled on day after day, sometimes making a few miles, sometimes compelled to lie up while the wind howled and the drift snow hurtled by. Often at the end of the day he was so weak that he had to rest before undertaking the laborious task of erecting the makeshift tent. Then the soles of his feet came away in entire pieces, but with strips of clothing he bound them back in place and staggered on.

Ten long days came and went, and then on 17 January he had the most trying experience of all. Suddenly plunging through space in a hidden crevasse, in a fraction of time the thought flashed through his mind that this was the end. But, with a jerk that drove the breath from his body, he pulled up, swinging round and round at the end of his sledging rope. A few feet above him was the half sledge, wedged at the top of the crevasse, on either hand two sheer walls which went down to the depths below, and affording neither hand- nor foothold by which to climb up. He hung for a while taking in his surroundings. Weakened by his previous trials, it seemed hopeless to reach the surface, but at least he would make the effort. Hand over hand he hoisted himself up; then, when at last he had his arm over the edge, it again collapsed, again precipitating him to the length of the rope. Then came the greatest temptation of all. His knife was in his belt – one cut, and his suffering would be over. He wrestled with the idea, but putting it behind him, he again essayed the climb. Inch by inch he went up, until it seemed he would never reach the top. With the last ounce of his strength he seized the sledge, then painfully, feet foremost, pushed himself out on top. For a while he lay exhausted; then, resting every few minutes, set about the task of erecting the tent, finally to crawl into his sleeping-bag for another day.

Out of this adventure came the idea of making a rope ladder from the alpine rope, for he knew he could never negotiate such a climb again. Several times during the passage of the glacier he had similar experiences, but by the aid of the rope ladder was able to extricate himself with much less difficulty.

Twelve more days passed – days which it seems incredible that he could have survived. A little stringy dog-meat, a little pemmican, an ounce or two of chocolate, entirely insufficient to keep up strength even without exertion in a less exacting climate. A review of the mileage covered reflects conditions, with occasional supreme efforts, which always brought their toll of added exhaustion: 2.5 miles, 3, 6, 3.5, 5.5, nil, 9, nil, and so on.

Then there came a day when, with Madigan Nunatak passed on the right, only 23 miles lay between him and the hut – 23 miles of comparatively easy going, which a man in good condition could walk in a day, yet an infinite distance to a man at the end of his physical endurance. He had a bare 2 pounds of food left, sufficient, if eked out, to last a day or two, but inadequate to see him through. This was 29 January, and no less than forty-eight days had passed since the loss of Ninnis, the last twenty-two of which he had been alone. It was the day of a miracle.

Through light drifting snow, a mound of ice, with something black on top, loomed across his path. He could not quicken his steps, but when he came up to it he found a bag of food. This had been left just on chance by a search party consisting of McLean, Hodgeman and Hurley only that morning, and the tragic part is that the two camps on the previous evening had only been 2 miles apart, well in sight in good weather, but hidden effectually from one another by the intervening drift.

To appreciate the one chance in a thousand that had led his steps to this spot, it might be likened to finding a buoy in a fog at sea, when even its existence was unsuspected.

It was not only food that Mawson found on that day, it was hope. It must be remembered that throughout the whole of his terrible journey, at no time had he ever thought that he might possibly win through. It was only an indomitable determination to carry on while strength remained, to reach the farthest possible point before he succumbed.

Even now his struggles were not over. On the hard blue ice of the glacier, and with a gale blowing, it was almost impossible to stand without crampons, and his crampons had been dispensed with weeks before in order to save weight. With ample food, he did 14 miles downwind, being blown along most of the time, and making much leeway, besides sustaining numerous falls. Here he camped, and spent much time fashioning crude crampons from the theodolite case which had been kept.

On the 30th he made 6 miles before these improvised crampons broke up; then, pitching camp, he was delayed another day by blizzard, to reach Aladdin's Cave on 1 February 1913.

Now only 5.5 miles separated him from the hut, all downhill over hard ice, less than two hours of easy travelling in good weather. But the weather was atrocious, the wind a hurricane and the air full of drift. Even now the ship was battling into it, waiting for the lull that would allow those of us returning to Australia to be picked up. Day after day passed and the lull did not come. Little we thought that only a few miles away Mawson waited and waited for that chance to cover the last stage of his epic journey.

The lull came, and even as the ship was steaming away, and while its smoke lingered on the northern horizon, he came in sight of the hut. He waved, and excited figures waved in answer. Then on the last slope came Bickerton, breathless from his uphill run, to support the staggering, emaciated figure down to the hut and safety.

CONCLUSION
from the 1947 volume

My own connection with the expedition ended with the return of the *Aurora* to Hobart in March 1913.

Of the experiences of those who were left in Adélie Land a further volume could be written, but this does not come within the scope of the present account. The Macquarie Island party, also, had many wide and varied adventures, some pleasant, others the reverse, and once again it is better not to tell these at second hand. They did valuable work. Blake completed a survey of the island, besides working out its geology, while Hamilton made large and valuable zoological and botanical collections. Ainsworth kept complete meteorological and other scientific records, while Sandall and Sawyer maintained wireless communication throughout.

When, during the second winter in Adélie Land, the receipt of wireless messages from here necessitated the maintenance of the Macquarie Island base, the party there were given the option of remaining or returning to Australia. They all volunteered to stay another year, but Sawyer, becoming ill, returned to New Zealand in the *Tutanekai* in August 1913.

The *Aurora*, on her way to the Antarctic, picked the other four up on 25 November in the same year, reaching Cape Denison on 12 December. Hunter, Hurley and Correll accompanied her again, to greet Dr Mawson and his six companions. The ship, with all on board, sighted Kangaroo Island on 28 February 1914, and this might be said to conclude the expedition.

The combined scientific results of the three bases exceeded anything that had previously been done by any other expedition. In addition to the work of the land parties during both winters, the *Aurora* had carried out much oceanographic work in the intervening seas, particularly in sounding and deep-sea dredging. The great mass of material thus obtained has been dealt with by specialists in all parts of the world, and the published results in themselves made a considerable scientific library.

Dr Mawson received a well-earned knighthood for his great work, but to all those who were with him he will never be known by any other name than the Doc or D.I. Subsequently in his two summer cruises, with the aid of aeroplanes, many of the gaps in the map of this sector of Antarctica have been filled in. All in all, through his and other expeditions, what until a few years previously was the largest area of unexplored land in the world fast began yielding its secrets to the seekers for knowledge.

This is as it should be; but even if a day should come when modern science brings these regions almost to our doors, and a journey to them becomes only a traveller's incident, it will not dim the memory of hard times, but good times, and the company of the best.

SHACKLETON'S
ARGONAUTS

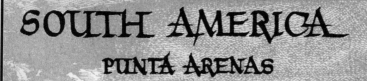

SOUTH AMERICA
PUNTA ARENAS

CAPE HORN
The final escape

ELEPHANT I

The boat voyage to Elephant Island

The drift on the icepacks

WED

ENDURANCE *crushed and sunk here*

The ship's dri

GRAHAM LAND

route from
Buenos Ayres

SOUTH GEORGIA

GRYTVIKEN

750 Miles

ackleton's boat voyage
to bring relief

DELL SEA

*The ship's course
through the icepacks*

COAT'S LAND

*The ENDURANCE
frozen in here*

THE STORY OF
THE PICTURES

It was in a spirit of good sportsmanship that a syndicate of friendly supporters advanced a large sum of money against the precarious security of the picture rights to help finance the expedition.

If all went well and the plans matured, there was a fifty-fifty chance of repayment: if they did not mature then it depended, to a large extent, upon the initiative and resource of the official photographer to retrieve the situation.

The amazing adventures which followed the destruction of our ship provided a grand theme for pictorial interpretation, but the circumstances placed the party in such desperate straits that the official photographer's major problem was to rescue the photographic records.

Sealed in containers, many of the negatives were submerged beneath the mushy ice, deep in the bowels of the wreck, for a fortnight. Rescued after some sensational diving, the cases experienced the perils of a six months' drift on an ice-raft. During the boat voyage, when a choice had to be made between jettisoning rations or negatives, the negatives survived. At Elephant Island these negatives, many undeveloped, were buried beneath snow-drift for five months and were practically the only records that were saved when the party was rescued.

The films and still photographs were eventually shown throughout the world. It is gratifying to relate that not only were they an inspiration to the millions who saw them, but the earnings repaid the 'good sportsmen' and went a long way towards disbursing the financial obligations of the expedition.

FRANK HURLEY

CHAPTER 1

OVERTURE TO ADVENTURE

Yet all experience is an arch wherethro'
Gleams that untravell'd world, whose margin fades
For ever and for ever when I move

TENNYSON

The staccato 'click-click, clack-clack ... click-click, clack-clack' of the boomerang orchestra ended with a *roulade* as the corroboree dancers, decorated from head to toe, disbanded to cook their evening meal. Francis Birtles began to put away the cameras as I made my usual diary entries on the day's 'shooting'.

We had journeyed to this remote jungle haunt on the shores of Carpentaria, north Australia, to film a story of primitive Aboriginal life, and had just 'shot' the concluding scene. While I was writing, our bulldog, Wowser, began to growl and to strain at his chain. Presently there emerged from the undergrowth a semi-clad Aborigine, holding in his hands a short, cleft stick, in the end of which a letter was clamped. This unexpected visitor caught me unawares. I stared back inquiringly as I recognised the broad, grinning features of Jacky, a tracker from the Burketown Police Station. In the lingua franca of north Australia, he spoke: 'Boss, Jacky bringem big white-fella talk along you.' I took the proffered letter from the stick. It was a cable from London. I opened it; it was from Sir Ernest Shackleton. As I read it, I could only express myself in spasmodic ejaculations. It offered me the post of official photographer to his Antarctic expedition, which was about to set out from London. I jumped and shouted for joy. Birtles joined in my glee. Jacky looked on, and, no doubt, sensing that the white man's magic talk called for a dance, he joined in. Soon all our 'artists' went into a pantomimic rapture that lasted well into the night.

The excitement, the heat, the irritating hordes of mosquitoes, interspersed with meditation, did not permit sleep. I meditated long over the enigmatic spin of fortune's where which had turned Sir Ernest's thoughts to seek me out for so privileged an appointment. It was not until some months later that the riddle was solved. Short of funds to the tune of £25,000 to complete his expedition's finances, Sir Ernest was offered this sum by an influential syndicate on condition that he secured the services of the recently returned Mawson expedition's cinematographer. When in the south with Sir Douglas Mawson, I made a remarkable cinema film which aroused worldwide interest. In any case, such a film would be a very precarious security for such a large amount, and I was determined that such good sportsmanship as the syndicate displayed, would not find fortune's wheel had stopped on a losing hazard. But I knew nothing of all this as I dozed off at last in the rosy dawn of Carpentaria.

I awoke in warm sunshine from a nightmare. Birtles was up to his tricks. My hammock, suspended between two trees to avoid ants, was swinging violently as he pushed it to and fro. Is it any wonder that I dreamed I was a castaway on an ice-floe in a surging sea? It was a prophetic dream.

Breakfast of fish, baked Aboriginal-fashion inside a mud envelope, was served, and then the car was packed ready for the homeward journey via Burketown.

I had not the slightest idea of what Shackleton's offer might involve or whither he was bound. The great explorer had long been my hero, and I was game to join him in anything that smacked of high adventure. The cable intimated that I should join the expedition ship at Buenos Aires in five weeks time. That meant a race to Sydney of 1500 miles, over bad roads, and a ship voyage halfway across the world. Could I make it in time? I sent a cable from Burketown saying that I was on the way.

The long tedious voyage to Buenos Aires has no significance in my present story. I arrived in Buenos Aires two days after Shackleton's *Endurance* was moored alongside the quay. I transferred my gear to the expedition ship. The leader was on board. He was standing on the after-deck, scanning the trim lines of the barquentine rig with a mariner's keen appreciation of the beauty of a well-found ship. And this was his flagship, the ship in which he and his 'Argonauts' must brave the world's wildest seas and win the battle against the warring ice-packs.

Sir Ernest Shackleton's greeting and warm handshake made me feel a welcome arrival and an important addition to his team. He fulfilled all the preconceived ideas and ideals that hero-worship had enshrined in him. Shorter by half a head than Sir Douglas Mawson, in many other ways also he bore little resemblance to my former leader. His strong face with its square chin, masterly nose and broad brows, was in sharp contrast to the finely chiselled features of the Australian, whose high forehead and longish chin made the face appear narrow and thin; but they had some characteristics in common. Both possessed the fearless, indomitable will of the born leader. Both were strong men, physically and mentally, able organisers, and accustomed to having their own way. Shackleton planned on broad lines, and while exercising the greatest thought for the comfort and safety of his men, delegated the responsibility of carrying out details to others. Mawson also saw far ahead, but planned elaborately and had almost a mania for minutiae.

Shackleton was an explorer of the type who has carried the Union Jack over uncharted seas and planted it in the heart of unknown lands for sheer adventure's sake. Mawson was first and foremost a scientist, but, not content merely to interpret the data gleaned by roving adventurers into strange lands, had gone forth to gather them himself. Shackleton grafted science onto exploration; Mawson added exploring to science.

Frank Wild, my old comrade of the Mawson expedition, was second in command, and of him I write in admiration. With more Antarctic experience to his credit than any living man, he was a tower of strength to his commander, and a capable substitute when the responsibility of leadership fell on him. Wild was not a big man, but for sheer grit, tenacity of purpose and comradeship he would have been difficult to match.

My first impression of the men with whom I was to be intimately associated for the duration of the expedition was pleasing. They were a genial and lusty crowd of young fellows, mostly from Oxford and Cambridge, and they differed from my comrades of the Australasian Antarctic Expedition only in accent and manner.

After the introduction to my new shipmates and home, Frank Wild briefly outlined to me the objects and plans of the expedition. From Buenos Aires we were to proceed to the sub-Antarctic island of South Georgia, and, after recoaling at one of the whaling stations, the *Endurance* was to push southwards through the pack-ice to the head of the Weddell Sea. There a base would be established and the scientific party would land. This unknown quadrant was to be extensively explored, and a party of five members would be chosen to accompany the leader in an 1800-mile sledge journey across the Antarctic continent, via the South Pole, to the Ross Sea. In the meantime, the *Aurora*, which Sir Ernest Shackleton had purchased from the Mawson expedition, would sail from New Zealand to the Ross Sea and pick up the transcontinental party. It was a plan that only a daring leader with wide vision and strong faith in his ability to inspire and endure would conceive. Those were the qualities that suggested themselves when I met Sir Ernest Shackleton for the first time, and those were the qualities which were continually impressed upon me as time passed.

In comparison with Mawson's sturdy and powerful ship, the *Aurora*, the *Endurance* appeared light and frail at first glance, but, upon going below-decks and investigating, I was gratified to find a mighty frame of oak and a hull of massive pine and greenheart. She was originally built by Christensen, the famous Norwegian constructor, for tourist work in the Arctic, and in consequence was provided with more comfortable accommodation than the *Aurora*, which was built for sealing. She was approximately 350 tons burden, barquentine rigged and capable of steaming up to 10 knots. The *Endurance*, festive in fresh paint, radiant in her dress of spotless sails, was a creature of elegance and shapely beauty. She was embarking on her first voyage – a bride of the sea.

The supercargo may have known that twenty-eight human beings intended to travel aboard the *Endurance*, but he gave no evidence of the fact. It was rumoured that the expedition might extend over three years, so he took no risks and accepted everything that could possibly be stowed aboard.

The crowded hours of our brief stay at Buenos Aires sufficed to infatuate most members of the scientific staff with the charm and hospitality of the Argentine's splendid capital. I suppose, too, that it was not unnatural that our vessel should become the centre of interest; that it should be meticulously inspected, freely autographed and bits of it souvenired; and that we ourselves should be scrutinised and discussed, to the accompaniment of nudgings and remarks such as 'That's one of them.'

Temporarily, attention is diverted from us to the port shipwrights, aloft in the heights of our rigging, dismantling the yards from the mainmast. In the far south these spars would present too great a surface to the blizzards, and might make the ship unnavigable.

A faint scent of attar of roses causes one to turn to ascertain the origin. Ah, yes! It wafts from a group of daintily clad females clustered about the gangway. They are deliberating over the 'No Admittance' sign. They linger and smile confidently. The *señoritas* have evidently made up their minds to look over the *Endurance*. Not even Frank Wild can resist this gentle zephyr of perfumed appeal. The waft passes and the smell of boiling pitch comes from the decks. The caulkers are pouring the molten stuff into newly caulked seams. The decks are strewn with debris, and vulgar for dainty steps and pretty shoes.

At last the official sailing time is set. From early morning a festive crowd of friends and sightseers begin to assemble and, by the time four bells are struck, the dockside is crammed with a congregation worthy of Buenos Aires and the occasion.

Before the sonorous ring of the bell has faded, the pilot gives the order to cast off. The heavy coir springs are let go, and the two tugs on our port side begin their labours. As the breach between the wooden walls and the wharf widens, there arise three glorious cheers. That vast concourse of silent watchers becomes suddenly electrified. Hats wave, handkerchiefs – dainty, man-sized, white and gaudy – dance above cheering heads in a joyous flutter. Farewell messages are shouted across the steadily growing breach to where we are gathered on the fo'c'sle head. We ourselves are doing our best to out-bellow the glad noises of tooting whistles and siren wails. All too quickly the faces of friends merge into the blurred impression of a distant crowd.

The engine-room telegraph on the bridge clangs as though to mark the closing of an overture. Our engines begin to turn on their great effort. The man at the wheel turns the spokes of fate.

CHAPTER 2

SOUTHWARD HO!

It's 'Gang-plank up and in,' dear lass
It's 'Hawsers warp her through!'
And it's 'All clear aft' on the old trail, our own trail, the out trail,
We're backing down on the Long Trail – the trail that is always new.

RUDYARD KIPLING

A gentle swell from the waiting sea sways the ship before the last cheers fade in memory. They echo like a far-off call from the whole world, and, to us, this was their significance. The good wishes of the world go with you, but civilisation sits in judgment on your actions and achievements. Go forth, therefore, 'to seek, to find, and not to yield'.

As we sever connection with our fellow men to follow a mirage in the frozen south, the mind falls into reverie; doubt, apprehension, inspiration and determination come crowding. What tremendous events may transpire while we are locked away in the Great White Silence? But it is impossible to feel other than optimistic and elated under such experienced leadership, aboard a vessel so splendidly equipped and ably manned.

Gently our bows part the waters, churning them into white foam, which, lapping against our sides, makes pleasant whisperings. We clear the mouth of the great Rio de la Plata and head south. The wind being fair, the order is given to make sail. The sails are shaken out, and to the words of the old sea-chanty, 'Sally Brown, I love your daughter', we haul on the halyards with a will. Soon, under a full press of canvas, the *Endurance* is bounding south over the deep blue hills of the south Atlantic Ocean.

As the wind began to freshen, all hands turned to, to lash and stow the deck cargo securely. Tom Crean and I were helping the sailors, when I noticed a boot partly obscured by some boxes and barrels. Fearing that someone had been crushed beneath the cargo, I called Crean, and together we began to investigate. To our surprise, the boot began to move. Crean grabbed it and began to pull hard. Another boot came into sight. Then we heard a muffled voice saying 'Hold on, don't pull, I'll wriggle out.' The boots backed out, a body wriggled next, and then a head. It was a young stowaway. We helped him out and then, to our further astonishment, another stowaway followed. It was his pal – a black cat.

Looking down from the bridge, keenly interested in what was going on, was Sir Ernest Shackleton. There was nothing left for us to do but take the stowaway up to the leader. Sir Ernest, with characteristic Irish humour, feigned austerity. The cat purred and rubbed contentedly against Sir Ernest's legs, as if to help the cause for which the stowaway pleaded. He wanted to go with the expedition in any capacity. Sir Ernest patted the youngster's shoulder and spoke to him in a fatherly way. Blackborrow – for that was his name – was made the ship's steward.

So time begins weaving. Days and incidents are entered and many pages turned in many diaries. Each morning Blackborrow tears a date off the wardroom calendar. We pay little heed. There are no weekend bills to meet, no appointments to keep, one scarcely stops to ponder at the effortless glide of time. Gradually, almost imperceptibly, we have drifted into a rut – a thing that we have been striving to avoid. We barely give thought to the fact that our razors have been laid aside, that beards, ten days old, have played havoc with the debonair complexions that were once our pride.

Water aboard ship must be conserved, and there is little for bathing and laundry purposes. We have been transferring coal from deck to bunkers, and our clothes and complexions bear witness to the fact. It is rather astonishing that even those with highly trained intellects can fall so quickly into primitive habits. There is nothing and no one with which comparisons may be made. The one who purloins enough hot water from the engineer or the cook to shave and scrub looks incongruously out of place among this hirsute assemblage.

We are steaming through the notorious 'roaring forties'. A callous, omnipotent foe encompasses us, merciless to the weak and wrathful to the strong. For a week he has flung magnificent power at our starboard quarter, but, beyond an occasional monster leaping aboard to flood our decks, we have ambled buoyantly south. This 'ambling' is as provoking as it is uncomfortable. Flung from side to side, plunging, lurching, staggering, rising, falling, gyrating, groaning, creaking, wailing: it was as if the constructors had specially designed our ship to indulge in these elfish pranks and to emit these hobgoblin noises. An hour of it is more than enough; a day, an exasperation; a week, almost unbearable. So it is not unnatural that we should have an interest in the promised land apart from its natural lure and our scientific purpose. We tolerate these annoyances with the best stoicism we can muster, but we all look forward to regaining paradise by stepping on solid rock.

It was not until the tenth day that we obtained a fleeting glimpse of the towering ranges of South Georgia peering above banks of dense fog. As we headed for land, we entered a heavy mist that obscured all vision. Though unable to observe the island, we were able to navigate a course by the aid of our noses: there was no doubt that we were drawing closer as there wafted out to us the growing smell of the whaling factories.

Since we were unable to determine a harbour entrance in the enveloping fog, our siren was sounded incessantly in the hope of attracting a whale-chaser. It was not long before we received an answering blast, and soon a small vessel emerged through the mist and ranged alongside. Captain Michelsen, of the *Sitka*, piloted us into Cumberland Bay and then into a miniature haven, King Edward Cove, where anchor was dropped off Grytviken, the shore station of the Argentina Pesca Company.

Ashore, clouds of steam were ascending from an extensive collection of sheds to the mists that wreathed the snow-clad heights. Numbers of whale carcasses, inflated like balloons, were moored to a buoy just off the cutting-up platforms, or 'flensing plan'. Derelict carcasses, stripped of blubber, drifted about the greasy waters and lay stranded on the beaches in vast profusion. We received a noisy welcome from the factory whistles, and a noisome one from the floating carcasses that drifted alongside. Our senses divided our impressions of Grytviken. Slimy waters lapped foreshores polluted by offal and refuse – the accumulation of years. Viewed through the reeking atmosphere, with the nose firmly gripped, even the magnificent inland scenery seemed to grow tainted and to lose its splendour. But first impressions are apt to be misleading. We were destined to spend an enjoyable month in South Georgia.

The dogs were landed and chained out on an adjacent hillside under the care of half a dozen of our men, who for a time, took up their abode in the station hospital. The animals, after their confinement aboard, were exceptionally frisky and broke loose continually, greatly to the consternation of the station pigs, which the dogs took a wolfish delight in rounding up.

Although South Georgia belongs to Great Britain, the men engaged in the whale-oil industry are mostly Scandinavians – seamen of the hardiest type, willing to risk their lives to effect a 'kill', and taking the good with the bad in weather or men. Vikings in feature and physique, they worthily uphold, though in another sphere, the best traditions of the hardy Norsemen.

South Georgia possesses some of the grandest and wildest alpine scenery in the world. Its storm-bound coasts rise precipitously to jagged scarps divided by crevassed glaciers and covered with perpetual snow and mist. The heart of the island has never been penetrated. Round the irregular shores are many fine natural harbours and beautiful fjords, and on the most sheltered of these are based the land stations of seven whaling companies. The industry is prosperous, well organised, and carried on scientifically on an extensive scale, over 100 men being employed during the height of the season. During the year of our arrival no less than 6000 whales were captured, and the value of the whale-oil and by-products approximated £1.25 million.

The whale-chasers range through a radius of 100 miles from the island. Reports, brought back by skippers operating to the south, indicated that ice conditions were severe and an abnormal season was forecast. The skippers strongly advised a month's delay, when the ice-packs would be more scattered and penetrable. The season was still young and, since these navigators had had years of experience in these seas, Sir Ernest Shackleton decided to stay for a month at South

Georgia. The field was almost a virgin one for scientific research, and most suitable for the investigations of our whaling experts, and Sir Ernest's decision met with general approval.

We soon found among the whaling companies many adventurous spirits after our own hearts. Most friendly relations existed between us, and we became the recipients of an almost embarrassing hospitality. A chaser and launches were placed at our disposal to tour the coasts and explore the fjords, and passages were always available for journeys to the whaling-fields.

Years of depredation by sealers and greedy oil-seekers had depleted the numerous sea-elephants and seal rookeries that had once thrived on the island. Through unremitting slaughter, the fur seal, or 'clap match', as it is known, has long since been exterminated. Since it is no longer profitable to exploit the amphibious life, sea-elephants and other members of the seal family have begun to multiply, but they are not as prolific here as in the more inaccessible sub-Antarctic islands I have visited.

Like whaling, the unrestricted massacre of any form of seal life should be most rigorously controlled by international agreements, and poachers should be subject to the severe penalty of confiscation of plant and ships. During a visit to the Crozet Islands with Sir Douglas Mawson's last expeditions, in 1930 and 1931, I witnessed the complete extermination of sea-elephants at American Bay beach by a South African company. Not only were the mature animals slaughtered, but cubs were clubbed to death with a cruelty bordering on sadism. I mention this as a warning to Australian and New Zealand governments, to prevent any such calamity in their sub-Antarctic and Antarctic possessions and dependencies.

King weather is the tyrant of these latitudes, and he rules South Georgia with ruthless despotism. Calm, sunshiny interludes are rare, but fortunately we arrived in fairly good weather. To take advantage of the calm, all hands were astir early and, with motor-boat and pram loaded with scientists, cameras and collecting paraphernalia – not forgetting lunch-baskets and camping gear in case of emergency – we set off to explore the ramifications of Cumberland and nearby bays and to make inland excursions.

Southward Ho!

As we left the 'Scent Bottle', as we facetiously dubbed our anchorage, flocks of Cape pigeons, like giant mottled silvery moths, swept to and fro across our wake. The chugging of our motor-boat put to flight a rookery of cormorants, and they came wheeling round in quick flapping flight, scrutinising our craft with blue-ringed eyes, mystified as to what manner of bird, beast or fish we might be. Of course, there were penguins in plenty. They plopped about in the water, squawking and entertaining us with their quaint antics. Then, as we entered a distant reach, there came to meet us diving petrels, skuas and Dominican gulls. Their cries, though discordant, sounded good to our ears. This symposium from the crags, fens and cascades was nature's welcome.

The glorious sun smiled brightly down upon us, and burnished with a silver lustre the snow-covered crags. The questing arms of the sea entwined moss-covered islets, and led on to distant glooms to embrace the naked feet of snow-crowned monarchs. Nature's gallery encompassed us. Her masterpieces confronted us at every turn. The dropping of the anchor and our wave-wash broke the 'mirror of reflections', and made it dance in a whirl of white mountain and blue sky.

For those members of the expedition who had not previously made the acquaintance of sub-Antarctic fauna in its own habitat, the scene aroused new sensations, and they stood gazing with amazement. The mating season of the sea-elephants was at its height, and the broad strand facing us was congested with wildlife. A few of the more aristocratic citizens – a deputation of gentoo penguins – waddled down, headed by a pompous little chap whom I took to be the mayor. Grouping themselves at a deferential distance, they squawked a dubious welcome. A flock of more inquisitive plebeians, known for some reason as 'paddies', alias sheathbills, but recognised generically by our ornithologist as *Chionis alba*, flew close and, after regarding us furtively, began pecking audaciously at our boots, instruments and paraphernalia. The first flush of excitement subsided, the members formed into little groups and set about their various missions. I found plenty of subjects for my cameras on the seashore: for instance, a comparatively small rookery of sea-elephants, comprising some 200 cows, presided over by one or two bulls.

The animals are at their best at this time of the season. The bulls attain a length of 20 feet and, in their prime, weigh fully 3 tons. During the mating period the animals, especially the bulls, resent interference of any kind. As we approach, they rear up and regard us balefully. Observing that this hostile display does not scare us, they inflate their characteristic proboscis, a sort of short trunk, open wide their mouths and emit a reverberating roar that sounds not unlike the massed snoring of a herd of hogs. This challenge is generally more than sufficient to put to flight other bulls with designs on the harem. The display rather pleases us. We pick up small pebbles and indulge in schoolboy pranks. Thoroughly enraged and evidently believing the sting of pebbles to be an attack, the nearest bull, with astonishing agility, swings round and charges with a headlong rush. This time we are put to flight, but the unwieldy creature is easily outpaced and soon becomes completely winded. Wearing a my-word-if-I-catch-you expression, he flops into the sand and puffs asthmatically. Meanwhile, an alert bull, fresh from the sea, seizes his opportunity to invade the harem. Recognising this would-be usurper as a more serious threat, the thoroughly infuriated lord charges angrily, and generally succeeds in so demoralising the intruder that he bolts pell-mell without showing fight.

Frequently, however, there are fierce fights between the bulls, terminating when one of the antagonists, torn and bleeding, is driven into the sea. On many occasions I stood turning my camera within a few yards of these laborious conflicts, but the rivals were so engrossed in the struggle that they paid no heed to me.

The animals rear up till only the after-quarter of their bodies is on the ground, in which rampant attitude they look fearsome sparring partners. For a moment both glare savagely, then snorting and grunting, butt into the fray. Seizing an opportune moment, one of the bulls attacks in an endeavour to bury his tusks in the blubbery neck-folds of his foe, but the latter is on guard and receives the thrust square on the chest. The impact has as little effect as butting at a stone wall. Hurriedly withdrawing, the attacker braces himself to receive a reciprocal blow, and so the bout progresses. The thick hides become gashed, and blood flows copiously.

If the opponents feel pain they give no sign of it. The conflict continues for an hour or more, and finally one of the bulls becomes tired out. This is the supreme moment. The victor bellows his triumph and the vanquished bull, keeping his eye warily on the winner, flounders seaward. Once out of reach he turns tail and hastily flops down the beach into the sea.

In the harem, the bellowing of the fighters disturbs the sleepers. The cows express their annoyance in staccato barks and snorts, the pups yelp, and the rookery grows restless. But beyond this, the harem takes little interest in the fortunes of its protector.

So the days passed swiftly, profitably and pleasantly at South Georgia. Whenever the weather permitted, keen parties went out, gathering valuable scientific data, and accumulating bulging collections of specimens which they brought lovingly back to the ship, to further strain the capacity of the confined cabin space and congested wardroom.

When blizzards held up these energetic enterprises in the field, the scientists diverted their activities to the ship, where the work of sorting, labelling and preserving went ahead with an alacrity in which the hands of time played no part. The deck laboratory was piled high with birds, and with buckets containing marine life dredged from the shallows. Two 'bird-men' conducted a methodical hunt through the feathers of the birds for ticks, lice and other parasites.

The wardroom is the battlefield of more scientific thrills. The dining table resembles a section of richly verdured South Georgian terrain. Sir Ernest Shackleton, Jock Wordie, Robbie Clark, Hussey, Dr Macklin and one or two helpers, armed with forceps and magnifying lenses, bend over a heterogeneous profusion of grasses, mosses, lichens, azorellas, etc. They are searching the tangled mass, blade by blade and leaf by leaf, for tiny springtails, diminutive spiders, beetles, slaters and other lowly insects.

Though I sympathise with the scientists, I am afraid I have not the patience to enthuse over these microscopical 'bug hunts'. Evidently they stimulate in the scientific mind some highly specialised emotion which I lack. However, I admire the zeal and indefatigable patience of these learned men.

I am greatly perturbed that some of the more ferocious mites – notably the springtails – may hop up into the luxuriant beards as they sweep across the mosses and grasses and, in this well-fed seclusion, breed a more formidable species that may hunt the scientists.

The intensive sorting invariably makes mealtime long overdue; the biologists seem to be playing at hide-and-seek with some microbe whenever the stewards come in to lay the table. During meals, amid much small talk, chiefly about insects, it is not uncommon to observe numerous uninvited guests making their way across the bare spaces of the table, while a scientific hunter dashes off for forceps and a preserving bottle.

While one section of our scientific staff prosecutes the search for life beneath a microscope, another branch finds even greater interest scanning the sea with a telescope in quest of the largest creatures that ever lived – but that is the fascinating subject of the next chapter.

CHAPTER 3

'THAR SHE BLOWS'

A wanderer is man from his birth.
He was born in a ship
On the breast of the River of Time
Brimming with wonder and joy.

MATTHEW ARNOLD

Whale-hunting is big-game hunting *in excelsis*. As far as is known, whales are the largest creatures that have ever lived on earth. The largest that has been officially taped was a blue whale captured near South Georgia, measuring 92 feet 5 inches. Such a monster would weigh about 80 tons, equal to the weight of sixteen full-grown Indian elephants. It is quite possible that larger whales have been taken. Specimens measuring over 100 feet have been reported but, as in many fish stories, they shrink under the measuring-tape.

Incidentally, the whale is not a fish, but a warm-blooded mammal belonging to the order Cetacea, which is believed to have had its origin in a group of carnivorous marsupials that roamed the earth some millions of years ago. On shore, the animal could never have grown to such gigantic proportions, because the legs could not have supported so ponderous a body. In the sea this problem does not exist and, because of this supporting medium, the young attain an almost unbelievable size at birth. Observations made by South Georgia whalers over many years show that the length of the average blue-whale calf at birth is 25 feet. Such a bonny baby would weigh a mere 8 tons. Twins? Well, very rarely. I did see a pair on the cutting-up platform at Grytviken and they measured 11 feet and 10 feet.

The calf grows at an amazing rate; in six years it will be full-grown and, if a female, will attain sexual maturity at the age of two years.

Two years later it may give birth to its own offspring. Sea legend is responsible for the belief that whales live for a thousand years, but scientists have reduced this fine old age to round about eighty years. All these facts are astonishing enough, but it almost savours of a true fish story when it is known that the food which supports these mammoth creatures is a variety of insignificant shrimp barely 1 inch long. These tiny shrimps, known to science as *Euphausia inermes*, and to the whalers as 'krill', subsist on diatoms which are invisible to the naked eye. So the food of the largest creature ever known is removed but one stage from microscopic life. These tiny shrimps are very abundant in Antarctic waters, and I have seen five barrels full of them taken from the stomach of a blue whale, and it was nowhere near full. These whales are incapable of swallowing large food, since their small throats measure only 8 inches across.

The seas surrounding South Georgia have been fished for many years, and are still being exploited profitably. At South Georgia all the subsequent processing operations, such as the extraction of oil and by-products, are carried out on shore at established stations. This limits the sphere of operations and, if the whales left the area, the shore stations would face ruin. To meet such an exigency, and also to exploit the pursuit farther afield, the floating factory was developed; a pernicious arrangement, which permitted a complete unit to follow the migration of whales from one feeding-ground to another.

At first, superannuated vessels up to 12,000 tons were fitted out with makeshift plants, and the cutting-up process was carried on alongside the vessel. Competitive ingenuity and abnormal profits evolved leviathan mother-ships of up to 34,000 tons, with a tank capacity of 25,000 tons. The obsolescent method of cutting-up was superseded by the inclusion of an immense stern port in the vessels' construction, which made it possible to haul the carcasses from the water up onto the spacious main decks. There power-saws and other dissecting devices reduced the time of cutting-up from half a day to half an hour. These modern vessels carry every conceivable refinement in plant and machinery, and, as aids to navigation, mother-ship and accompanying chasers – generally six to eight in number – are equipped with wireless telephones and direction-finding apparatus. Problems of navigation during the frequent blizzards are thereby eliminated.

The methods employed in pursuit and catch at South Georgia are similar to those used elsewhere, but since this industry is of interest to Australia, I will change the scene to those regions, explored and mapped chiefly by Australians and New Zealanders, which are now the richest whaling-fields of the seven seas.

In the glamorous days of whaleboat and hand-lance, only three species, the right whale, the sperm-whale and the bowhead were hunted. The mighty finners and blue whales were immune from such hunting and, furthermore, if a kill were made the prize generally sank. A Norwegian sailor, Svend Foyn, revived the waning industry through the invention of the bomb-harpoon.

But we shall visit one of these modern mobile factory units. Drawing close, we read the name *Sir James Clark Ross*, a doubtful tribute to the illustrious navigator who discovered the Ross Sea. The vessel is of 22,000 tons, with a productive capacity of 2500 barrels a day and a carrying capacity of 135,000 barrels. At least 2000 whales must be captured to fill the tanks of this ship. Six chasers accompanied the vessel to maintain a continuous supply of whales. These operate within a 60-mile radius.

The unusual design of the *Sir James* at once arrests attention. As we draw closer, the sight of this monster abattoir, with blood cascading from its scuppers into a red sea covered with oil and grease, turns interest to revulsion. The dissection of carcasses and the extraction of oil on an unrestricted scale is too colourful for description. We cannot, however, avoid contact with it as I transfer my paraphernalia from the exploring ship, across steel decks littered with blankets of blubber and hunks of flesh, and awash with blood, to the chaser moored alongside.

We go aboard the chaser, *Star X*, and meet Captain Jacobsen, crack gunner of the fleet, and his mate, Als Larsen. These is no doubting the jovial sincerity of the welcome that makes one feel at home. We cast off and sheer away through the congestion of blown-up whales which rise from the sea like partly inflated balloons. Once clear we leap away at 12 knots.

By a happy coincidence I was acquainted with mate Larsen's father, the distinguished Captain C.A. Larsen of the Nordenskjöld Expedition, founder of the South Georgia stations and pioneer of the whaling industry in these waters.

Larsen escorted me over the *Star X*; a workable, sturdy craft, stoutly designed to withstand rough weather and usage, 90 feet long, and equipped with an oil-fired steam unit developing 750 horse-power. Full fuel tanks give the vessel a 4000-mile range.

The principal object of interest is, of course, the harpoon gun. A few steps lead up from the main deck on to the gun platform, which is set well above the bows. The gun is a short, powerful, muzzle-loading cannon, 22 inches long, with a 3-inch bore, pivoted to train in any direction by means of a small wooden handle-grip at the butt end. The harpoon weighs 116 pounds and is equipped with four 12-inch flukes. When the harpoon enters the whale, the pull causes the flukes to open and prevents the iron from drawing out. The harpoon's function is not only to make the whale fast, but to kill it.

A conical-shaped bomb is screwed onto the tip and charged with high explosive. The bomb explodes a few seconds after striking, generally causing instant death. The shaft of the harpoon is slotted to receive a sliding shackle or ring, to which the line is secured. Immediately beneath the gun, 40 fathoms of line is coiled on a flat tray to afford slack for the harpoon during its aerial flight. This forerunner passes over suitable fairleads to a powerful braking device on the winch, and then leads down into the hold. Larsen mentioned that the coiled line was a mile long, and had a breaking strain of 25 tons. This arrangement makes is possible to 'play' a whale much as the angler uses his rod and reel.

Larsen continued: 'If we happen to make fast to a big blue or a finner and the bomb-harpoon is a dud, the whale goes wild. Then the fun begins; that's when you should be here with your camera. He might turn and ram us or dash off – that reminds me – last season we had nearly the full coil out and were towed along at 6 knots with the engines at half astern. After a four hours' tow we came to ice. The weather was pretty thick at the time and we couldn't see far ahead. Unexpectedly we came to ice. The engines were put full astern but that made no difference. The whale dived under the ice and we had to cut away quickly to avoid getting smashed up.'

We climb up onto the bridge where we are greeted by a seemingly gruff fellow, who nods drowsily at us as if dozing in a sleep-walk. Later I found Captain Jacobsen a most cordial host; at the time he was weary to the point of apathy through ceaseless vigil and lack of sleep.

All this time the *Star X* has been speeding through open spaces of water or, with undiminished speed, has been thrillingly manoeuvred through loose pack-ice. Exciting navigation, this, rushing a steel ship through a maze of 'white, floating rocks'. In and out, round and about, we dart and swing. It seems inevitable that we will crash into the masses ahead; then, as one wonders whether those bleary-eyed watchers have dozed off to sleep, and old Johann at the wheel gone crazy, over she heels and round we swerve into an ice-free pool. So the engines throb, the sea rushes past.

The lookout in the crow's-nest shouts down, 'Thar she blows – whale on the port bow.' The chaser swerves as if swinging sharp round a hairpin bend, and the hunt is on. Jacobsen points to a short plume-like spout about 2 miles ahead.

'A sperm,' announces Larsen. 'No use to us, but we'll run close so that you can film it.'

Very few factory-ships are equipped for storage of sperm-oil, and the sperm-whale is not sought after at present because the oil will not mix with other varieties. Sperm-whales were once eagerly hunted and the species is only now recovering from those early depredations. Finners and blue whales comprise 90 per cent of the present-day catch.

As the *Star X* draws closer, I make out the outlines of old-man sperm, idly wallowing as if thoroughly enjoying himself in the glorious sunshine and calm sea. I hasten down onto the gun platform and begin shooting – with my camera. The engines stop and we drift noiselessly, which enables us to get a good close-up of one of the strangest creatures that has ever existed.

I judge him to be about 60 feet long, with an enormous box-like head that takes up one-third of his length. The body is criss-crossed with scars as though the monster has been indulging in a furious battle. I have observed similar injuries on sperm-whales captured near

South Georgia. These were relics of mighty contests with the giant squid, on which the sperm, the largest of the toothed whales, feeds. In the stomach of a sperm we found the mangled sections of huge tentacles as thick as a man's thigh, which must have been torn from a giant squid measuring at least 30 feet across.

We are almost on top of the sperm-whale before he senses danger, when, in a great churning flurry, he disappears, throwing the flukes of his powerful tail high into the air – an indication that he has sounded deeply. Apart from its extraordinary shape, the head presents another strange feature. It contains a spacious cavity filled with cells containing a liquid called 'spermaceti'. Up to fifteen barrels of this fine-quality waxy oil can be obtained from the one whale. The function of the oil-filled cells is conjectural, but they probably serve as a store of energy to sustain the animal when food is scarce, and also over the breeding periods.

Spermaceti must not be confused with ambergris, which is also found only in sperm-whales. Ambergris is never found in healthy whales, but is due to a pathological condition of the intestines. It is a grey, cheesy-looking substance, which is extremely valuable and much sought after as a fixative in high-grade perfumes.

The low evening sun is dappling the clouds and casting reflections on the oily vastness of the deep. It is difficult to see any moving thing among the dancing shapes. Then, as unexpectedly as before, the eagle-eyed lookout calls our attention to a number of tall silvery columns of vapour which spout from the northern skyline at a distance of about 5 miles. Larsen announces, 'All blues, and feeding; we are in luck.' Asked how he knows they are blues at that range, Larsen explains: 'The spout is the telltale. It differs in each variety. The blue whale exhales a powerful column about 50 feet high, the sperm a short thick plume, and so on.'

Warm-blooded sea animals must rise frequently to breathe, and just before the animal reaches the surface it exhales breath under considerable pressure from its lungs. This warm, moisture-saturated vapour condenses in the cold atmosphere, forming a column of finely atomised spray. At a distance of 2 miles, the sound of the spouting can be heard clearly in the still Antarctic atmosphere. The rush of air through the pipe-like nostrils produces a sound not unlike the escape of steam under pressure from a valve.

The distance from the whales is now rapidly narrowing, but they seem quite indifferent to our approach. The waters about us are pink with vast shoals of krill on which the animals are intently feeding. Moving along with mouths open, the whales take water and shrimps into the great caverns of their mouths to be strained by the bristles of the whalebone plates attached to the roof of the mouth. Then, the lower jaw is raised and the entrapped water strained through the baleen by the action of the great soft tongue, leaving the shrimps behind to be swallowed.

This interesting sight is interrupted as we draw almost within harpoon range. The animals sense danger and sound before Jacobsen can get in a shot. We heave to. 'They'll be up soon,' says the gunner. We can follow their course by the oily swirls on the surface.

Now all eyes are focused on the gunner who is intently following the swirls as they change direction. The teamwork aboard is faultless. A hasty word from aloft. 'They're coming up!' The helm is spun hard over, the ship swings, and an explosion of vapour, followed by a dark heaving mass, swells up almost beneath out bows. The gun dips and challenges with a deafening roar. The line leaps through the smoke and haze towards a mighty vortex of blood-dyed foam, from which comes a sullen thud as the bomb explodes in the body of the whale. Hurrah! We're fast. It's a blue leviathan, 85 feet of him if there's an inch. The line is rushing out, turning the brake-drums like spinning-jennies, and the brakes can't hold. The gun is quickly reloaded with a killing harpoon, which carries a larger bomb. The desperate dash for freedom slackens, and the winch-man takes advantage and applies the brakes. We begin to move. The tachometer registers a strain of 15 tons on the line – 10 tons then 5 tons – the *Star X* is being towed. This certainly is sensational sport, being towed over the Antarctic seas at 8 knots by a whale.

The burst of speed soon eases as the terrible injury inflicted by the bomb begins to tell. Soon the dying mammoth rises to the surface, spouting columns of blood-dyed mist. Still there is plenty of reserve energy left. The winch hauls in until we are within easy range. The second harpoon is fired; again that horrible sound of the delayed action bomb – and then the end. The winch clanks in the loose line as the carcass slowly begins to sink. Soon the line becomes taut with the weight of the dead whale. At last it appears, the winch stops, and the gunner pushes a hollow lance attached to a flexible air-pipe down through the blubber into the body cavity. A hissing noise indicates that air is being pumped in.

The carcass beings to swell, to float, to become awash. The lance is withdrawn and the wound caulked with oakum to prevent the air from escaping. A wire strop is next placed round the powerful tail, and made fast to the forepart of the *Star X*. Two of the crew cut off the flukes, which are of no value and would obstruct the towing.

All this was neatly timed, for the capricious Antarctic weather suddenly changed, and heavy mists rolled down over the sea. Then the wind began to pipe and with it came flurries of whirling snow. The *Star X*, deeply laden with her prize, plunged valiantly into the rising blizzard. Vision ahead was limited to 20 yards. But those aboard did not worry. Larsen went into the chartroom, turned a few dials and was able to speak to the factory-ship, and to get precise bearings and directions by wireless signals. So through the storm we headed, maintaining a close lookout for drifting ice. Captain Jacobsen went below to resume his nap, but the fascination of it all kept me awake, although I had already been on deck for 40 hours.

We burst from the fog and snow and confirmed the infallibility of the directional beam. The *Sir James Clark Ross* was directly ahead. As we drew close, she loomed above us through the mist like a gargantuan monster, from which blood, caught in the snow-flurries, rained down on our decks.

I had marvelled at the devices that enabled man's ingenuity to triumph over nature's moods and most powerful creatures, but I marvelled still more that man was unable to triumph over the seemingly more potent monster of his creating: its name is greed.

During the last week of our stay at South Georgia, my whaling experiences terminated in a sensational experience which won for me the expedition's 'Jonah' medal. This rare distinction was awarded for some ludicrous happenings or unusual *faux pas*. It was an outsize leather medal, featuring on one side two whales rampant on a sea azure, and on the reverse side the impress 'JONAH' in large letters.

The presentation took place with appropriate levity during the farewell banquet tendered to the expedition members by the whalers. The citation referred to 'a similar experience having befallen a Hebrew prophet who, as holy writ records, was swallowed by a whale'. Here is the unique experience which befell me, or to be more precise, the experience into which I fell.

It happened on my way to keep a dinner engagement at Captain Jacobsen's. The night was exceptionally black, blowing hard and snowy. The sailors had rowed me ashore and returned to the *Endurance*, and I made my way along the waterfront by the feeble flutter of a hurricane lamp to the 'flensing plan', across which I intended to take a short cut. Halfway over I found the path barred by a huge carcass that had recently been hauled up. I tried to make my way round the head but, as the tide was full and it was deep in water, I tried the tail end. There was too much offal that way, so I decided to climb over the obstacle. This was made possible by several small ladders which the flensers had left alongside the carcass. I reached the top safely, but then the ladder began to slide and, before I knew what had happened, I was precipitated into something yielding and horribly clammy. The lamp went out, and I had no matches, so I could not see my surroundings – which was perhaps fortunate – but I realised that I had fallen literally into the bowels of a whale. The flensers had been at work dissecting the opposite side, and the chasm they had dug was not visible when I climbed. The absurdity of my loathsome predicament was aggravating, yet grimly amusing. The more I struggled to get free, the more entangled I became and the deeper I sank. Though naturally anxious to avoid the publicity, there was nothing for it but to call for assistance.

In response to repeated bellowing, I heard the sound of footsteps, and a lamp was thrust over the opening, revealing an astonished face which, peering at me, muttered a Norwegian oath. The face vanished and I heard my rescuer hurrying off. A little later half the factory-hands turned up with ropes and lamps. I was hauled out amid boisterous laughter and cries of 'Jonah'. In my filthy condition I felt like him, but after a hot bath and clean clothes I was ready to laugh at the experience, which, as far as I know, has only once befallen another person – but on that occasion the whale was alive.

South Georgia must ever be to us, who were Shackleton's men, the home of memories. Its whalers were not only ready to lend a helping hand at the outset of the expedition but, as will be seen later, when disaster and calamity overtook us in the far south, they came hurrying to our relief.

At Grytviken there is a little Lutheran church with a tiny graveyard, looking out over the peaceful blue of Cumberland Bay. Behind tower the mountains that Sir Ernest loved so well – the mountains that two years later he attacked and conquered in order to bring relief to his castaway comrades on Elephant Island; the mountains that stand as nature's imperishable monument to his memory.

In the little graveyard is a cairn built by the hands of Frank Wild. It marks the earthly resting place of our beloved leader, who passed away aboard his ship, the *Quest*, on 4 January 1922, while making his last voyage to the Antarctic.

CHAPTER 4

THE SEA OF CALAMITY

The ice was here, the ice was there,
The ice was all around:
It cracked and growled, and roared and howled,
Like noises in a swound!

COLERIDGE

Information gathered at South Georgia from whaling captains corroborated the records of the few expeditions that had visited the region of our forthcoming activities – the Weddell Sea – and indicated that its waters were so congested with ice as to be almost unnavigable. They averred that we had only a fifty-fifty chance of being able to reach the head of the sea, and a fifty-fifty chance of ever being able to get out again. Failure and disaster had beset ships attempting to penetrate this forbidding, ice-ridden sphere, which they dubbed 'Weddell's white hell'. As we were to discover, through bitter experience, the whalers knew what they were talking about.

Sir Ernest Shackleton determined to exercise every precaution commensurate with reasonable risk, and to modify his plans accordingly. He would force the *Endurance* to our intended destination at the southernmost limit of the sea and, if a suitable anchorage could be found, he would winter the ship there. This would avoid doubling the risks by a return voyage to pick up the land party the following year.

According to the whalers, the ice-fields extended as far north as the South Sandwich Islands, an indication that the season was unusually severe. If their information was correct, it meant that the *Endurance* would be compelled to force a passage through more than 1000 miles of pack-ice, in order to carry out the first stage in the plans of the expedition.

Every pound of coal that the vessel could carry would be required, and extensive additions would have to be made to the clothing equipment. We were fortunate in being able to procure the coal from Grytviken station and the clothing from the stores of the various whaling companies.

On 5 December 1914 we drew away from Grytviken, amid farewell cheers, blasts from factory whistles and salvos of harpoon-gun fire, which echoed and rolled among the mountains until we rounded the bluffs of Mount Dusie and headed for the open sea. Outside the weather was, as usual, dull, and there was a high sea running, but the wind blew fair. Sails were set, the order 'full-speed ahead' was rung down to the engine-room, and the ship's bows were turned to the south. As we drew away from the lee of the land, the wind increased. Under steam and sail and with a heavy following sea, our deeply laden vessel proved splendidly seaworthy, riding the combers steadily and buoyantly, and shipping no water.

The scientific staff combined with the sailors in forming three watches, under the charge of Sir Ernest, Frank Wild and Captain Worsley. The work ranged from sailor-man's duties to stoking, and from helping the cook to attending to the dogs. After the freedom ashore and the ample diet of whale-meat, the dogs resented their confinement and grew savage and quarrelsome. A fight between two of them – and these scuffles were frequent – was sufficient to induce in the whole pack a tumult of snapping excitement. They were chained in kennels arranged fore and aft along the port and starboard sides of the main deck, and we had to move cautiously along the narrow passages, because many of the beasts snapped slyly, generally attacking just after one had passed them by.

Thus time scores from our programme the first stage in our plans, and in the reckoning column writes 'satisfactory'. I turn from the ship's wake, with past associations indelibly printed on my memory, to the bows, now toiling determinedly over the intervening swells that lead on to the future and all it holds.

Here no ships pass. Here 'the besom of God is the wild west wind that smites the sea-floor white' or sweeps it up into mighty heaves that roll, unimpeded by landmass, round the globe. But these storm-swept latitudes, ruthlessly inhospitable to man, are the dominions of prolific bird- and sea-life. In their ceaseless quest for food, the feathery wanderers come wheeling and fluttering about the *Endurance*. Here the elegant mollymawk vies with its lordly albatross brother in perfection of flight. These magnificent creatures attain a wing-spread of 10 feet and are truly the supreme rulers of the air. They move in their glide with flexible outstretched wings, which they rarely flap, and they warp almost imperceptibly to adjust their balance or to perform some evolution. They follow the ship tirelessly, day after day, ever ready to pounce down on refuse thrown overboard. Floating garbage scarcely passes the ship's counter before the birds hasten to it. They hover to inspect for a brief moment, slightly retract their wings, and hastily flop down. Almost before they begin to settle, they start gobbling up the titbits ravenously. Other birds, seeing their rivals alight, quicken their speed in anticipation, but invariably just too late. Then they all squat in council, no doubt to argue over the meal, oblivious to the rise and fall of the breakers. When the ship draws well ahead, they resume the chase. This they do in a most interesting way. When heaved to the crest of a wave their wings are quickly outspread, and the birds impulsively dart forward into the breeze, making use of their webbed feet to 'run down' the wave until flying speed is attained.

This observation carries the story to a few hundred miles below South Georgia, where we sight the first ice. A colossal berg comes into view, gleaming like an island of marble surrounded by indigo swells. Sapphire rollers are curling in green billows over its base, and as they break they fling shimmering showers of spray high up its white perpendicular cliffs.

Two days after leaving Grytviken, we reached the South Sandwich group, drawing abreast of Candlemas Island towards sunset. A belt of pack-ice surrounded the shores, which were wreathed in cloud. This impenetrable pack prevented us from landing on these little-known volcanic outcrops.

At intervals, rifts in the mist yielded glimpses of snow-clad heights and scarps of black rock – the last rock we were destined to look upon for sixteen months. At 10 p.m. we received the first check – our first actual encounter with ice. This was disconcerting, since we had hoped to find open water for at least another 200 miles to the south. Sails were furled and, as the pack appeared to be only a narrow belt, we proceeded under steam along the margin, looking for an opening.

The swell was breaking along the edge of the ice, which was crushing and grinding wildly. Conditions were much too hazardous to permit an attempt to force the ship through. The thunder of the surf and the tumult of the battling masses seemed to utter an ominous warning that the barriers of the Weddell Sea were set against us.

'And then there came both mist and snow and it grew wondrous cold.' Gazing through the snow-flurries at the grey curtains of fog that rolled up from the south, we felt like Argonauts whose quest had led to the edge of the world. Slowly we crept on, filled with wonder and expectancy. The weather improved and the sea became calm. For three days we skirted the sea-edge of the ice, which trended away to the east, and, since it then showed favourable indications of thinning, the ship's bows were swung to the south, and the conquest of the Weddell Sea began in grim earnest.

During the ensuing five weeks, we nosed through heavily ice-laden waters, threading a careful course down narrow ways, or ramming a path, yard by yard, through stubborn ice-fields. The passage became a combination of intricate navigation, subtle seamanship, and engine-room tactics. The ship became a floating ram. The problem was how to reach a determined point by the shortest route, without consuming coal unnecessarily in ramming the ice, and without jeopardising the vessel by getting her 'nipped' between the floes.

Although barely embarked upon our adventure, we had already passed into a world of peril and wonder. From the crow's-nest at the stern mainmast, our eyes surveyed a vast inhospitable waste – a stupendous and soul-perturbing scene. From horizon to horizon the sea presented itself as a vast plain, tessellated with dazzling, irregular sheets of ice, resembling a colossal jig-saw puzzle with pieces varying in area from a few square yards to expanses of square miles. The sections were seamed with the endless ramifications of a maze of waterways and pools. Each waterway or 'lead' was a treacherous trap, gaping like the jaws of a titan's vice, ready to close and crush the intruder.

Looking towards the sun in the vessel's wake, the leads formed a mesh of waterways – chains of silver which linked together burnished lakes, like jewels on the bosom of the world. Yet how capricious is nature's expression in these latitudes! Her enchanting smiles, in a matter of minutes, change to scowls of devilish malice. In less than an hour frowning clouds could drape the skies, and the blizzard, let loose with awful wrath, could set the packs in thunderous motion, thousands of square miles of ice driving north, millions of ice-floes in the crush. Pity the ship caught in the devastating turmoil.

Let us observe how the ship is navigated through the treacherous labyrinth. Viewed from aloft, our vessel resembles a huge wedge. Captain Worsley is standing on the bridge, one hand on the engine-room telegraph, the other manipulating a semaphore which directs the man at the wheel. The lead through which we are steaming is narrow and winding. Worsley signals the direction, the helmsman instantly responds, and we swing through. Too often the lead narrows, or is blocked by an impenetrable floe, perhaps a mile across. If the floe is not more than 3 feet thick, the *Endurance* can split it and wedge her way through.

Our vessel is now coming to such an obstruction. Worsley selects a point of attack that promises a line of weakness. 'Full-speed ahead' is rung down to the engine-room. The engines throb and the ship quickly gathers speed. Hold on in readiness for the impact. There is a mighty collision as though we have run onto a reef. The ship is brought to a standstill. Her massive bows rise up on the ice nearly clear of the water. Then, as if dulled by the violence of the concussion, she slides slowly back, reeling from side to side. The steel-shod prow has inflicted a deep scar in the floe, but it has not yielded. We must try again. We go astern and prepare for another charge. This time the ship's bows will be directed full and square into the 'V'. The dogs have been stirred from sleep by the violent shock and are taking a yelping interest in the proceedings. Once more we forge ahead, gaining speed. The helmsman watches the semaphore keenly. One wonders whether the ship will split the floe or the floe will split the ship. Anxiously we watch and wait. Again the floe receives a 500-ton thrust from our wedge-like bows. The vessel reels under the encounter – a moment of suspense – and then to our joy a dark streak runs from the bows, marking a jagged course, far out across the floe. It is a noble sight.

The engines throb and the tapering bow drives into the cleft. But we are not always able to force a passage so readily. Sometimes the floes are too massive and all our battering is futile. Then the best that can be done is to make the ship fast to a hummock, and await the opening up of the floes under the influence of winds or tides.

The further south we progressed, the heavier the ice became. The great slab-like floes gave way to floating ice islets, gnarled and contorted by terrific pressure. We contemplated these surroundings with some anxiety and wondered ruefully whether the power that could crush ice 10 feet thick to powder, would likewise crush our small wooden ship.

When the novelty of our surroundings and method of progression wore off, we chafed under the exasperating delays. The season was rapidly advancing, and we had a herculean task before us.

Christmas festivities afforded diversion and cheer – especially since we made an excellent run of 71 miles before noon. In honour of the day, the wardroom was decorated and the tablecloths were 'turned'. The Christmas dinner came chiefly from tins, the menu being mock-turtle soup, whitebait, jugged hare, Christmas pudding, mince pies, dessert and crystallised fruits.

Some guests dropped in for a visit after dinner: a bevy of Adélie penguins came from a neighbouring lead and waddled over to contemplate the ship. Hussey entertained them from the poop with his banjo. The birds seemed to enjoy the music, and occasionally expressed their feelings with croaks of 'Clark, – Clark'. Clark was our biologist, and it amused us to hear the penguins apparently calling him. Clark, a patriotic Scot, endeavoured to entertain our little visitors with the melodies of his native highlands; but his amiable intentions failed, for when the penguins heard the bagpipes, they fled in terror and plunged back into the sea. Later in the afternoon a number of beautiful emperor penguins came strutting towards the ship in stately dignity. When they observed us, the strange creatures formed into a group and repeatedly bowed their heads with human-like familiarity.

Later on, we observed that they extended this politeness to one another, and even to their smaller cousins, the Adélies.

I saw New Year's Day 1915 in at the wheel, under cold, snowy conditions. A group of enthusiasts assembled on the bridge to 'ring out the old, ring in the new' on the ship's bell, and all joined hands and lustily sang 'Auld Lang Syne', accompanied by a chorus of piteous wails from our sixty dogs.

The new year augured well. We had established a record run, since entering the pack, of 120 miles for the twenty-four hours. The prospect was improving. A few more such spans and our destination would be in sight.

The 10th of January was a notable day. We reached Coats Land, discovered in 1904 by Dr W.S. Bruce, of the *Scotia* expedition. The 'land' was a barrier of sheer ice-cliffs, rising from the sea to a height of 70 feet, and trending away to the south-west. A light breeze was blowing offshore and this had the effect of drifting the ice away from the barrier and keeping open a wide lane of 'land-water'.

As we proceeded down this imposing waterway, we observed large numbers of seals swimming about and basking on the pack-ice to windward. Immense schools of several hundreds of seals were attracted to the ship, and they entertained us with wonderful displays, gambolling, racing, diving, and sporting like shoals of porpoises. Then they turned about and headed north. This migration of the seals was a warning that winter was falling. They were hastening north to escape before the leads froze and turned the pack into one huge, unbroken field, trapping them in a prison of ice.

On 16 January we sailed along the seafront of a majestic glacier, to which Sir Ernest gave the name 'Caird Coast', in honour of Sir James Caird, a staunch supporter of the expedition. Mighty walls of ice rose perpendicularly to a height of 200 feet from the sea, sloping gradually upwards to the hinterlands, which we estimated to be about 3000 feet in altitude. The ice-sheet looked bleakly inhospitable and was seamed with impassable crevasses. Not a vestige of rock was visible. We passed a large bay where the ice sloped down to the water, offering a possible location for a base, but in view of the great distance to be traversed in the projected transcontinental sledging journey, the leader decided to try to win still farther south. Noon gave our position as latitude 76°27' south, longitude 28°51' west – indicating a remarkable gain of 124 miles in the past twenty-four hours.

We were held up by a blizzard, after this magnificent run, and took shelter in the lee of a grounded iceberg. It was the beginning of our calamities. When the blow was spent and the atmosphere had cleared, a disturbing sight met our eyes. The wind had not only filled the bay before us with ice, but all the sea was jammed with closely pressed pack-ice.

We succeeded in winning a few laborious miles on 18 January, but the wind, blowing hard from the north-east, drove the ice before it, filling up the bight at the head of the Weddell Sea. No water was visible in any direction as far as the eye could reach. The ship was a helpless atom, locked in, and drifting helplessly with the pack.

The rising slopes of the inland ice came clearly into view on the 22nd, about 20 miles to the south. We were in a desperate predicament. The ice-packs were rapidly freezing together and we were utterly powerless to extricate the vessel. There was nothing to do but to wait patiently for a southerly wind, in the hope that it might scatter the pack. Only two hours' steaming through open water, and we could win through to our destination.

CHAPTER 5

IN THE GRIP OF THE PACK-ICE

Out of whose womb came the ice?
And the hoary frost of Heaven, who hath gendered it?
The Waters are hid as with a Stone,
And the face of the deep is frozen.

At midnight next night (23 January 1915) I climbed into the crow's-nest at the head of the mainmast. The midnight sun in glorious spendour threw the shadows of our ship over the snows. We were the only black speck in the dazzling, white panorama of ice that extended to the horizon.

In the absence of even a breath of wind, the air was wonderfully mild, and up there, alone in the intense silence and vastness, I realised the helplessness of our vessel and our utter insignificance. The will that gives man might to rule and dominate avails nothing here. The breeze which wafts the snowflake, the ripple which stirs the lead, the tiny crystals which in countless millions build this gleaming ice-world, are all indifferent to man's word or will. But when the passive tranquillity changes to scourging blizzard, wrathful sea and driving ice-packs, then puny man may well feel overwhelmed by a sense of his abject impotence.

We had one faint hope – that the land, which even then I could see from my lookout, might be reached in a series of forced marches across the pack. In anticipation, the motor-tractor was assembled and tried out on the ice. It proved, however, to be a failure, and quite unsuitable for such a rough surface. To be imprisoned in the ice within view of our intended goal was a heart-rending disappointment. We strained our eyes constantly towards the land to which our hearts yearned, sorely exasperated by its closeness and the impossibility of reaching it. A careful survey of the ice showed that to attempt a journey in the dog-sledges or on foot would be suicidal, since the surface was utterly impassable. As the currents and winds drifted the ice-bound ship to the north, and the shore grew more and more remote, our hopes of landing that season were abandoned. Nevertheless we did not despair, and we looked optimistically towards the future, hoping that the ice might carry us speedily to the open sea. Once free, the *Endurance* would return to South Georgia to be refitted, and would then make another attempt. But these hopes of freedom grew daily smaller and smaller, and we began to realise that it was as impossible to escape to the sea as it was to set foot on the land. We were in a predicament that would test us and our ship to the full. As January ended, we faced the gloomy prospect of autumn and winter as hopefully as we could.

One exciting incident broke the monotony of the first month. During lunch on 25 February we were surprised by a violent shock. All hands rushed on deck to find that the floe in which our ship was embedded had split across, leaving the vessel in the line of the crack. Cheers went up at the sight, but their echoes mocked us, for the ice came together again, leaving us in the same position as before. Four hundred yards ahead, however, lay a reasonably large lead of open water, and Sir Ernest determined to make one more desperate effort to burst our icy shackles. All turned to and attacked the ice with picks, chisels and saws.

In my keenness to secure records of these efforts and of the ship charging the ice, I had a narrow escape from being crushed to death. Putting my camera in a waterproof case, I stood on a small floe immediately in the vessel's path. My programme was to show the vessel making her charge, then to hop aside with the camera a few seconds before the impact. 'Taking movies' while the vessel bore down on my floe was a thrilling experience. She grew larger and larger in the viewfinder. Two seconds more and I must jump. But I didn't jump, for, as I was preparing to spring, there came a mighty bump, and I was thrown into the mushy brash-ice with the ship almost on top of me. The *Endurance* had been diverted from her course by a deep-sea ice-tongue, and had split the floe I was standing on. By the greatest of luck neither I nor the camera was any the worse for the crash or the ducking, and the film I secured was worth the experience.

For two days and nights every endeavour was made to cut the ship free; but the temperature continued to fall, the ice that was broken froze again, and conditions were worse than before.

Although we had known our fate for some time, it was not till the end of February that it was officially admitted. We were ice-bound, and on the 24th all hands were formally put off ship's routine. New forms of duty were allotted to each man. In alphabetical order we took turns as nightwatchmen, coming on duty from 8 p.m. until 8 a.m., and being responsible for the safety of the ship, the keeping up of the bogie-fire, and the taking of meteorological observations. The ship ceased to be a 'nautical vessel' and became practically a shore station. These conditions were observed for a full eight months, 24 October 1915 being the date on which the *Endurance* again became a ship and ship's watches were resumed.

We began the transformation by first housing all the dogs in igloos on the ice in an extended circle round the ship – greatly to their delight. These huts were called 'dogloos' by the men. Some tender-hearted members of the crew made straw mattresses for them, which amused the dogs immensely; they did everything to them except sleep on them.

We next discharged all the stores and cargo from the main hold, and in the space thus made we erected a series of cubicles along both port and starboard sides, leaving room for the mess-table. The bogie for keeping up the temperature was placed near the after-end. The new quarters were christened 'The Ritz', and the occupants – two to each cabin, except the centre one in which Dr Macklin, McIlroy, Hussey and I were berthed – adopted such fancy names for their apartments as 'The Anchorage', 'Auld Reekie', 'The Knuts', 'The Poison Cupboard', and our own, 'The Billabong'. The wardroom was also turned into a double-ender and became 'The Stables', tenanted by Wild, Crean, Marston and Captain Worsley. Sir Ernest occupied his original cabin aft, and if the roasting bogie fell below its normal radiance – as when, for example, some luckless being mistakenly dumped into it a piece of ice instead of a lump of coal – the temperature in the immediate vicinity was raised several degrees by the heat of his comments. The fitting and furnishing of the slightly less than 6-foot cubicles was entered into in an amusing spirit of rivalry, and the relative merits of our dens, the degree of our capacity for entertainment or annoyance, and our hospitality or close-fistedness, provided matter for unending debates throughout the following months. The Ritz was an unostentatious abode, in which one might study the anatomy of the ship – no attempt being made to disguise its strong ribs and stout timbers – but it made a snug home, and was more comfortable than a hut, though eventually we paid the same price as the man in the Bible who built his house upon sand, our abode being founded upon something even less stable.

In the meantime, the sailors had been at work 'ashore', encircling the ship with mounds which were afterwards linked together by a wire hawser. This acted as a guide for those who strayed away from the vessel in the dark of winter or in the fogs and blizzards. The mounds also marked a track to the lead ahead, and this was called the 'Pylon Way'; later the 'Khyber Pass' was added to the local topography.

Life on the ship was varied enough with its duties and exercises. While the light was good enough we played football and hockey on the ice to keep ourselves more or less amused and in good fettle. Work was organised and although the scientific work was naturally limited, there was plenty to do, particularly for the photographer, whose services were requisitioned in every department for making records. This, my own particular field, was one with limitless pictorial possibilities. The ice-sheet, stretching away a thousand miles to the north, was always changing. Its ice-blocks, contorted and thrown up into every conceivable fantastic form, presented a boundless range of subjects. The more prominent ice-pinnacles and unusual formations were fittingly christened and photographed. Several icebergs, which had become temporarily stranded in the pack, became alluring objectives and, later on, serious menaces. These gigantic masses, drawn along by deep-sea currents, forged invincibly ahead, ploughing their way through the fields, and on one occasion our doom would have been sealed but for a blizzard coming up, favourably for once, and driving the ice-packs before it.

The vessel itself was the connecting link between the vast, lifeless solitudes of the south and the living humanity of the north. It was a symbol to all of us, but to me it had a double interest, for, as a factor in any pictorial composition, it was invaluable, giving point and interest, perspective and comparison to many a picture. In itself, too, the ship was an object to muse over. As time went on it became more and more evident that she was doomed. I conceived the ambition of making some pictures of the *Endurance* that would last, and I spent weeks studying her from all angles. She was never twice the same. She was, indeed, a lady of infinite variety. But perhaps she never looked quite so beautiful as when the moonlight etched her inky silhouette, transforming her into a fairyland vessel. During the winter months, when for ninety days we caught no glimpse of the sun and everything was encased in ice, I took a series of flashlight pictures, the temperature being 70°F below freezing point.

Meanwhile, by daylight, the skies were a sublime spectacle. At times the dome of heaven was iridescent, like a lustrous shell in which the mist-veiled sun reposed like a dazzling pearl. There were times when the sky was a rainbow, flaming with radiant mock suns, and one's very heart and soul cried out in rapture, 'These things are not earthly; this is heaven.' There was such a day, just before the sun went down and the long polar night began, when the ice split up in gaping leads and laid bare the sea. The extremely low temperature of the air meeting the comparatively warm sea-water set up a process of condensation. Immense clouds of dark vapour rolled skywards from the water, as if from a boiling lake. These mists solidified into crystals, which fell in shimmering showers from the clear blue sky – a rain of jewels. The sun shone through the glinting fall in great rainbow circles, which spanned the sky. The crystal showers carpeted the pack-ice and ship until she looked like a tinselled beauty set on a field of diamonds.

It was not only the contemplation of the vastness, painted by the sun with scarlet, purple and gold, the dawn flushed with pink, magenta and lilac, the stars which, like celestial lamps, glittered from crystalline skies and lit the infinite spaces that enraptured us. There was as much to be discerned in the smallest things about us – even the most minute crystal. Things the unaided eye could not see became worlds beneath the microscope – worlds conceived with that perfection and love with which the Almighty Sculptor has fashioned the universe.

Our nights, which grew longer and longer, were frequently enlivened with homemade entertainment. At first the gramophone proved a godsend. Many an hour we lay in our bunks listening to its music. Memories of other days were awakened by familiar tunes; we speculated as to when we would hear them again. Curiously enough, the 'talking machine' became the object of one of those superstitions to which men fall victim under unusual conditions. After a time it was noticed that as soon as the music began the ice-pressure commenced, and the vessel began to quiver and creak. The fact was that the pressure recurred at regular intervals, but nothing would convince certain members of the party that the music did not conjure up the elements and originate the pressure. The belief became so strong that eventually the gramophone was placed under a ban. When the ship broke up, the instrument, as it happened, was forced up to the top of a pile of wreckage, and there it was left when we took to the ice-floe, not a soul attempting to salvage it.

Birthdays were, of course, celebrated in proper fashion, but our most ambitious entertainment occurred on 22 June 1915 in celebration of midwinter day. A close holiday was observed. After an excellent breakfast and lunch, we partook of a 'feast' dinner, after which we all retired to our cubicles to dress up. I erected a stage, complete with acetylene footlights, and decorated it with bunting. Sir Ernest opened the evening with a satiric harangue, which was admirably responded to by the Reverend Dr Bubblinglove (Lees). An overture, 'Discord Fantasia' in four flats, by the 'Billabong' band worked the audience up to concert pitch, the band then opportunely retiring to its retreat. Rickinson made an admirable flapper, and McIlroy a gay grisette, highly perfumed, and bewigged with oakum. Greenstreet, the dashing 'knut', was a great success. James's humorous dissertation on the calorie, delivered in a broad brogue, was loudly applauded. Marston, as a country farmer, was superb. The programme comprised some thirty items, and concluded with 'God Save the King' and 'Auld Lang Syne'. Afterwards we sat down to a midnight supper.

I might mention that at that time we had only two hours of very poor twilight each day, in which we could see stars of the fifth magnitude; our ship was embedded in a frozen sea, stretching away to the open ocean, 900 miles to the north. Below us the waters were 2000 feet deep.

Individual hobbies also helped to pass the time. Our library was fairly extensive and varied. Vast imaginary sums were won and lost at dice and cards. The daily round and nightly tasks were summarised in the diary thus:

> *My turn to nightwatch. The duties of the nightwatch are to keep the Ritz bogie glowing, the Stables roasting, and the Boss, who is right aft, at an equable temperature. The latter is a difficult job, as the Boss's room is but a small cabin. The temperature within is either ninety degrees or well below freezing, according to the wind, which greatly influences the bogie draught. Sir Ernest's temper oscillates inversely with the room temperature. The nightwatchman also arouses friends, and they sit around the bogie fire, discoursing in subdued whispers, and partaking of the watchman's bounty, to wit, sardines on toast – a great favourite – grilled biscuit and cocoa or tea. Frequently, a special 'perk', reserved for the occasion, is produced, and the visitors, termed 'ghosts', are appreciative. All hands are called at 8.30 a.m.*

The weather during the six months we had been encumbered by the floes was on the whole quite good; compared with the climate of Adélie Land it was heavenly, though blizzards were not unknown. The temperature ran as low as 70° below freezing point, and those of us whose occupation necessitated dabbling in water found our fingers splitting and our hands nipped with frostbite. But within the shelter of our stout vessel, with a perfect lighting system, a well-stoked bogie and a generously stocked galley, we cared little about the driving snow and shrieking gales. The uncomfortable work of attending to the dogs during blizzards and the job of cutting ice for drinking purposes, and of removing the accumulations from the ship's sides and propeller, only heightened by contrast our appreciation of the comforts of our station.

Yet during the whole of this period, we were conscious of many dangers. Sometimes, as we lay snug in our bunks, the wind, roaring across the hummocked spaces and shrieking through our top hamper, would set the vessel trembling from stem to stern till we wondered if the masts would be torn out like uprooted trees. Sometimes a towering berg would be seen ploughing a drunken passage through the ice, as if bent on crushing the intruding ship; and always, away to the south and east, could be heard the infernal growl and groan of the pressure-tortured ice. We were, however, at this time, alert rather than anxious, assuring ourselves – perhaps bluffing ourselves if the truth were told – that the time would come when the ice would open naturally and our staunch little craft would fight her way clear of the pack.

CHAPTER 6

SLEDGE-DOG PALS

To Shakespeare, the leader of my team and the king of the pack.

How dreary the frozen captivity of our life would have been without the dogs. They were born, bred and trained in the Hudson Bay territory. When we first made their acquaintance on board the *Endurance*, they were fierce, sullen and shy, and appeared not many degrees removed from wolves. We had fifty-four dogs when we reached the Weddell Sea. Six pups were born after we had been frozen in for some months. Four, belonging to Sally, became great favourites, not only with their foster-father, Tom Crean, but with the entire company, who watched their development through frolicsome puppyhood to sturdy doghood with the interest usually bestowed upon an addition to the human family. Sue, of Macklin's team, was not so successful with her family, for, of a litter of eleven pups, only two opened their eyes upon a white and troublesome world.

The dogs were housed on deck in individual kennels, and they stood the outward voyage remarkably well, though naturally they lost condition. As soon as the *Endurance* became embedded in the ice, they were transferred to the floe alongside. When seal-meat became plentiful, they quickly recovered their spirits and eagerness for work. The average weight of our sledge-dogs was 85 pounds – the smallest weighed 70 pounds and the heaviest, a powerful brute named Jasper, 132 pounds. Shakespeare, who was four years old, weighed 115 pounds.

At first the dogs were, to us, just dogs, a mere pack. Certain members of the expedition were responsible for their feeding and others for their care. But later, Sir Ernest adopted the wise plan of dividing them into six teams and apportioning them, by lot, to the members of the party who were to accompany him on his proposed transcontinental journey. It was expected that this would take about 120 days, and each driver was instructed to train his team for a march of that duration.

The feelings of proprietorship and the competition thus set up were speedily reflected in the improved condition of the dogs. I was singularly fortunate in drawing what was probably the best team, and I certainly had the best team-leader. Rival teamsters asserted that I started with an unfair advantage in once having served a brief apprenticeship to a bullock-driver in the backblocks of Australia, while few of them had driven even a golf ball. Nevertheless, I maintain that, though language is important, leadership is paramount; and so I pay tribute to Shakespeare, the finest sledge-dog that ever wore a leader's harness. He was irreverently called 'Tatcho', because his tail had been shorn of all hair by his brother, Bob, in a historic fight. In the north he had been called 'Light', possibly on account of his wonderful learning. Others had called him 'The Holy Hound', because no matter what mischief was afoot, he was the leader; yet, when it came to an investigation of the trouble, no saint ever presented a more innocent face, no dog ever wagged a more virtuous tail. But when his energies were applied to breaking the trail, in sledge-harness, he showed a sagacity that was uncanny, and as a companion he was better than some humans. All in all, his wisdom and knowledge of men justified his new name; he was the Shakespeare among dogs.

The erection of dogloos gave us considerable amusement. At first they were strictly utilitarian, but later, when we were able to secure flat slabs of newly formed ice from a neighbouring lead, the teamsters were as keen to outdo each other in the building of dog-kennels as in the improvement and training of the tenants. The slabs of thin ice could be readily chipped into any desired shape, and cemented together by pouring sea-water over the joinings. Snow, mixed into a mush with sea-water, also made an effective cement, and, in order to secure the dog-chains, it was only necessary to cut a shallow hole in the ice, insert the end of the chain, and pour in a little water. In a few moments the chain was frozen in, and it held so strongly that the combined efforts of a whole team could not wrench it free.

Crystal villages quickly sprang up round the ship and the facilities afforded by the endless supply of building material, and the ease with which it could be assembled, afforded much diversion. Architectural design was limited only by the imagination of the builders. The crystal homes were provided with wooden floors and door-frames – windows being unnecessary, because a faint, blue light filtered through the walls. 'Sailor' was the tenant of a model church, which boasted an icy spire and portico. He, like many another sailor, preferred to curl up outside its precincts. It was, in fact, only when the weather was specially bad that the ice-kennels were used as sleeping quarters. Only then would the dogs retire within them to sleep peacefully, while the wind howled and the snow piled up above them. Some of them, by scratching away the snow, maintained little peepholes through the doorway, either for fresh air or to watch for the hoosh. They also regarded their houses as useful sanctuaries when the stings of conscience troubled them and they had a foreboding that retribution would be exacted by the driver's whip.

Our teams were generally made up of a leader and eight dogs, who were clipped to the main hauling-trace in pairs, each dog having its own particular harness. The training and handling of a dog-team is a fine art. The wise driver first gets to know his dogs and teaches them to know him, and to recognise his mastery. Then he learns to use his words of command with decision, and his long-lashed whip with precision. He practises hour by hour with the whip, until, with unerring accuracy, he can flick a coin from the ground at the length of his 20-foot lash. Driving a dog-team then becomes as simple as driving a motor car; but the man who gives confusing commands, or makes mistakes with his whip, has a sorry time. One of our party was an exponent of the 'rule-by-kindness' theory, but it was proved beyond a doubt that the only way to handle these dogs is by enforcing rigorous but just discipline, under which the animals thrive and work perfectly. Weakness, unkindness and, above all, injustice, will destroy efficiency. A good dog will see that the one in front of him keeps up to his work, snapping at his heels if he shows signs of 'slacking'. Every dog is capable of hauling about 115 pounds when in good fettle.

The only dog in my team who was a consistent slacker was Sailor. He was a powerful, cunning creature who performed all the actions of a hard worker, but exerted only just sufficient energy to keep the trace taut. While on the move he would peep furtively over his shoulder, watching his master and the whip. At the swing of its thong, Sailor would halt instantly, so that the lash would expend its flick in the air – just where Sailor ought to have been, but was not.

We followed the established method of driving. The dogs, when clipped to the trace, are trained to sit absolutely still on their haunches. At the word 'Ready' they leap to attention. At the order 'Mush', they give a quick jerk to break the runners free of the ice, and then move off at a steady gait, each dog putting his back into the work. In turning the team, the order 'Ha!' swings them to the right, 'Gee!' turns them to the left, and the universal 'Whoa!' brings them up standing. During the winter months, when there was no sun, and the whole world was grey and trackless, when an ice-hummock was indistinguishable from a hole, it was impossible for a human being to keep a direct course without a compass; but an intelligent leader – such a dog as old Shakespeare – once put on a set course, would pilot his team unerringly, swinging round hummocks in detours to avoid rough ice, without losing a point of direction.

Astonishing, too, was the complete understanding and sympathy that grew up between dog and man. Time and again, during some moment of acute danger – especially after the wreck of our vessel, when decisions and immediate compliance with them became matters of life and death – the dogs responded to orders with an alacrity they had never displayed before. I am confident they apprehended the danger in our desperate circumstances, and just as each member of the expedition instantly obeyed the instructions of his leader, so did these sagacious creatures eagerly respond to the command of their masters.

My dog-team greatly widened my field of operations. With a comrade on my sledge, I would scout the pack-ice far and wide, in quest of subjects for the camera. These trips were not without a certain risk, for frequently the ice would open up between us and the ship, and then we would be compelled to await a closing up, or to ferry ourselves across on a loose floe. But the dogs' sagacity was by no means infallible. One day, after a solo drive with my team, I was returning to the ship, lying back on the sledge, deeply engrossed in studying an atmospheric phenomenon, the dogs scampering back over the beaten trail, when suddenly I felt myself falling, and before I had time to collect my thoughts I was floundering in icy waters. The cold immersion quickly brought me to my senses, and I realised what had happened. The ice had broken away into a lead right across the track, and the dogs had gone in with the sledge on their heels. On either side, the fractured ice-walls rose perpendicularly from the water, which looked like an inky river running east and west, 20 yards wide. The dogs swam for the opposite bank, towing the sledge, to which I clung for dear life. My life, and the team's, was saved by a large watertight box which I had attached to my sledge for carrying the photographic instruments. On reaching the opposite side, I guided the sledge close against the ice-face. It had just sufficient buoyancy to bear my weight, and, standing precariously on the top, I managed to clamber to safety. Securing an emergency line to a hummock, I hauled out the first three dogs, who pulled the rest of the team onto the floe. On regaining safety the dogs turned on Shakespeare and attacked him for having led them into the lead, and I had to rush to his rescue and stun half the team with the whip handle, to save him from being torn to pieces.

The Antarctic explorer has one foe in the water that he fears – the dreaded killer-whale. With its cruel double row of teeth and its wicked eye, it looks like a huge shark, only more terrifying. The killer – or *Orca gladiator* – is a constant menace to the seal, and the traveller over the ice has always to be on guard against it. When we set out on our sledge journeys, this danger always lurked beneath the ice. Once I was out with one of the sailors, and we were crossing a wide lead that had just frozen over. We had not gone 50 yards when we heard whales blowing close by. Quickly I wheeled the dogs on the thin and treacherous ice and, swinging as sharply as possible, made a dash for safety. No need to shout 'Mush!' and swing the lash. The whip of terror had already cracked over their heads, and they flew before it. The whales behind – there were three of them – broke through the thin ice as though it were tissue-paper and, I fancy, were so staggered by the strange sight that met their eyes, that for a moment they hesitated. Had they gone ahead and attacked us in front, our chances of escape would have been slim indeed; but fortunately we reached the solid ice and made for a big hummock. The killers charged the floe, and poked their heads over the edge. Never in my life have I looked upon more loathsome creatures. Yet, being now in comparative safety, the one thought that came to me was, 'What chances one misses in venturing out without a camera or a gun.'

The sledge-dog is a most accommodating animal in regard to his diet. When pressed by hunger, he will cheerfully consume his brother in harness, and will even make a meal of the harness itself. Fortunately the dogs of the *Endurance* were never reduced to such desperate straits, for early in January we began to collect seal-meat, securing enough to last through winter till the seals reappeared in spring. Variety of food being essential to dogs and men alike, a routine diet was arranged, each dog receiving on one day 1 pound of seal-meat and half a pound of blubber, on the next day 1½ pound of dog biscuits, and on the third day 1 pound of pemmican, which, being designed for sledging rations, is very concentrated. This routine was altered to suit the circumstances and the condition of the dogs. Nourishing hooshes were regularly given, and, when available, bones for gnawing. On one occasion the cook, when the dogs were kennelled aboard, unfortunately put some salt-beef brine into the hoosh by mistake. This drove the dogs nearly mad with thirst, and kept the drivers busy all day melting ice to quench it.

About mid-June 1915, when the teams were at their best, a Canine Derby was arranged. The racetrack was the Pylon Way, the starting line 200 yards away, and the winning-post by the ship. All hands were given a day off to see the race, and all entered thoroughly into the spirit of the meeting. Bets were freely laid in the currency of the Antarctic – chocolate and cigarettes – and some of the sailors dressed themselves up as bookmakers, Wild's team having, in racing parlance, a shade the best of the odds. It was a strange event, run in the short, dim twilight of the Antarctic winter. The teams had all been trained over the course, and seemed to enter into the fun. Sir Ernest, who was also the judge, started the competitors by flashing on the electric light that stood at the head of the Khyber Pass. The teams were sent off to the accompaniment of encouraging cheers from their backers and shouts from the drivers. The dogs seemed to realise what was expected of them, judging by their barking. Wild's team won, covering the distance in 2 minutes 16 seconds. Shakespeare led in his team-mates ten seconds later, and Macklin's team, with Bony Peter in the lead, was third. Next day I challenged the favourites to another spin, 'with passenger up', and won on a protest, Sir Ernest, who was Wild's passenger, having been ignominiously pitched off the sledge en route.

Towards the end of July a three-day blizzard, accompanied by a heavy fall of snow, raged day and night. No one was allowed to leave the ship, except to attend to the dogs. When the wind dropped the aspect of the entire landscape was changed. A huge dump of snow had collected on the port side, depressing the floe and completely covering the kennels. All hands were engaged with shovels, and the dogs emerged none the worse for their experience; in fact, they were unusually active. My own sledge was loaded with five cases of benzine, each weighing 100 pounds, yet when I sprang on top, bringing the load up to 681 pounds, they started off as if pulling an empty sledge and I had great difficulty in restraining them.

A few days later heavy ice-pressure was observed south-west of the ship. Sounds like the breaking of surf could be heard, and during the days the decks were cleared and chains secured so that the dogs might be brought aboard at any moment. A constant lookout was maintained throughout the day and an hourly watch during the night. A crack started from the lead ahead and ran to within 30 yards of the ship. A bare 400 yards away, on the port bow, the ice became very active, crunching and rafting. Huge fragments, many tons in weight, were forced up, and balanced on the top of pressure-ridges 15 feet high. On the morning of 1 August the floe in our vicinity began to move. The dogs were hurriedly brought aboard and the gangways were raised just in the nick of time, for shortly afterwards a pressure-ridge was thrown up close to our starboard quarter. The edges of the floes came together with such force that huge blocks of ice were thrown up and the dogs' crystal palaces were crushed to powder. Next day wooden kennels were constructed on the deck, and thenceforward the dogs were kept on board.

Let me record, as a conclusion to this chapter on the dogs, a typical drive. August was ushered in, and the black darkness of winter skies was beginning to brighten, for the sun was hurrying south. It was gloriously calm when Macklin and I harnessed up old Shakespeare and clipped my team into the sledge. The air was crisp and very keen, for the temperature was 70°F below freezing point; but how exhilarating it was to be alone on the drifting pack-ice at the edge of the world! A dawn of rose and gold lay over the northern sky. Writhing mists ascended from an open lead. The northern sky flared, brilliant and radiant, but over the south the wings of night were still spread, and the full moon was rising, painting an alluring silvery path across the glinting ice. Into this shining way I swung my team, allowing the old leader to meander and to pick his own track through the maze of hummocks. As we drove towards the moonlit south, the northern side of the pack which faced us glowed with reflected pink from the bursting dawn. Looking back we saw the southern side illuminated by the bright moonlight, which converted fantastic ice-ridges and fangs into ghostly shapes. The silence was profound; we were in a dead and frozen world. Then the short day ended. Dawn in the north waned to sunset; northern stars added their jewellery to the skies. We wheeled about in our tracks, and the team sped merrily homeward to the jingle of Shakespeare's bell. We were soon back at the ship, whose hull, ropes and shrouds, heavily coated with rime crystals, stood in gaunt detail, etched sharply against the dark sky and glistening in the moonlight – a spectre ship. We tore ourselves from a phantom world to reality. We unharnessed the dogs, kennelled and fed them – and then went down noisily to the warmth of the Ritz, where the others sat around the bogie fire, carolling merrily to the strains of Hussey's banjo.

CHAPTER 7

THE DEATH OF THE SHIP

Nor dim, nor red, like God's own head,
The glorious Sun uprist.

COLERIDGE

On 26 July 1915, for the first time in seventy-nine days, the sun peeped above the horizon and, after winking at us for nearly a minute, sank in glorious majesty, painting the northern sky with crimson and gold. It was a sign we all had been eagerly awaiting, and we gathered on deck and lustily cheered 'Old Jamaica' on his reappearance.

Condensation crystals were falling on the ice-fields from a cloudless sky, the sun's beams converting them into showers of scintillating gold. At last dawn was breaking and the long polar night had ended. The dawn was also a signal that the siege of the *Endurance* was about to begin in earnest.

The dogs were brought aboard on 1 August, and on that day the surface of the ice, seen from the masthead, was a chaos of hummocks, ridges, needles and broken blocks. The north-east drift had been accelerated – doubtless on account of the vast 'sail area' presented to the wind by the surfaces of millions of ice-hummocks – and the ocean depth increased rapidly from 2712 feet to 6876 feet. That the pack was breaking up and that leads were opening everywhere was evident from the clouds of condensation vapour that rose in all directions, some resembling burst of smoke from a grass-fire, others looking like trails of smoke from a slowly puffing locomotive.

The nights became times of great anxiety, for the ship now lay in the heart of an icy battlefield. We heard terrifying noises of grinding ice and creaking timbers. The floor buckled under the strain, and the tongues of boards in the wooden partitions between the cubicles sprang from their grooves with sharp reports. For ten weeks the ship was in continual danger, but it was not until early October that its position became desperate. On 14 October the ice was in convulsions ahead of the ship, and a splitting crash suddenly caused all hands to rush up on deck, where we found that a crack had opened from the lead ahead, and had passed along our starboard side to another crack that had opened aft. The ship was free for the first time in nine months. At midnight she drifted from her cradle and fell astern, leaving her form moulded in the splintered floe. The spanker was hoisted, and we actually sailed 100 yards.

We were now in a narrow lead, double the width of the ship's beam, but blocked immediately ahead. Our position caused the gravest anxiety as the floes came gradually together. With silent, irresistible force, they nipped the ship in their terrific jaws. She creaked, shivered and protested in agony, but the grip became tighter and more relentless until, just when we expected to see her sides stave in, she slowly began to rise above the ice. At this critical juncture the pressure fortunately ceased – as suddenly as if an arresting hand had been placed upon the controlling lever of some gigantic machine. We were balanced on the top of a pressure-ridge, and in imminent peril of toppling over on our beam-ends. For several hours we remained thus, and then the floes gradually drew apart and we resumed a normal position.

The ice remained quiet throughout that night, but late the following afternoon it was seen to be again in motion. Watching from the deck the grinding of the floes against our sides, we could not but feel apprehensive. Every timber was straining to breaking-point. The decks gaped; doors refused to open or shut; floor coverings buckled; and the iron floor-plates in the engine-room bulged and sprang from their seatings. The ship groaned, whined and quivered like a tortured creature in agony. Shortly after 5 p.m. she began to rise from the ice. In the short space of seven seconds we were ejected from the floes and flung 30° to port. There was great chaos on deck – snapping dogs, kennels, sledges and emergency gear were thrown into confusion. Below deck, the men were pitched from their bunks, the cook's range was upset and all unsecured gear went the same way as the deck cargo. Laths were nailed to the deck to give footholds and order was finally restored.

The Death of the Ship

Despite our predicament, dinner in the wardroom that evening was an occasion of great hilarity. We all sat on the floor with our feet jammed against the laths to prevent sliding, while the steward performed miracles of balancing passing round the plates of soup. Unthinkingly, somebody would put down an empty plate or vessel on the floor and away it would career to port. We were all fervently thankful when the pressure was relieved at 9 p.m., and we once more swung back to an even keel. During the last week of October the climax was reached in another act of our Antarctic drama. We had at this time twenty hours of daylight, and the weather, though calm, was piercingly cold. I quote from my diary:

October 24th: *The floes, which have been in motion during the afternoon, were assailing the ship on the starboard quarter with great energy. At 6 p.m. all hands go down onto the floe with picks, shovels and chisels, and cut trenches to try and relieve the strain, but we are miserably impotent. As fast as the ice can be hacked away new masses are hurled forward. At 7 p.m. an oncoming floe impinges on the helm, forcing it hard over to port and wrenching the rudder-post. The ship's stern-post is seriously damaged, and the hidden ends of the planking started. Soundings in the well announce the gloomy tidings that we are rapidly making water. The pumps are manned, but it is a great task keeping them going as the water continually freezes and clogs the valve. The carpenter set to work on a coffer-dam in the shaft tunnel in the hope of sealing off the damaged stern of the vessel. Watches keep the pumps going vigorously. Their clickety-clack resounds throughout the night above the ominous creaking of timbers. The position is serious.*

October 25th: *Went down into the engine-room this morning to see the progress made by Chips on the coffer-dam. The water is level with the engine-room floor but is still being held in check and we still hope to bring our staunch craft through. Outside, the configuration of the ice has undergone another complete change, most of the pools in our vicinity have been converted into pressure-ridges, while there is an extensive lake half a mile away. Heavy pressure-ridges menace us on starboard quarter and astern. The ship is in a highly dangerous situation, with a heavy list to starboard. If the ridge advances it is obvious that the assailing ice will impinge above the sheer of the bilge and, as the ship is beset on every side with great masses of shattered ice, she will be unable to rise above the pressure. However, all is quiet for the present.*

October 26th: *Fine clear day. The ice in a state of turmoil all the morning subjected the ship to terrific strains. I was assisting Chips on the coffer-dam down in the shaft tunnel when the pressure set in and the creaking and groaning of timbers mingled with the pounding and scrunching against the ship's sides produced a hideous deafening din and warned us to make for safety. As there was a likelihood of the ship's sides crushing in and trapping us in the tunnel we hastened up on deck. All were actively engaged clearing the lowering-gear of the boats and stacking the emergency stores in case of compulsory disembarkation, which now seems inevitable.*

The dogs, instinctively conscious of the imminent peril, set up distressed wails of uneasiness and fear. Sir Ernest stands on the poop, surveying the movements of the ice, and giving an occasional peremptory order. Sledges and all gear are being rapidly accumulated on deck, without confusion, as though it were ordinary routine duty. At 6 p.m. the pressure develops terrific energy; apparently our vicinity is the focus, as the ice, a short distance off, remains motionless. The ship shrieks and quivers, windows splinter, while the deck timbers gape and twist. The brunt of the pressure assails our starboard quarter and the damaged stern-post. The ship is forced ahead by a series of pulsating jerks, and with such force that the bows are driven wedgewise into the solid floe ahead. This frightful strain bends the entire hull some 10 inches along its length. At 7 p.m. the order is given to lower the boats. They are hauled some distance away from the Endurance and out of the zone of immediate danger. At 8.15 p.m. there is a welcome cessation in the ice movement, and all go on board to take their turn at the pumps, and secure what rest they can.

October 27th: *Chips expects to complete the coffer-dam tonight and great hopes are still entertained that he will be able to. All, including Sir Ernest, continue turns with the pumps, which are able to keep pace with the inflowing water. We have just finished lunch and the ice-mill is in motion again. Closer and closer the pressure-wave approaches. Immense slabs are rafted, balance a moment, then topple down and are overridden by a chaos of crunched fragments. Irresistibly this stupendous power marches onward, grinding through the 5-foot ice-flow surrounding us. Now it is within a few yards of the vessel. We are the embodiment of helpless futility and can only look impotently on. I am quickly down on the moving ice with the cinema, expecting every minute to see the sides, which are springing and buckling, stave in. The line of pressure now assaults the ship and she is heaved to the crest of the ridge like a toy. Immense fragments are forced under the counter and wrench away the stern-post. Sir Ernest and Captain Worsley are surveying the ship's position from the floe when the carpenter announces that the water is gaining rapidly on the pumps. All hands are ordered to stand by to discharge equipment and stores onto the ice. The pumps work faster and faster and someone is actually singing a chanty to their beat. The dogs are rapidly passed out down a canvas chute and secured on the floe, followed by cases of concentrated sledging rations, sledges and equipment. The ship is doomed.*

By 8 p.m. all essential gear is 'floed', and though the destruction of the ship continues, smoke may be observed issuing from the galley chimney – the cook is preparing supper. All hands assemble in the wardroom to partake of the last meal aboard the good old ship. The meal is taken in silent gravity, while the crushing is in progress and an ominous sound of splintering timbers arises from below. We have grown indifferent to dangers for we have lived among them so long, and our sadness is for the familiar surroundings from which we are being expelled. The clock is ticking away on the wall as we take our final leave of the cosy wardroom, that has for over twelve months been connected with pleasant associations and fraternal happiness. Before leaving, I went below into the old winter quarters, the Ritz, and found the waters swirling in and already a foot above the floor, the ribs disrupting and tongues of ice driving through the sides. Our ship has put up a valiant fight and done honour to her noble name, Endurance.

Sir Ernest hoists the blue ensign on the mizzen-gaff to three lusty cheers and is last to leave. All equipment and boats are moved some 300 yards as the floes are in active commotion in the vicinity of the ship. During the dim hours of midnight, the calm, frigid atmosphere is resonant with the grinding of the pressure-ice, and the hideous noises coming from the dying vessel. By some curious happening, the electric emergency light becomes automatically switched on and for an hour or more an intermittent making and breaking of the circuit seems to transmit a final sad signal of farewell.

CHAPTER 8

ADRIFT ON THE SEA-ICE

... to reside
In thrilling region of thick-ribbed ice;
To be imprisoned in the viewless winds,
And blown with restless violence round about
The pendent world!

SHAKESPEARE

So ended our twelve months' sojourn on the *Endurance*, so began our five months' drift on the precarious sea-ice.

During the 281 days in which the *Endurance* had been beset, we had drifted on a zigzag course approximately 1500 miles – an average of about 5 miles a day. Actually we were 570 miles north-west of the position where our vessel had first been imprisoned, and could no longer say: '*Man made me and my will is to my maker still.*'

Our first night on the ice was bitterly cold. We were harassed by the working ice, which split up beneath the tents or rafted into hummocks and pressure-waves. Sir Ernest was ever on watch and, as I took refuge in one of the tents from the stabbing wind, the last sight I had that night was of a sombre figure pacing slowly up and down in the dark. I could not fail to admire the calm poise that disguised his anxiety, as he pondered on the next move. What was the best thing to do? How should he shape his tactics in the next round of the fight with death, with the lives of twenty-eight men at stake? I realised the loneliness and penalty of leadership.

Early next morning, before the others were astir, Wild and I rejoined our leader, and together we went aboard the *Endurance*. Poor old ship, what a battered wreck she was. All the cabins along the starboard side had closed up like the bellows of a folding camera. The alleyways were underwater and blocked with debris and ice, while the wardroom was crammed to the ceiling with ice-blocks and splinters. Riding on the top of all, among wrenched timbers and twisted steel, were two objects that had survived without a scratch, the gramophone and a glazed picture. On the lower deck a veritable 'hummocking' of timbers had taken place, the entire upper deck had been sheared off and had fallen away to starboard, so that we could step from it onto the floe. Fore and aft resembled a switchback. The jib-boom had snapped off, the fo'c'sle was overridden with ice, the foremast had splintered at the cross-trees, the mainmast was shattered 6 feet above the deck, while the mizzen, with the blue ensign still floating at the gaff, remained staunch. The refrigerating chamber, which had once served as my darkroom, was a wreck of timbers filled with mushy ice. Somewhere in the icy waters lay submerged the hermetically sealed cases containing my films and negatives. I had been warned not to remove them from the ship, owing to the desperate struggle which now lay before us in a march to the land – a march on which food alone could be carried.

With her stern cocked high in the air, it was difficult to recognise the *Endurance*, the acme of man's ingenuity in shipbuilding, and his challenge to the might of the polar seas. It was evident that the wreck would sink as soon as the pressure relaxed and the piercing tongues of ice acting as supports were withdrawn. We returned with several tins of benzine, kindled a fire and roused the camp.

For the past two months most of us had realised that the vessel was doomed. The inactivity aboard had become a dreary monotony, and though the exile into which the destruction of the ship had thrown us was desperate enough, we looked forward to the future optimistically. The last weeks had been filled with anxiety and uncertainty, and we felt relieved when fate proclaimed the verdict, cruel though it seemed.

Sir Ernest decided that an attempt must be made to reach Paulet Island, 350 miles to the north-north-west, where there was a small hut and a cache of food, left in 1902 by the Swedish expedition under Otto Nordenskjöld. Before setting out, each man was provided with his share of the salvaged clothing, into which he changed. It was so evident that we could win through only by the barest margin, that every superfluous ounce was seen to be a handicap and everything beyond the barest necessities was abandoned.

Before setting out, Sir Ernest addressed the party, thanking them for their loyalty towards him during the trying conditions of the past, and asking them to continue their faith in him during the severe trials that threatened the future. His simple words, nobly spoken, touched the heart, and put every man on his mettle. It was a sad scene. The leader with his men around him; the discarded gear strewn about on the snow; the sledges lashed, and the whining dogs harnessed, ready for the march; the cheerless sky; and, in the background, the grim outlines of the crushed ship, surrounded with ice and debris.

We started for Paulet Island full of hope and vigour, for the general health of the party was good and the dogs were in fine condition. They seemed to realise the straits we were in and behaved magnificently, working as I had never seen them work before. My team generally took the lead, because Shakespeare – good old fellow – was unrivalled for picking out a track. The orders issued for the march were as follows:

A path-finding party of three will start at 7 a.m. with a light sledge, and demolish hummocks, bridge cracks, and smooth out the track. This party has a couple of hours lead on the main body. Then follow seven sledges, each drawn by seven dogs and with an average load of 100 pounds per dog. Five teams to return and bring up the balance of the gear loaded on five sledges. The remaining two teams, Wild's and Hurley's, will link together and bring up the light boat. The balance of the party, eighteen members, will manhaul the large boat – the James Caird.

The arrangement dispensed with the disheartening relaying by the men, this work falling to the lot of the dogs, which even with the double haulage, were working at about half their capable efficiency. However, almost from the start the going was so hard that we had to go over the ground three times to bring up the loads. Then the weather grew so thick that we were forced to camp for hours at a time. The surface was terrible, being covered with deep soft snow, through which we trudged, and treacherous with pitfalls, into which we fell. There were deep holes to be negotiated, and sharp ice-blades to avoid. A patch of rotten ice would give way, plunging us into the sea. Water-leads and hummocks barred the way. On the third day we toiled like titans, and advanced a single mile. The fourth day was a little better. At the end of the day Sir Ernest called a halt, and announced his intention of abandoning the attempt and of establishing a permanent camp on a piece of old floe-ice. The sledges were beginning to break under the rough going, and the boats were showing signs of damage. The other members consulted wished to push on and try to win through, but the leader was firm. It was one of those crises in an expedition when the true leader proves himself, and Shackleton stood the test. On his decision hung the lives of the party and his judgment was that the ice-fields which barred the way to Paulet Island were impassable.

The positive plan of escape having definitely failed after heroic efforts, we settled down to the only alternative, a negative policy of watchful waiting. Our hope now was that the ice-pack would drift northwards to the open sea, when the boats would be launched and an attempt would be made to reach one of the whaling stations on South Shetland Island, 450 miles away. It was a slender-enough thread of hope for twenty-eight men to hang upon; yet like a golden strand it sustained us during five wretched months. We knew that the prevailing winds were generally from the south, and that the tides were setting in a northerly direction. Moreover, we were aware that even while we had been confined to the ship the whole vast field had been in motion; for every day our position had been determined by the theodolite, and we knew it to within a few hundred yards. In brief, we were on a gigantic raft of ice, which, in due course, must inevitably go to pieces, and our problem was to travel as far as it would carry us, and then get clear of the disintegrating material without loss of life or stores, and without damage to our final resort, the boats.

Our first duty was to form a more or less permanent camp, and the second was to furnish and provision it. The point at which further progress on our march to the land was blocked seemed to offer a favourable site, and there one section was set to work while another, under Wild, sledged back to the ship for salvage.

'Ocean Camp', as we called it, was situated about 4 miles from the *Endurance*. Here the boats were drawn up, tents to accommodate the party were pitched, and the sailors erected a canvas hut measuring 23 by 11 feet for galley and shelter, which was christened 'the Billabong'.

In the smallest tent, the leader, James Hudson, and myself took up our crowded residence, while those who had formed close friendships aboard the vessel likewise clubbed together.

Meanwhile, the dog-teams and their drivers were busily employed, and without exception relished the activity. We proceeded to salve the wreck systematically, and to transfer from the 'dump camp' beside her all the gear that might prove useful. This adventure was liberally spiced with danger, owing to the fact that the *Endurance* was suspended above 2060 fathoms of ocean by the great tongues of ice that were thrust through her ribs. Having removed the overhanging spars and cleared away many tons of ice and snow, Wild and his men rigged up a reciprocating drill, made from a large ice-chisel lashed to a spar, and cut a hole in the deck just above our old living quarters. As soon as the planking was removed, there was an outrush of walnuts, onions and small buoyant articles. By diligent probing around with boathooks, case after case was directed to the opening, from which they emerged buoyantly to the surface. A great cheer arose whenever a case of high food-value came to light. I arrived on the scene just in time to see a keg of sodium bicarbonate greeted with groans. The party worked at high pressure all day, taking advantage of the tranquil state of the ice, and by evening practically all the cases were retrieved. All the flour was saved, as well as a large quantity of the sugar – the two commodities we regarded as most essential. The teams, loaded to full capacity, were busy transporting the ice-covered cases, timbers and salvaged sundries to the camp all day, each team averaging five trips.

Next day, after the salvaging was completed, I went down to the wreck, unknown to the leader, with one of the sailors, to make a determined effort to rescue my films and negatives. We hacked our way through the splintered timbers and, after vainly fishing in the ice-laden waters with boathooks, I made up my mind to dive in after them. It was mighty cold work groping about in the mushy ice in the semi-darkness of the ship's bowels, but I was rewarded in the end and passed out the three precious tins. While Seaman How was massaging me vigorously to restore my circulation, the vessel began to shake and groan ominously. We sprang for our lives and leaped onto the ice – almost into the arms of the astonished leader, who demanded, 'What the hell are you up to?'

However Sir Ernest at once accepted the position with his usual good humour, and, I fancy, was glad of the salvage. A large sum of money had been advanced against the motion-picture rights to help finance the expedition, and these were the assets.

I might mention in this connection that when it came to a question of selecting such negatives as might be taken with us, so as to keep down the weight as much as possible, I had a painful hour. Sir Ernest and I went over the plates together, and as a negative was rejected, I would smash it on the ice to obviate all temptation to change my mind. Finally, the choice was made, and the films and plates which I considered indispensable were stowed away in one of the boats, having first been placed in double tins, hermetically sealed. About 400 plates were jettisoned and 120 retained. Later I had to preserve them almost with my life; for a time came when we had to choose between heaving them overboard or throwing away our surplus food – and the food went over. All my photographic gear was compulsorily abandoned, except one small pocket-camera and three spools of unexposed film. I wonder if three spools of film ever went through more exacting experiences before they were developed.

While on the subject of salvage, I might add that I recovered the volumes of the encyclopaedia from the chief's cabin, and a large part of my personal library, as well as several packs of cards. Many a day we had cause to bless the fact. What tedious hours were whiled away in reading; what wonderful and purely imaginary fortunes changed hands at poker-patience.

One of the last objects hauled from the wreck was the steel ash-chute, from which I constructed a blubber-fed cooking-range, cutting potholes through the quarter-inch mild steel with a tiny chisel. Sundry oil-drums and empty cans completed the contraption, which added materially to the cook's comfort, and to our well-being.

Thus, well sheltered and amply provisioned, we settled down to what was surely one of the most extraordinary cruises in the history of deep-sea navigation. Around us spread, as far as the eyes could reach, fields of snow, which not even the most fertile imagination could conceive to be the frozen bosom of the sea. We ourselves could scarcely realise that we were dwelling on a colossal raft, with a few feet of ice separating us from 12,000 feet of ocean. Our motive power was the mighty forces of nature, which we could neither regulate nor control, and our pilot was the originator and director of these forces.

On 8 November 1915 we paid the final official visit to the remnant of the *Endurance*. From the shattered poop we fired a detonator to salute the ensign, which still fluttered over the heap of fragmentary timbers and twisted rails. And so we left her. It was not until a fortnight later, however, that the derelict escaped from further tortures and dived to her last resting place. It was evening, and we were all in our sleeping-bags, when Sir Ernest called from the lookout, 'She's going, boys.' We hastened out of the tents and climbed to the lookout and other vantage points. Sure enough, a mile and a half away, the poor old ship was in her final death-throes. The stern rose vertically in the air, then she dived quickly below the ice. A little later the ice-floes came together and threw up a high pressure-ridge – a monument to her. Her name, *Endurance*, was a fitting motto to inscribe upon our banners as we moved forward into the unknown future.

The disappearance of the ship cast a temporary gloom over the camp. Although battered beyond recognition, she still stood as a symbol of civilisation and a link with the outside world. Now that she had gone, a feeling of intense isolation and loneliness fell over us. But it passed, and later, at mealtime, all were as cheerful and bright as ever, and Sir Ernest was bantering the cook over the thinness and smallness of the bannocks. The cook, with ready wit, replied that the disappearance of the ship had given Lees, the storeman, such qualms and doleful visions of the party perishing through starvation that he had issued him only half a ration of flour for the bannocks.

'Oh! Well, issue double the number of bannocks and get more flour from Lees,' responded Sir Ernest.

From this date till the close of the year, our camp, in good or bad times, reflected good leadership and fine comradeship. We were healthy and had ample food, which was further supplemented by stray seals and penguins.

In six weeks we drifted 120 miles. During the last week of the year we struck camp and made another desperate effort to reach the land. This attempt also had to be abandoned. The surface was a chaos of hummocks, ridges, fissures and hidden treacheries, which made progress absolutely impossible. A new camp was then established – 'Patience Camp'. It was some 10 miles west of Ocean Camp and was in a stronger strategic position in relation to Paulet Island, which now bore north-west 189 miles.

We hailed the new year with a cheer. Leads and pools on every side gave satisfactory indications that the ice would break up and afford us an early chance of launching the boats. But during a fortnight of abominable weather, the floes closed up again, and the drift and adverse winds forced us back upon our tracks for a distance of 7 miles.

Then came a sorrowful incident. For some time it had been felt that the ranks of our dogs must be thinned out. It was a painful thought, but owing to the increasingly broken nature of the surface, their use was becoming more and more limited, and they were becoming a grievous tax on our larder, as the supply of seals diminished. On 14 January I made a laborious search for seals – the going was very difficult over the broken and cracked ice – and reached Pinnacle Berg. From its summit I closely examined the floes for miles around with twelve-magnification prisms, but there was not a sign of a flipper at any point of the compass. This report finally settled the fate of the dogs, and during the afternoon four teams – those of Wild, Crean, Marston and McIlroy – were shot. They were thirty-five magnificent sledgers and they had done us good service, but it had to come sooner or later, and, since they consumed an entire seal a day, enough to last the whole party for three days, the decision was unavoidable. My team and Macklin's were under sentence, but execution was suspended upon my suggestion that we should first make an attempt to reach Ocean Camp, to retrieve what was left of the farinaceous food and odd stores.

Macklin and I spent the afternoon cutting a road from the camp to an adjacent large floe, to give us an unencumbered start to Ocean Camp. At 6.30 a.m. we set out, and after 2 miles of desultory going came across an extremely difficult area of leads and pressure-ridges. We had to bridge the leads with ice-blocks and cut a way through the ridges. After some four hours of solid pick-and-shovel work another mile was covered. The surface then became disheartening, the dogs sinking deep to their bellies in soft snow and having to paddle their way. At every few steps we sank in to the thighs. Finally, the two teams were linked together while I went ahead on skis and broke trail. This answered much better, but travelling was still so heavy that frequent rest spells had to be allowed the dogs. We arrived at Ocean Camp at 4.30 p.m. It had taken us ten hours to cover 10 miles. A good brew of coffee and a meal of tinned cauliflower and Irish stew, which we selected from the stores that we had been obliged to abandon when we left this spot, cheered us up immensely. We then set about collecting our load.

Ocean Camp presented a forlorn appearance, resembling a deserted Alaskan mining village that had been ransacked by bandits. The abandoned gear was half buried in snow, and pools of water had formed everywhere. The billabong itself was surrounded by a lake 3 feet deep. We gave the dogs a full ration of pemmican and, after a couple of hours' rest, made a much easier run back in spite of the heavy load, having the advantage of the track we had broken down on the way to the camp. We returned to camp after a six-hour run, having added an additional 900 pounds to the larder – nearly an extra month's supply of concentrated rations.

Sunday was an easy day in camp, and Macklin and I were not sorry to make it a day of rest. Wild shot my team during the afternoon – a sad but imperative necessity. I said goodbye to my faithful old leader, Shakespeare, with an aching heart. It seemed like murdering in cold blood a trusty pal, but, alas, there was no alternative. Food was running short and the end was inevitable, for the dogs could not be taken in the boats. Macklin's team was held in reserve for emergency transport.

A fortnight later it was decided to try to bring in the third boat, the *Stancomb Wills*, which had remained abandoned all this time at Ocean Camp. Observations showed that the distance between our old

Ocean Camp and our new Patience Camp had decreased from 10 miles to 6, owing to the shuffling of the ice-floes. Since it was still light all night, Crean and I with the dogs left camp at 1 a.m. to path-find, and a party of sixteen men followed our trail, covering the distance in a couple of hours, as against the ten hours which we had taken on our first trip. The venture was entirely successful. On the return journey, Crean, James, McIlroy and I went ahead as 'trail-breakers' – demolishing ridges, breaking down hummocks and bridging gaps in the ice, while the others dragged the boat on runners. The dog-team hauled a load of stores and sundries. Sir Ernest, with one of his brilliant inspirations, sledged out to meet us a mile from camp with two cans of steaming tea, and, with lusty voices, if husky from fatigue, we all cheered and sang, 'For He's a Jolly Good Fellow'. Nothing in the whole of the world's 'wet' resources could compare with that jorum of hot tea. Nothing stimulates and heartens a weary body like tea. Like the famous Dr Johnson we could all have consumed twenty-seven cups. Renewed and refreshed, we made light of that last mile, and in less than an hour the boat lay on the floe at Patience Camp. How she served us in a pinch will be told later. A few days afterwards Ocean Camp was observed to be several miles farther away; the ice had opened out, and an attempt to reach it with the last dog-team was frustrated. We never had the opportunity of visiting it again. The boat had been salvaged just in the nick of time.

Our meals were now cooked on a portable 'bogie', which I improvised from two oil-drums and sundry scraps of metal. This small range would consume anything combustible, but roared away like a miniature furnace when fed with seal-blubber or penguin skins. Green, our capable cook aboard the *Endurance*, continued his duties undaunted. A 'galley', or, more correctly speaking, a windscreen, had been rigged up, by pushing four oars into the snow and straining round them an old sail. Green's never-ending activities among the flying soot gave him the appearance of a merry chimneysweep who had not washed for many months. He did his cooking thoroughly – too well at times – and if chided about the leathery toughness or cinder-like crispness of a seal steak, had a ready fund of wit which always completely exonerated him and laid the blame on the seal.

Each man took his turn to act as mess 'peggy' for his tent. His duties for the day were to go to the galley, collect the steaks in the hoosh-pot, and return with them to his hungry tentmates. The 'peggy' then proceeded to sort out the steaks into portions as equal as possible, and 'whosed' them. One of the occupants turned his back, so that he might not see the steaks, and the 'peggy', skewering a portion, would demand, 'Whose?' The questioned one then pronounced the name of one of his tentmates, and so the steaks were 'whacked out'. This method entirely dispensed with any suggestion of favouritism or unfairness.

Table furniture was of the simplest. Our tent possessed a sheath-knife which was common property. Each man had, in addition to a tin-lid which served as a plate, a spoon, either a souvenir from the *Endurance*, or one carved from a piece of wreckage. To lose a spoon or a knife was a calamity. By this time we had begun to fear a shortage of food and rations had to be used economically. It was therefore customary to dally as long as possible over meals to that their meagreness might not be so apparent, and mental satisfaction might at least be stimulated. With a sigh the last morsel was sedulously scraped from the tin-lid, and spoons were licked and put by into the indispensable pocket on the chest of the jersey. The 'peggy' then took the hoosh-pot outside and scoured it with snow. Occasionally meals were modified with a ration of dog pemmican. This was canned by the makers in 1-pound tins, and the 'peggy' for the next day took the tin into his sleeping-bag overnight to thaw it out. For breakfast the square of pemmican was cut into four equal cubes and 'whosed'. A beverage was concocted from powdered dry milk and hot water, its redeeming quality being its warmth. This potion, mixed with the dog pemmican in proper proportion, and vigorously stirred, produced a doubtful mixture not unlike haggis.

Mealtimes, too, were times of conversation, especially after the evening dinner, when pipes were lighted.

Weather, a commonplace topic in the cities of civilisation, meant life to us. Weather was the paramount tent-topic. Wind was the propelling and guiding influence that held our freedom in its breath. If the breeze was fair and there had been sunshine, talk was gay and hopes ran high. Adverse weather, false winds and setback drifts were received with silent gravity. 'What is the wind's direction?' was the never-ending query in the camp. Every puff or caprice was given as much attention as if it were a delicate mechanism to be cajoled. Temperatures, blizzards, inconveniences, worried us not, so long as the wind was with us. Every four hours, Hussey, the meteorologist and the bringer of good or bad tidings, reported at our tent and gave Sir Ernest the weather forecast. Worsely, with the sextant, and James, with the theodolite, had a competition at noon each day to determine the latitude and compute the distance the sea-ice had drifted during the twenty-four hours. Their report was anxiously awaited by all. If it was exceptionally favourable, our scanty ration would be increased; if we had been set back, the gloom was doubled by shrinking economy.

Second in importance as a subject of conversation, came 'grub'. When there was a dearth of seals, hunger pinched and conversation waned. Much speculation ensued over the compilation of prospective menus, though all were agreed that their desires were for good and plenty, rather than a procession of 'tantalising' flavours, devoid of substance, even if they could be served on silver salvers. For such repasts as we craved the descriptive name of 'gorgie' was coined.

At rarer intervals there were poetic outpourings; and though we loved to hear snatches from Tennyson, Service, Keats and Browning, strangely assorted companions in that wilderness, I recall an amusing incident which indicated forcibly the real trend of our thoughts.

Sir Ernest, reciting Browning's 'Rabbi ben Ezra', came to the well-known lines:

> *But all the world's coarse thumb*
> *And finger failed to plumb.*

He was interrupted by a muffled voice from a sleeping-bag saying, 'Couldn't we do with plum duffs now?'

And what a grand tentmate Sir Ernest was. A close friendship had sprung up between us, and always when things were blackest he rose to his best. He was the very soul of encouragement, though in those days he seemed to have grown old. I could read in the furrowed lines behind his smile, that his mind was never at rest, but was always working to devise plans for our safety or to anticipate the unexpected. He was completely unselfish and wonderfully tolerant – never thinking of himself, and, in spite of his constant anxiety, he had regard for our most trivial wants. It is in these circumstances, stripped of the veneer of civilisation, that one sees the real man. Living in such intimate contact, under conditions of ever-present peril, one senses one's fellow men's thoughts, nay, scans their very souls. And whatever dangers or hardships I may have experienced were generously repaid by having had this man's confidence and comradeship.

In spite of his heavy burdens, Sir Ernest retained all that wholesome boyishness of spirit that had endeared him to all. When elated by a favourable happening, he would discourse enthusiastically on such subjects as the recovery of the treasure of Alexis, or of King John's train. Then he would lead imaginary expeditions to the Indies and the South Sea Isles in quest of buried treasure and pearls. He would even give us the exact latitude and longitude where they lay buried. Often in imagination I wandered with him in some glorious adventure, excited by the lust of the treasure hunt, not for the sake of the booty, but for the sheer joy of winning it.

Sir Ernest's memory was inexhaustible. He had a ready phrase or a quotation for everything. A born poet, through all his oppressions he could see glory and beauty in the stern forces which had reduced us to destitution, and against which he was fighting.

Sometimes conversation glided into strange channels, such as the development of commerce on the Yenisei, the arts and crafts of ancient Egypt, comparisons of the social life of London, New York and Paris, etc. Then we had debates on such varied subjects as the birthrate, the liquor question, the mysteries of lighthouse optics, ship construction, the elusive unknown quantity x, and so forth, and disputes were referred to the arbitration of the *Encyclopaedia Britannica*. But by far the most popular of tent-topics were talks of other lands and unknown places. I told of travels in the East Indies and of wanderings in hidden Australia, and delighted to hear in return of the tinkling temple bells of Burma, and about the homeland, from the heaths of bonnie Scotland to London, with its 'stream of liquid history' – the Thames. After evening hoosh had set the blood coursing and the body aglow with tingling warmth, we would lie in our sleeping-bags and meditate. We longed to feel the exquisite sensation of donning the latest style of clothes. Our pockets (if we had any) burned with desire to patronise the refinements of civilisation and its gaieties. Darkness quickly came in the tents when winter drew near, and with a final prayer of 'Blow, good breezes, blow', we turned over in our bags to dream of safety, home, dances, and dinners, which would afford food for tomorrow's conversation.

Each afternoon, Sir Ernest and I made it a regular practice to play six games of poker-patience, and at the end of ten weeks our aggregate scores were within a few points of each other. I had become the possessor of an imaginary shaving glass, several top hats, enough walking canes to equip a regiment, several sets of sleeve-links and a library of books. Moreover, I had dined, at Sir Ernest's expense, at Claridges, and had occupied a box at the opera. Sir Ernest had become the owner of scores of fine linen handkerchiefs, silk umbrellas, a mirror, a coveted collector's copy of *Paradise Regained*; and had been my guest at dinner at the Savoy and visited, at my expense, most of the theatres in London.

During our life at Patience Camp it fell largely to my lot, as being an expert on skis, to be the hunter of the party, and to keep the larder and fuel supplies going. Seal-hunting can hardly be classed among the nobler sports, but when twenty-eight men are dependent upon the chase for fresh meat, firing and lighting, there is a keenness about the hunt that no mere sport can give. Equipped with a pair of reliable skis, the hunter would sally forth to look for game and, if none was within sight, a visit would be paid to one of the bergs – Flat Berg or Pinnacle Berg – and from that vantage point the ice-field would be minutely examined through a pair of powerful glasses. In the distance, a dark slug-like object would be seen basking beside a hummock or lying on the edge of a lead. Perhaps two or more would offer and, choosing the one most accessible to camp, the hunter would lope off and, taking care to approach without being seen, come up with his quarry. Sometimes, indeed, no precautions were necessary, for the Weddell seal, though a superb swimmer and the embodiment of sinuous grace in the water, is, when on the ice, very slow-moving and easily killed. The ski makes a handy weapon, and, pursuing the orthodox method, the hunter stuns his victim with a shrewd blow on the blunt nose and cuts its throat with a sweep of the knife. It is a brutal, messy business, but one of dire necessity.

Hunting on the solid floe presented no danger, but when scouting among loosening pack one needed to be cautious. Skis were then indispensable, for cracks 4 and 5 feet wide had to be crossed. The negotiation of these cracks and of the brash-ice developed in us a cat-like delicacy of tread.

Penguin-stalking is much the same as seal-hunting. But while neither seal nor penguin puts up any defence, the element of risk is supplied by killer-whales, which are apt to poke their ugly heads through the thin ice with a snort that immediately imparts to the hunter a marvellous speed and a keen desire to get back to a solid floe. I had many narrow escapes during these excursions. Occasionally the ice would open up into a wide lead, and I would ferry across the water on a small floe, using my skis for paddles. I soon abandoned the habit of taking these short cuts, when one day a school of seven killer-whales began blowing in the lead around me, giving me the fright of my life.

Occasionally I came upon large convoys of penguins, too numerous to cope with single-handedly. Then I would heliograph to the camp with a small pocket-mirror, and all hands would turn out, armed with clubs, to the slaughter. One day we added 300 penguins to our depleted larder. The birds were evidently migrating from the southern rookeries to the northern pack limits. The skins were reserved for fuel, the legs for hoosh, the breasts for steaks, and the livers and hearts for delicacies. A seal was consumed by the party with restrained appetites in five days – just as long as his blubber lasted to cook him. Twenty penguins, cooked by the fuel of their own skins, was a fair daily average. The floe had, by pressure, formed ice-ridges and hummocks. These had discharged the brine of their original sea-water, and the fresh-water ice that remained was the source of our supply of drinking water. Through all our experiences on the floe, game never entirely failed us. At times we were compelled to go on short rations, but when we were hard-pressed, something had a curious and providential knack of turning up. At the end of March 1916, for example, when a severe shortage was felt, a huge sea-leopard was secured and it its stomach were found some fifty fish in excellent condition. These were eaten with much gusto. Immediately afterwards a second leopard, 11 feet long, was enticed from a lead by several of our men, who hopped about on its icy shore like penguins. The same night a crab-eater seal blundered into our camp in the dark.

All through these times we kept an anxious watch on the weather. It was not the wind's roar and buffeting that worried us, but its absence. There was one particular period of exasperation. For one tantalising month we zigzagged a score of times across the Antarctic Circle. It really seemed as if the spirit of Antarctica held us in durance and refused to permit us to cross its borderline, the 67th parallel. At last a blizzard confined us in our tents for several days, while the wind roared constantly from the south-west. When the weather cleared enough for an observation, we awaited the verdict of the navigating officers (Worsley and James) with anxiety. It was not merely favourable; it was amazing – latitude 65° 43'. We had been positively bowling along. In four days we had averaged nearly 20 miles per day. The spell was broken, the sun came out, and the camp assumed the appearance of a laundry. Clothes, sleeping-bags, gear, sundries of all kinds swung on lines in the warm sunshine, and as the soggy conditions of the past few days gave place to dry comfort, spirits rose and visions of the open seas formed in our minds. But the caprice of Antarctic weather soon exhibited itself again and we were blown back 3 miles by adverse winds.

The disappointment, monotony, inactivity and the return of wretched weather now made life well-nigh unbearable. To add to our plight, food was scarce and we were always hungry. The biting cold of the blizzards pierced through our threadbare garments and deluged us with wet snow. When calms fell and the temperature rose, conditions were scarcely better, for the warmth of our bodies thawed the soft snow beneath our sleeping-bags into puddles, and everything became soaked. When the temperature fell again our clothes and sleeping-bags froze as stiff as boards.

We seemed to be in an icy maze. When the floes opened up, a dense, wet fog rose from the water and obscured everything 50 yards away. Then, when the south wind came and dispersed the fog, and we looked eagerly for a chance to launch the boats, the temperature fell rapidly and the open water froze over again.

On 17 March, Paulet Island lay abreast 60 miles to the west, but the surface, which had barred us previously by its insurmountable hummocks and ridges, was now very much worse through decay. We turned our hopes to the Danger Islands, mere pinnacles of rock 35 miles distant, said to be inaccessible, but a possible refuge to castaways in our predicament.

On 2 April, Wild shot the remaining dog-team. The carcasses were dressed for food, but we found the meat extremely tough, for the poor creatures had been on very scanty rations for some time. We had dearly hoped that the ice would carry us close to the land so that we could save their lives. But the culminating struggle lay close before us, and it would have been quite impossible to take them on such a voyage as we would soon be forced to undertake.

Sir Ernest, who was on watch on the night of 22 March, called me early the next morning to corroborate his view that a point lifting its bulk through the fog was land. It was one of the Danger Islands, and, later in the day, we sighted a range of misty peaks on Joinville Island. Only 40 miles separated us from it, but the 40 miles were over impassable ice-fields, and might as well have been 40,000. A single day at the oars would have taken us there, but our boats might as well have been bicycles. Nevertheless, our eyes had seen that which confirmed our faith. That point of land looming through the mist was evidence that there was still something solid in the universe. It was a peak of actuality in a landscape of uncertainty. It was the seal upon the knowledge of our scientists; the assurance that we were not to spend the rest of our lives in nightmare wanderings inscribed like a gigantic fever-chart upon the map of this desolation.

However, the precise landing-place which was to be our stepping stone to the world of men was still, and for many a day to come would remain, a matter of conjecture. We knew for certain that 40 miles west lay Joinville Island and the Danger Islands. One hundred miles to the north were Elephant and Clarence islands, and King George Island lay a little farther north-west – which was it to be? A sweep of 28 miles in a single day pointed to Clarence Island as our possible destination; then a strong north-west drift turned our thoughts to Elephant Island; but again a current carried us so strongly westwards that Elephant Island was placed beyond the range of our hopes, King George Island – best of all, on account of its accessibility to the whaling station at Deception Island – seemed to lie directly in our path.

The first unmistakable intimation that we were approaching ice-free waters was the opening and closing of an insignificant crack round the margin of the floe. Although only just perceptible, it indicated that the swell from the open ocean was working through, and that the ice was swaying under its influence.

The news caused a sensation in camp and, throughout the day, we loitered by the working crack, noting with intense satisfaction that the action was gradually increasing. It was a welcome sight – an omen that our long tedious drift on the floes was at last drawing to a close.

Visions of the wide ocean, rolling deep, blue and free, filled our minds, and we eagerly discussed the respective merits of various refuge points to which we might sail. Elephant Island sounded enticing; the name suggested the haunts of the succulent sea-elephant. Prince George Island, 80 miles farther west, was equally attractive; sea-elephants would doubtless be found there as well, and Sir Ernest informed us that the Admiralty Sailing Directions mentioned a cave. We were indeed fortunate. Sea-elephant for food and a cave for shelter – what more could any man desire? We unanimously agreed, however, that Deception Island, still farther west, was preferable, because the whalers made it their headquarters during the summer months. In its favour there were huts, a depot of stores and a small church. The stores would enable us to survive the winter months, and if necessity compelled, we could build a seaworthy vessel from the timbers of the church. The carpenter drew designs in the snow, picturing to us a sturdy craft built from beams and pews. His dream-ship looked wonderfully alluring, with her swelling sails of threadbare tent-fabric bearing us over seas of fancy to freedom. How simple it all appeared.

But as day followed day, and the surges of the Atlantic surges drew closer and the ponderous ice-floes drew apart, only to crash together thunderously and splinter, we ceased all comparisons and came to the conclusion that any bit of rock capable of affording refuge would be a glorious haven after all our tribulations.

Our long spell on the floe had lulled us into a sense of false security. We had scarcely thought of the icy plain on which we were camped for what it was – a treacherous layer covering the surface of an ocean 2 miles deep. Now that the white floor began to shatter and to disintegrate beneath our feet, feelings of helplessness and utter dereliction crept insidiously over us. We had cherished hopes that the floes might carry us close to land, or at least open up into navigable leads that would enable us to reach the shore without facing the open sea. This was now out of the question, for the currents had carried us beyond the northernmost limit of the mainland.

How often we had buoyed our hopes on empty objectives and unrealised fancies. How often had mirages stirred up to excitement, followed by depression when the 'dream islets' turned out to be clouds or icebergs as we drifted closer to them. It was natural, therefore, that Captain Worsley and I should gaze uncertainly over the pack-ice towards the swaying horizon at a nebulous contour, to which Sir Ernest was pointing, under the impression that it was land. Even as we strained our eyes, anxious to confirm, yet sceptical, the haze cleared a little and we made out black patches of rock. The peak, which was about 60 miles distant, could be none other than Clarence Island. It lay directly in the path of our drift and, if the current and winds continued fair, in a few days we would be walking on solid rock. What a sensation! It was sixteen months since we had seen rock and walked on it at South Georgia. Oh blessed memory! Late in the afternoon a group of low peaks loomed up to the north-west, which our charts indicated to be Elephant Island. Elephant and Clarence islands were the last outposts of Antarctica. Between them the sea rolled as through a broad portal, and, if we failed to land on one of them, we would be swept through into the tempestuous spaces of the open ocean. We were indeed the forlorn playthings of colossal forces.

The daily spectacle of the disruption of the ice-packs on which we were living so precariously was appalling and terrifying. The swells of the ocean now came surging through the ice-fields from the north, in great undulations, from horizon to horizon. The floes bent under the heave, yet no open water was visible. When exceptionally violent swells reached the centre of the floes, they splintered like sheets of glass, and then, as the fragments drew apart, the inky waters showed through. A few moments later, the fractured pieces would batter and grind into one another, adjusting their new shapes to the oncoming waves.

As we continued on our northerly drift, the floe on which we were encamped shared the fate of its neighbours. Yet there was no water in which to launch the boats. We shuddered at the thought that the ice might spilt into fragments too small to carry the camp, and yet remain in a compact, grinding mass without opening up. Whatever might be in store for us, one thing was certain; it would call for the last ounce of our strength, and in order that our emaciated bodies might be more capable of enduring the coming conflict, extra seal steaks were issued, while everything was held ready for a hurried effort. Guards patrolled the camp day and night to give warning at the first sight of danger. Rest was not for us. The battering impact of the floes and the dread of the ice splitting beneath our tents and letting us drop through into the sea, was ever with us. We sat up in our sleeping-bags, fully dressed, shivering through the long nights, waiting for the dawn. Haggard faces and dulled eyes told a painful story of fatigue and anxiety.

In those times of bitter adversity, Sir Ernest's leadership was a supreme encouragement. He, too, felt as we did, but never a word or sign betrayed him. He sank his own distress. Although burdened with the knowledge that the lives of twenty-eight men depended on his judgment, he still had an eye to each man's smallest wants, and words of hope and cheer to inspire his followers. There were times, however, when his overwrought mind cried out against the strain and the tremendous responsibility. There were nights when, startled by a cry or a groan, I would rouse him from a troubled sleep. Sitting up in his sleeping-bag, Sir Ernest would then relate some horrible dream he had had of the boats being crushed between floes, the camp being engulfed, or some other nightmare. Plans would then be discussed to avoid these calamities, for he regarded these dreams as warnings. It was to his unrelaxing vigilance and planning that we owed our lives.

I shall never forget those cold, hideous nights in our tent and those discussions of the problems of the future, with the floes hammering sinister warnings a few paces away.

It was now 8 April 1916. The Antarctic winter had already set in and the nights were rapidly lengthening. Shortly after 6 p.m. the watchman raised the alarm that the floe was splitting. We hurried from the tents in the gloom and observed a dark, jagged line gradually broadening through the centre of the camp. It passed directly under the *James Caird*, separating the other two boats from us. In a few minutes we rushed the boats across to the section where the tents stood. Our camp was reduced to an overcrowded, rocking triangle, and it was evident that we must take the first opportunity to escape, no matter how desperate the chances might be. During the night a strong breeze sprang up from the south, and under its influence the pack began to scatter.

On 9 April we found that the previous night's wind had loosened the ice, but it was impossible to launch the boats, for the leads were opening and closing so rapidly that if we had attempted to navigate them we would have been crushed like eggshells. Changes took place so rapidly that a clearing which appeared to offer an excellent opening at one moment, was a grinding ice-mill a few minutes later. In our awful dilemma we all turned our eyes to the leader, who was standing surveying this baffling maze. Action was imperative at the first opportunity. After a hurried breakfast, tents were struck and all made ready to launch the boats. Crews were allotted. The leader, Frank Wild and eleven men, of whom I was one, manned the *James Caird* – the largest but frailest boat. Captain Worsley with nine others formed the crew of the *Dudley Docker*, and Tom Crean had charge of the *Stancomb Wills* with the remainder of the men. These preparations proved to be opportune, for, as we stood by, the ice parted beneath our feet. Hastily we hauled the boats and gear to temporary safety on the larger piece, which was barely big enough to accommodate everything. The ice had cracked in an uncanny fashion through the old camping-site, which the leader and myself had vacated but an hour previously. We stood on the brink of the widening fissure and watched the depression in which we had slept for four months drift away amid the churning ice. How insecure it had been! The warmth of our bodies had thawed the ice, until we were sleeping, happily unconscious of the fact, barely a foot above the surface of the sea.

The first desperate chance came just after lunch. At one o'clock a treacherous lead opened up through the heaving ice. Sir Ernest gave the order to launch the boats. We slid them over the jagged edge of the floe into the inky waters. The gear and supplies were hurriedly stowed and we rowed for dear life through the winding channel and entered a vast lake of gently heaving deep blue water in which floated a solitary mammoth berg. At last we were free. No longer idle captives with capricious winds and tides for gaolers, but free to shape our own destinies. Our adventures during those 159 days on the floe had come to an end. How thoroughly the happenings of the next six days were to eclipse them, and indeed all the experiences of the preceding sixteen months!

CHAPTER 9

THE ESCAPE IN THE BOATS

. . . the tempest screamed
Comfort and warmth and ease no longer seemed
Things that a man could know: soul, body, brain,
Knew nothing but the wind, the cold, the pain.

MASEFIELD

The *James Caird* took the lead, and as we bent to our oars we sang joyfully – we were bound for Elephant Island at last. But we sang too soon.

We had covered only a few miles when we observed the eastern horizon of pack-ice in violent agitation and rapidly bearing towards us. The noise of the oncoming water and ice sounded like the rush of a tidal bore up a river. We stopped rowing for a brief moment and observed that the whole surface of the sea was covered by a mass of churning ice and foam, which was driving towards us in a broad crescent in the grip of a furious tide-rip. The horns were converging, and it seemed as though we would be trapped in a rapidly closing pool. Sir Ernest shouted to the boats to make for the lee of the mammoth berg. Tossing, plunging and grinding, the ice-laden surge swept after us, and though we pulled with all our might we could not draw away. It was only 100 yards behind, and tongues of ice were flicking out ahead of it. One of these reached to within a few yards of the *Stancomb Wills*, which was bringing up the rear; disaster was averted only by the greatest exertion of her crew and by Crean's skilful piloting.

After a fifteen minutes' race for life, the phenomenon ceased as quickly as it had begun. All became quiet, save for the groaning and creaking of the floes as they fretted in the swell. The waters were littered with ice and, night falling swiftly, the leader decided to rest his weary men on an old floe. The cook with his small stove and his assistant were put 'ashore' first, and, by the time the boats were discharged and hauled up, and the tents pitched, hoosh was ready. The hot meal set our cold bodies aglow and, with the cheerful prospect of a night's rest, laughter and song came from the tents.

We had lived so long in this perilous vortex that we had become almost indifferent to hazards and dangers. We cared little that our camp was pitched on a brittle ice-raft, scarcely more than fifty paces across, adrift on an unplumbed sea. Nor did we heed the schools of killer-whales patrolling the neighbouring waters in search of prey. Guards being set – each man taking an hour's watch – we snuggled down into our sleeping-bags, and were soon rocked to sleep by the swaying floe. But the hope of a night's rest was shattered. Shortly after 11 p.m. a loud cracking caused us to hasten from our sleeping-bags and to investigate. A minute examination of the floe by the light of hurricane lamps displayed nothing more than a subsidence of the surface snow. Once more we turned in and had just dozed off when another report aroused us.

It was no false alarm this time – the watchman was yelling that the floe was splitting. The crack passed beneath the tent occupied by the sailors, and so quickly did it draw apart that before the men could escape one fell through into the sea. By marvellous good fortune the leader was near, and, rushing to the breach, flung himself down by the brink and hauled Seaman Holness, who was floating in his sleeping-bag, from the water. An alarm was raised that a second man was missing, but, before a search could be made, the fractured floes came together again with a terrific impact. The *James Caird*, which had been separated from the body of the camp, was hurried across the rift, which was opening again. So rapidly did it widen that Sir Ernest, who was waiting on the far side till the boat reached safety, was unable to leap across. A few minutes later he drifted away and was swallowed up in the darkness and falling snow. We heard a voice calling for one of the boats, but Wild had already anticipated the order and had manned the *Stancomb Wills*.

Owing to the darkness and the congestion of the ice, we had great difficulty in rescuing the leader. The roll was called, and with deep relief all hands were accounted for. A roaring blubber-fire was kindled and, since the floe was rocking badly in the increasing swell and might fracture again, the tents were struck. We huddled close to the fire and spent the rest of the night longing for the dawn and praying that our camp would remain intact. Dawn came at 6 a.m. and the sight it revealed was disturbing, for the sea was closely packed with ice. A good hot hoosh and a cup of hot milk banished our fatigue to some extent, and we stood by, waiting for an opportunity to get under way. At 8 a.m. a lead opened and the boats were launched and loaded. The previous day's experience showed that the boats were too deep in the water, so we left behind some cases of dried vegetables, a number of picks and shovels, and sundry oddments which we considered could be dispensed with. A strong east wind was blowing, which gradually increased to a moderate gale. At noon we won through to what appeared to be the open sea. Heavy rollers were running outside and breaking on the margin of the pack-ice, and the deeply laden boats began to labour badly. Sprays continually broke over them, freezing as they fell. Everything became sheathed in ice, and our soaked garments froze as stiff as mail and cracked as we moved.

It was too hazardous to face the dangerous sea, and we were reluctantly compelled to run back to the shelter of the pack, where the sea was broken down by the weight of ice. We continued sailing westwards until late afternoon, when we entered an extensive, calm pool in which drifted a massive, friendly floe – an excellent camping place. Soaked to the skin, weary through lack of sleep, and utterly worn out, we were thankful for any place on which we might lie down and snatch a few hours' rest. Guards were set to watch over the safety of the camp, and we managed to get more sleep than we had had for a fortnight.

The dawn broke, foggy, cheerless and sinister. A piercing wind was blowing from the north-west, bringing sleet which froze in a glassy veneer. While we were making ready to get under way, fields of pack came rapidly driving down from the north. There was no choice. Our floe appeared capable of withstanding a buffeting, and Sir Ernest decided to remain and await events.

Driven on by the swift tides and heavy swell, the ice swirled round our floe, bearing it along, rolling and rocking alarmingly. In less than an hour the bosom of the sea was obscured by a seething expanse of crushing pack-ice. Climbing to the top of a reeling knoll, we gazed spellbound on a terrifying spectacle. Furious warfare was raging on one of nature's age-old battlefields. We had reached the northern limit of the ice-pack, where the endless streams of ice cast adrift from the polar continent were being lashed back remorselessly by temperate seas. Here the conclusion of a cycle in nature's equilibrium was taking place. The ice-packs, pounded up and eroded by the action of the waves, were returning to their primal element. Around us churned the mill of the world. Gnarled old ice-floes, weather-worn bergs, fragmentary stumps, and decayed ice-masses were crowded together in one heaving, rolling grind. To the girdling horizon stretched this tempest-ridden, battling confusion. It was sublime, irresistible, terrible. Our rocking floe was suffering the fate of its neighbours. We experienced a series of sickening impacts as its ramparts were torn asunder. What helpless atoms we felt – mere human flotsam, caught in a maelstrom of unlimited power, and separated from eternity by only a thin partition of crumbling ice.

We stood by the boats, ready should our frail raft shatter. A large section of it sheared from its margin, and a broad ice-foot formed, over which the surf swirled and on which masses of ice were stranded. It would be difficult to launch the boats over this lunging ice reef. Sir Ernest and Wild stood on the peak of our foundering berg, patiently watching and waiting for a chance. There was a cry of 'She's splitting.' We manned the boats, waited, but nothing happened – it was only the surface snow subsiding. Our floe was wallowing like a sinking ship before the last plunge, and the end seemed near.

The leader called out that a lead was approaching, and that we were to stand by to launch the boats. On the horizon we noticed a dark line cleaving through the tortured ice – a narrow, open lead. Would it never hasten? A flock of sea-birds circled over us like messengers of freedom, a few seals drifted past, sleeping peacefully and safely on rocking floes; but we, in spite of our superior intelligence, were in peril, powerless to help ourselves; how anomalous it seemed. Slowly, stealthily, with exasperating deliberation, the lead crept closer. At last it reached our floe. Sir Ernest stood by the rising and falling ice-foot, directing the launching, which was extremely hazardous. When the floe rolled favourably, the order was given, 'Launch boats'. The *James Caird* had barely swung free when the uprising ice caught her bow and she was nearly swamped. We flung stores and gear aboard, leaped in and rowed desperately. The three boats in procession headed along the lead to the west, and soon entered large stretches of water, sufficiently open to allow the sails to be hoisted. Light snow and biting winds numbed us to the bone, but our spirits were cheered by the excellent progress.

Wild was at our helm and Sir Ernest stood up in the stern keeping a watchful eye on the two boats following in our wake, and occasionally shouting words of direction. As night drew on, we ranged up alongside a floe that promised shelter, and made fast. The cook was put ashore just long enough to prepare some hoosh. We had had enough of the floes, and preferred to remain in the boats until daylight. We were compelled to cast off in the dark, for streams of ice threatened to hole the boats. It was a stern night – snow and sleet fell; killer-whales skirmished round, and we dreaded that they might rise to 'blow' beneath the boats, or capsize them with their massive dorsal fins. We had seen the killers charge and upset heavy masses of ice on which luckless seals basked, and we had little doubt that these voracious monsters would appreciate a variation in their diet if a boat overturned.

Dawn rose on a pitiful scene. Haggard, drawn faces, with beards encrusted with ice, peered out from garments shrouded with snow. The boats were drifting idly on a stagnant, mushy sea. Before getting under way we set about looking for a suitable floe on which the cook might land to prepare breakfast. Such a floe was difficult to find without running into the body of the pack, and it was interesting to note the keenness that was displayed in searching for a friendly ice island. At last we drew up alongside one. The cook – excellent fellow – though stiff with cold, soon had a hot hoosh ready, which heartened us for what the immediate future might bring.

The day proved to be clear, and radiant with sunshine. Sails were set and the purl of a silver bow wave sang merrily in our ears as we moved over the deep blue. For the first time for months we admired the callous beauty of the pack-ice, eroded by the waves into countless fanciful forms. Penguins rode on crystal gondolas, and countless seals basked on marble-white slabs, which swayed gently in the swell. Beyond the margin of the pack rolled the seas, deep-furrowed and white-crested.

Since embarking on 9 April, thick weather had obscured all view of land, and there had been no opportunity of determining our position by sun observations. All the time we had been sailing west, but, since we knew little about the set of the currents, our precise location was a matter of conjecture. We imagined, however, that it must be highly favourable as far as Elephant Island was concerned. With keen speculation we awaited noon, when Captain Worsley would check up our 'dead reckoning' by a 'sun-shot'. As the time approached we watched Worsley stand up in the *Dudley Docker*, put his arm around the mast to steady himself, for the boat was rolling badly, and manipulate his sextant. We then rowed the *James Caird* alongside the *Dudley Docker* and the leader jumped into it. After the observations were worked out, he returned to the *James Caird* and held a whispered discussion with Wild. The outcome was that our destination was changed from Elephant Island to Hope Bay – roughly 80 miles to the south-west – on the Antarctic mainland. Fearing the reaction it might have had on the party at the time, we were not made aware of Worsley's calculations, though Sir Ernest informed us that our progress was not as favourable as we had anticipated. In fact, we were actually 30 miles east of the position where the boats had been launched three days previously. Though sailing west during the day, the currents had carried the ice-floes on which we had rested during the night swiftly to the east. Not only had we lost all the distance sailed, but the drift had actually gained 30 miles on our efforts. This was heartbreaking.

Throughout the day we continued, until dusk made navigation dangerous, and we then set about finding a suitable floe behind which to shelter for the night. The ice was so broken and tossed by the surge that it was unapproachable. At last, in the darkness, we succeeded in making the boats fast to a large floe, tethering one behind the other. The swell prevented the cook from being put 'ashore', so hoosh had to be prepared with the aid of primus stoves. This was a lengthy business, for the boats were rolling violently, and sprays occasionally broke over them, extinguishing the stoves.

It seemed as if evil forces were arrayed to torment us. No sooner was one peril overcome than another arose in its place. Streams of ice fragments, borne along by surface currents or driven by the winds, were attracted to the lee side of our floe, and this became a new annoyance. For several hours we staved off the ice with boathooks and paddles, and then, shortly after midnight, the wind suddenly changed and began to drive the boats back broadside on to the ice-spurs of the floe. There was no time to cast off, so reluctantly we cut our valuable mooring-line and backed away, to save the boats from being holed.

So that we might not drift apart, we kept the boats tethered to one another, and all night long they lay hove to in the freezing sea. We huddled together, clasped in each other's arms, so that we might glean a little warmth from each other's bodies and consolation from whispered hopes. Where our bodies touched, the warmth thawed our frozen garments and, when we moved, the icy wind stabbed through us. Would the dawn never come – would the sun never rise again? Night seemed an eternity. Where our wet clothes chafed, boils swelled up, throbbing intolerably in the piercing cold. It seemed that the limit of human endurance must soon be reached.

Dawn came at last. We were denied the cheer of a hot breakfast, for everything was iced and the sea was running high. But there were compensations. No restraint was placed on the amount of cold rations we might eat, the sun was rising, and the wind had changed fair for Elephant Island. We had much to be thankful for.

The pack-ice had closed up to the south in the direction of Hope Bay, so the boats were again headed for Elephant Island, which now lay 100 miles to the north. Sails were hoisted, and with a strong fair breeze our three small vessels sped forward to the land of hope. The pack was rapidly thinning out, and it appeared as if we were nearing its northernmost limit. Shortly after noon we passed through a narrow belt of ice and unexpectedly emerged into the open ocean.

Had we not been driven by desperation, we would not have dared to venture into the heavy seas in three such frail boats. It was amazing that our spent and weather-beaten bodies responded so heroically to the occasion, and I doubt if any creature but man could have survived the excesses of exposure, fatigue, hunger and lack of rest to which we had been subjected. It was the will alone that made it possible – the will that enabled us to rise above suffering and to dominate and drive our jaded bodies.

Again, I cannot speak too highly of our leader. The piloting of the party through perilous adventures, from the time the ship was beset up to our escape from the ice, without loss of life, was a far greater achievement than the realisation of the original plans of the expedition would have been. If ever an environment was likely to breed pessimism, ill-feeling and revolt, it was that which surrounded us during the monotonous months on the floe. Scientists and sailors of widely diverse natures, training and outlook, cooped together in tiny tents, hungry, cold, with tempers exasperated by nature's despotism, betrayed neither enmity nor discontent. All this I attribute to the leader, whose magnetic personality inspired cheerfulness, hope and encouragement.

The three small boats and their weather-beaten refugees had proved themselves in the conflict with the ice – now they were to measure their worth against the sea. The ocean seemed an old friend and, though our vessels were mere cockleshells, their pilots were skilled mariners, and He who had directed the floe through its tortuous wanderings was surely still with us. In an indefinable way we felt that our escape was no matter of mere chance. Always, when on the brink of doom, an outlet of escape had saved us in some miraculous way. So our hearts swelled with exultation as our crazy boats bounded over the glinting seas, while the white-crested, sapphire combers chased us, passed us, and led on.

During the afternoon an icy wind lashed the water, and sails were reefed. Spray, dashing on board, froze and caked boats and men with ice, and the salt water saturated our garments, and provoked our split skin and boils to fresh miseries. Some of the men had sea-sickness

Frank Hurley, photographer, in sledging costume.

Frank Hurley

The *Endurance*, in the full pride of her youth, breasting the Antarctic ice-packs at the outset of the expedition in 1915.

Frank Hurley

The ship's wake through newly formed sea-ice, called 'rotten' ice, in the Weddell Sea.

Frank Hurley

Attempts were made to cut a passage through the ice, but as temperatures fell to 65°F below freezing point the ocean froze over as fast as the ice could be cut away.

Having forced a passage through 1500 miles of ice-encumbered sea, the *Endurance* became immovably trapped in ice. A few days later, a blizzard heaved the ice into a chaos of hummocks. Shackleton was only 30 miles short of his intended destination.

Frank Hurley

A flash-light study of the ghostly *Endurance*, with her hull and rigging encrusted with glittering rime-crystals.

Hurley distributing the midday meal – two pounds of seal meat – to his team of dogs in the midwinter darkness.

After 90 days the sun reappeared in the north and with it came a new danger: a mighty iceberg ploughed its way through the pack and bore down upon the imprisoned ship. A timely blizzard turned this fearsome mass off course and saved the *Endurance*.

Frank Hurley

Frank Hurley

The pressure of many millions of tons of ice made a toy of the helpless vessel.
The ship was squeezed up 10 feet above the sea and badly strained.

Frank Hurley

The floes crumbled, then came together again, and under their irresistible squeeze the timbers gave way and the waters rushed in. The ship was dead.

Frank Wild with Lupoid, one of fifty-four sledge-dogs to reach the Weddell Sea. Six pups were born after the ship had become frozen in ice.

A shelter was made by turning two boats upside-down and walling them around with fragments of canvas and snow. Twenty-two men lived for five months like semi-frozen sardines within the shelter's cramped, dark interior.

Frank Hurley

Shackleton's Argonauts – the men who remained behind on Elephant Island
while the leader set out to bring relief. For the nearly five months before rescue
came, they lived entirely on the meat of seals and penguins.

Frank Hurley

Rescue at last ... Ringing cheers greeted the approach of the boat put off from the Yelcho, a Chilean trawler dispatched by Shackleton for the rescue of his men. Four determined attempts had been made before the castaways were relieved.

added to their afflictions. Even under these conditions we were still capable of seeing the humorous side of things. One of the party, who had consistently skimped and saved titbits from his frugal rations, keeping them reserved in a bag against the day of starvation – of which he lived in constant dread – became violently sea-sick, and was unable to eat even a crumb of the liberal rations that were issued, and on which the more fortunate gorged themselves. This brought smiles to cracked lips, for we felt our doubting companion was doing just penance for his lack of faith.

Most of us were badly frostbitten, and it was notable that the old campaigners, Shackleton, Wild, Crean and myself, though not seriously affected by most conditions, were not immune from frost-bite. My hands became badly frozen through the continual wearing of wet mitts. The leader, noticing my endeavours to restore circulation, took off his warm gloves and handed them to me. 'Take these until your hands are right,' he said. Since he was suffering himself, I refused. But he was determined that I should have them. 'All right,' he replied, 'if you don't take them I'll throw them into the sea.' It was a brave action – characteristic of the man.

We had burst so unexpectedly into the open sea that we had not taken any ice aboard for drinking purposes, nor had we any drinking water. To alleviate our burning thirsts, we had eaten raw seal-meat, cut into squares, but this had unfortunately been drenched with salt spray, and only aggravated our condition. One wondered what additional anguish and suffering the body was capable of feeling and the mind of withstanding.

Night fell and, though we wished to continue and to take advantage of the fair wind, our leader decided to heave to. This was a wise policy, for it would have been impossible to keep the boats together in the darkness. Sails were lowered, a sea-anchor was hastily made by lashing the oars together, and the boats were tethered to it one behind the other. Owing to the cross-currents, the boats would not keep head on to the seas and kept continually bumping together. The temperature fell below zero, and as our vessels tossed and plunged the sprays broke over them and quickly froze. The added weight of the accumulating ice caused the boats to wallow, and we spent the night chipping the ice away, staving off the boats and trying to keep ourselves from freezing. They were hideous hours, and the flame of hope all but died in many a heart. Indeed, many of the party were unhinged by their agonies. It was a night of terror, horror and despair.

Sharp indeed are the contrasts in these latitudes. With the dawn came an abatement of the sea and a glimpse of land. It was a sublime revelation. I am convinced that nothing less could have brought the party from its state of death-like apathy back to life again. A grey fog had hung over the sea, screening all distant prospect. Then the sun burst through pink vapours. Like an enchanted curtain the mists rolled skyward, revealing a sun-gilt mountain, like a colossal pyramid of gold rising from the purple seas. It was Clarence Island. Magical had been its appearance, and magical the reaction on us. Our moribund party flickered into life again. A little later we observed on our port bow, some 30 miles away, seven domed peaks, the ice-clad summits of Elephant Island.

The tethering-lines were cast off, and our sea-anchor of bundled oars, which had grown to the thickness of tree-trunks through accumulated ice, was chipped clean and taken on board. Sails were hoisted with difficulty, for the ropes and pulleys were fouled with ice, and the sheets were frozen stiff like metal plates. With a fair breeze, the three boats headed for Elephant Island.

Breakfast rations were served, but we could only nibble at them, for our cracked lips bled painfully and our parched throats and swollen tongues would not permit us to swallow. The sun mounted in the sky and beat down on thirst-maddened men, but somehow we seemed indestructible in spirit and body. At last the land lay within our grasp – the land that we had been patiently longing to reach for sixteen long months. We could stand a few hours' more suffering. A few hours and we would be walking on good solid rock.

At noon the breeze died down and we took to the oars. How we laboured. How anxiously we watched the land gradually draw closer and the snowy peaks grow clearer.

'I can see rock!' cried one. And 'Look! The crevasses are now showing up!' said another. We strained our eyes towards the goal, measuring the distance by details gradually revealed as we drew closer.

The Escape in the Boats

At 3 p.m. we were within 8 miles of the island. Wild picked out a little bay, sheltered by white peaks, with rocks standing out boldly from the ice-clad shores. It was to us a sunlit, homely prospect. We rowed with joyful eagerness – tonight we would be camped on solid rock. Oh heavenly prospect!

The minutes grew into hours. The sea was calm, the water was rippling from our bows, but somehow, in spite of our efforts, we were drawing no closer. Then the terrible truth burst upon us – we were caught in an adverse current. It was only just possible to hold our own against it. Curdling despair crept into us, and all the agonies that hope had dulled throbbed with fresh acuteness. We could not row much longer. The reserve energy which the near realisation of freedom had called up was almost spent. It was cruel, uncharitable, relentless. There was not a man whose soul did not cry out in anguish to the controller of the winds and tides, not to forsake us. Throughout the dreary, suffering months we had quelled our heartaches with the consoling thought that the future would one day reward our hopes. That time, the panacea for all tribulations would solve the problem of our destinies as our hearts desired. Barrier after barrier had raised itself and had been surmounted, but now, on the very threshold of salvation, it seemed we must fail. Only a miracle could save us – the wind! A favourable wind, which would swell our sails and tear us from the merciless suck of the tide. Our plight had never been so desperate as now. Most of the party were at the last gasp, crazed and dazed, and could row no more.

Night shut down, black and pitiless. The open ocean lay to the right, and the tide was hurrying us into its greedy spaces. Down fluttered the snow, coming from the south-east in whirling flurries. It fell in a soft shroud over forms huddled down in the boats, listless and careless of death. An occasional moan came from the men. We were helpless. Then a great, black cloud filled the sky and the wind came. It came from the south, at first gently – it seemed like a sigh. Then the waters rippled under its caress. More strongly it came, till the sea swept up in the rolling waves – waves rolling to the shore. The miracle had happened. It was not chance – our prayers had been heard.

Shackleton called to the men in the boats to hoist sails. Those aboard the *Stancomb Wills* were too far spent, so we took them in tow. On through the dark, towards our goal, now swallowed up in the blackness, plunging through a void of waters swelling up in the gale. Those who were able trimmed the boat as she heeled to the wind's press – the others lay corpse-like. The noise of tumbling crests was all around, and the spume flung forward by the wind raked the boats.

Wild had not left the helm for forty-eight hours, and was now so frozen that his arms and hands would not function. He was relieved by Chips, the carpenter, but he, too, overcome by exhaustion, swooned at his post. Instantly the boat turned broadside to the seas and a huge wave leaped aboard, drenching everything and nearly swamping us. Wild carried on again. In the darkness and agonising cold the worn-out party fought the storm, chipping away the accumulations of frozen spray, and frantically bailing the boats to keep them afloat. Every billow brought a spasm of misery. Each black gulf, viewed from the crest of a spuming comber, yawned to swallow us. Scoured by the winds, mocked by the storm, we wondered if the night would ever end – or if there had ever been such a night.

With the *Stancomb Wills* in tow, we were making heavy weather. It seemed from moment to moment that we would have to part the line and leave her to her fate. Sir Ernest, in the stern, strained his eyes into the darkness, watching that black object tossing in the dark torment, and shouting at intervals words of cheer and inquiry. 'She's gone!' one would say, as a hoary billow reared its crest between us. Then, against the white spume a dark shape would reappear, and through the tumult would come, faint but cheering, Tom Crean's reassuring hail, 'All well, Sir!' So we lived through each wave and through the night. In the darkness we lost sight of our third boat, the *Dudley Docker*.

Anxiously we peered through the mists and snow-whirls towards the land. As we drew closer, the watery moon broke fitfully through the storm-racked sky, and shone on nebulous contours of peaks and phantom-like glaciers. The land seemed like a spectral fantasy conceived by our distressed minds. Our overwrought nerves were steadied when we heard the growl of surf on the reefs. It must be real! We stood off till the dawn, which came at last to reveal leaden clouds, great grey seas and ... the land.

Land! Land! Mountains and glaciers peeping through the mists – and blessed rock! We made into the lee, and rowed over the heaving surges which swirled at the base of mighty cliffs. Our boats were dwarfed to puny specks by the magnitude of mountain and sea. A thousand feet above, the rising sun was tipping with gold the summits of Elephant Island. Everywhere the land was burdened with ice. Snow was piled in masses on mountain crests, ice festooned the rocky terraces and filled the defiles with convulsed glaciers. And the perpendicular mountain walls rose, sheer and relentless, from the sea. We had reached land but, to our dismay, to set foot upon it appeared to be an impossibility.

CHAPTER 10

LAND! LAND! LAND!

We made the lee of the land, and rowed along the coast over inky reflections of beetling, black mountain-walls, searching anxiously for a breach or ledge that might afford refuge, but could find nothing that promised even a foothold.

Ahead, an avalanche had tumbled into the sea, littering the water with ice-blocks. From its margin we eagerly hacked fragments, hauling them aboard to quench our excruciating thirst. It was the land's first blessing, and seemed likely to be its last.

We reached Cape Valentine, on the north-east extremity of the island, and observed a small channel running up to a possible landing-place. It seemed our last hope. The *Stancomb Wills* rowed in through the surf and reported favourably. It was a mere foothold, yet it offered a temporary shelter. Her party landed, and those of us who were able began disembarking the stores and helpless men from the *James Caird*. While this was in progress, our third boat hove into sight. She had been blown into an adjacent bay during the night, where she weathered the gale with great difficulty. Her party and stores were landed, the boats hauled up and a camp made. We were a pitiful sight; the greater number of us were terribly frostbitten and half-delirious. Some staggered aimlessly about, flinging themselves down on the beach, hugging the rocks, and letting the pebbles trickle through their fingers as though they were nuggets of gold. It is hard to describe the joy we felt, walking on land, feeling and looking upon solid rocks, after having lived through the terrible experiences of the past sixteen months.

And then to fall asleep; to rest unperturbed; to turn over and hear the music of the surf, the swirl of the ice-blocks, the croak of the penguins; to dream with hope of the future; to experience the unspeakable joy of waking up to find we were on something solid, something that had not drifted miles in the night. It was the realisation of all our hopes. It was heavenly. Nothing else mattered. A terrible chapter in our lives had ended; we scarcely cared what was to open the next.

In the morning we made an investigation of the refuge to which the guiding hand had led us. It was a wild place. Behind us rose sheer cliffs of rock over 1000 feet high. At their base stretched the narrow strip of shingly beach on which we were camped, strewn with ice-blocks, and swept by the stormy billows of the wild Antarctic Ocean. High on the cliffs was a dark line, which indicated the encroachment of storm-flung seas, and farther along the beach lay piles of rocks that had tumbled down from the cliffs. It was perfectly obvious that the place would be untenable in bad weather, and that at any moment we might be buried by an avalanche of rocks. Sir Ernest dispatched Wild and several sailors in the *Dudley Docker* in quest of a new home. Early in the afternoon they returned, having located a promising site 9 miles to the west, on the north coast. The tides and weather being in our favour, the party embarked, having first lightened our cargo by making a depot of a quantity of stores in a cave above the sea's reach.

The weather in these latitudes is extremely treacherous. During our short trip to our new refuge we ran into a gale when rounding Cape Valentine. The south-west wind shrieked down from the mountains, lashing the sea white. Hour after hour we toiled at the oars. Sometimes the gale drove us back; then, while it seemed to pant for breath, we gained. We all knew our fate only too well should we be driven out into the wild west sea. Emaciated and worn-out as we were, the paralysing thought that icy death was still stalking us took possession of our minds. But the example of our leader and of Wild made men of us again, and we shook off our dread and fought our way through the storm inch by inch to the lee of the land. Painfully we rowed along, while the hurricane raged on the pinnacles 1000 feet up. The scurrying rivulets of snow rushing down the sheer faces of the cliffs were caught up in eddies and whirled out over the sea, where the tortured waters leaped to meet them. But with the evening the storm abated and we reached our new haven.

Camps were pitched, a hot meal was made, and the low-burning flame of life was fanned again. Once more, with gratitude for the stability of the good old earth, we lay down and stretched ourselves in the dreamless slumber of the utterly fatigued. But we were not to rest for long. The winds attacked again with diabolical malice, hurling gravel and ice splinters at us, and ripping the tents to shreds. Only the tent occupied by Sir Ernest, James and myself escaped, for we tumbled out and dismantled it before the blizzard reached its full height. In the troubled darkness we crept beneath the flapping folds, once more to seek sleep. Was there ever a place so pitiless and inhospitable?

At 4 a.m. we were awakened by a new alarm. This time the rising tide was creeping upon us, and the waves were washing our canvas covering. Turning out, we moved higher up the beach. It was bitterly cold, with a dense drift, and not a square inch of shelter. Making a feeble rampart of cases, we lit the bogie, laid our tent on the ground, and, weighting the skirting with stones, crawled beneath its folds. The silence was broken by shouts, and, looking out we saw the occupants of what had been no. 5 tent trying to make a shelter by overturning one of the boats. We also observed that the ringed penguins inhabiting the rookery near the camp, having had enough of the weather, were congregating on the beach. They migrated during the morning. Lucky, lucky birds! The homeless party from no. 5 succeeded in overturning the *Dudley Docker* and converting it into a safe and comparatively comfortable shelter.

A wretched day was followed by a miserable night and another day of bad weather, the air being thick with wet and drifting snow. During the evening the wind dropped, and we were treated to a magnificent moonlit night, which silvered everything with a mystic charm. The frowning coastline stood out in a dark silhouette against a starry sky. But morning ushered in a day of incessant, heavy snowfalls, which, however, could not make us wetter, for we were already soaked to the skin.

Those first few days on Elephant Island were hell, and it seemed at first that many of us would be unable to survive further worry and exposure. Our new refuge was named 'Cape Wild' – at once an apt description and a tribute to a great-hearted comrade. Cape Wild was a spit of rock thrust out into the sea, with a sheer ice-cliff on the land side, and a cluster of huge boulders just off its tip. The coast curved towards it on one side, and formed the bay where we had landed.

Land! Land! Land!

Food had been reduced to vanishing-point, and the party had no protection against the weather. What was to be done? To remain meant death from slow starvation or from exposure. The situation was desperate, but again our leader rose to the occasion. He consulted with Wild and decided that some of us must attempt to reach South Georgia, and bring relief to the others. He determined to make the endeavour himself, taking with him five men who were skilled sailors. The remainder of the party, twenty-two men, would be left at Elephant Island under the charge of Frank Wild. The decision was characteristic of the man, and was undertaken in the grand spirit which had distinguished his leadership from the beginning of the expedition.

Chippy, the indispensable carpenter, began to deck over the *Caird* with odd fragments of wood and scraps of canvas, in preparation for the proposed voyage, which now became our all-absorbing interest. Personnel, equipment, chances and the journey's duration were topics of keen discussion. During a let-up in the weather, penguins were slaughtered and skinned for their meat, while a fat Weddell seal that had waddled ashore also found its way into our larder. This solved the food problem temporarily.

We re-rigged our tent, and all hands turned to in the erection of a wind-shelter for the cook's galley. Green, our indomitable cook, showed signs of a breakdown, so I was appointed chef, and found ample occupation in serving meals at 8 a.m., 1 p.m. and 4.30 p.m. I quickly assumed a piebald appearance as the mixed blubber-soot and snow-drift formed a coating over me. Weather conditions still being wretched, we retired daily at 5 p.m. to our saturated sleeping-bags for fourteen long hours. The tent walls became thickly covered with condensation rime, showering us with every gust. Nevertheless, the invalids were recovering, frostbites were healing, and the general spirits of the party were rising with the prospect of the relief expedition – forlorn hope though it might be. All our apparel and equipment were in a deplorable condition, owing to the continued bad weather, and nothing would have been more welcome than a sunny day. On Easter Monday, 24 April 1916, the weather let up. A moderate sea was running, and Sir Ernest thought it wise to set out immediately. At any hour the pack-ice from which we had escaped might drift northwards, encircle the island, and make navigation impossible. With a rousing cheer we slid the *James Caird* down the gravelly beach and launched her through the surf. Disaster was narrowly averted at the outset, for the unballasted boat capsized, and McNeish and Vincent, who were on the deck, were precipitated into the sea. Relieved of the top weight, the *James Caird* righted, but was caught in the heavy undertow and carried towards the reefs. By a resolute effort, those aboard managed to row her out to safety beyond the breakers.

The *Stancomb Wills* carried out the ballast – bags made from blankets filled with sand – and the concentrated rations which had been reserved for the voyage. By midday the little vessel was loaded. It was a desperate venture, yet her crew, already spent, faced this terrible voyage with the hearts of British seamen. Those who risked their lives to succour their comrades were Shackleton, Worsley, Crean, McCarthy, McNeish and Vincent. We shook hands and sent them off with a cheer. We stood on the beach watching the tiny sail grow smaller and smaller until it diminished to a minute speck. How lonely it looked! Then it disappeared from sight. Before Shackleton and his gallant companions lay a voyage of 750 miles, across the most tempestuous ocean in the world; yet we never doubted the issue, for providence which had already guided and delivered us, would surely never forsake us in this hour of need. Our hope was that they would reach South Georgia in fourteen days, charter a steam trawler from one of the whaling stations, and return to us within a month. How opportunely their departure was timed may be gathered from the fact that the next morning a change in the direction of the wind filled the bay with pack-ice, blocking all access to the sea for many weeks. Regarding our comrades' escape from this as a favourable omen, we shut our eyes to the hazards, and fixed our minds on the hope. Great is the tonic effect of hope – and great was our need of its stimulus as the weeks passed. Here we were, a party of twenty-two men, maintaining a precarious foothold on an exposed ledge of barren rock, in the world's wildest ocean. Our leader had departed, taking with him the pick of the seamen. Of our party, one was a helpless cripple, a dozen were more or less disabled with frostbite, and some were, for the moment, crazed by their privations. Our refuge was like the cramped courtyard of a prison – a narrow strip of beach 200 paces long by 30 yards wide. Before us, the sea, which pounded our shores in angry tumult, would at night be frozen into icy silence, only to break up again under tidal influence with a noise like the churning of some monstrous mill. Behind us, the island peaks rose 3000 feet into the air, and down their valleys and across their creeping glaciers the wind shrieked, lashing us with hail and smothering us with snow-drift.

Inhospitable, desolate and hemmed in with glaciers, our refuge was as uninviting as it could be. Still, we were grateful. It was better than the ice-floes. Here before us lay our hope – the great, open, rolling ocean, which washed the shores of tropic and pole, the highway to lands of human beings, our homeland – and freedom.

CHAPTER 11

OUR LIFE BENEATH TWO BOATS

Our hut is double-storied, with bedrooms twenty-two,
A library and a drawing-room, although indeed 'tis true
We haven't any bathroom, at which perhaps you'll smile;
But we found it warmer not to wash in our hut on Elephant Isle.

TOPICAL SONG

Marooned, we devoted ourselves to making our lot as endurable as possible. We estimated optimistically that the *James Caird*, under the guidance of providence, might reach South Georgia in fourteen days, and that another two weeks, at the outside, should see the rescue party at hand.

It had been decided, after examining every square yard of the beach for possible shelter, that the only hope was to excavate a cave in the dead end of an adjacent glacier, and to this task we applied ourselves with a will.

In the meantime, since all gear was thoroughly wet, and no drying was possible, we had to turn into wet sleeping-bags, and after wringing out our soaked garments, take them into the bags with us so that they might not freeze stiff by the morning. We suffered no ill-effects from this practice, and attributed this immunity to the fact that we were absorbing considerable quantities of blubber, which thoroughly waterproofed us. A good seal hoosh with plenty of blubber just before turning in, induced a steamy heat, and we slept soundly, although pools of water were thawed from the ice beneath our sleeping-bags.

It may seem incredible that human beings could live in such circumstances. What is, perhaps, more remarkable is that our men, many of whom were at death's door when we landed, were making a rapid recovery in what was surely the weirdest and most unfavourable convalescent home that can be imagined. The fact was that we had been in these conditions for so long that we had become inured to them. We had gradually become broken into Antarctic rigours by our life aboard the ship. The *Endurance* was a nightly refuge in which we could repair the physical ravages of our daily exposure. Thus prepared, we were able to face the strenuous life on the floes, which might well have ended disastrously for untrained men. On the drifting ice we increased our powers of resistance to cold, and accustomed our bodies to assimilate the blubber and the seal- and penguin-meat upon which we had largely subsisted. Had we not been thus toughened during those five weary months, we certainly could not have faced the appalling boat journey. The human body's adaptability is marvellous. We had grown almost as fit to endure the climate as the seals themselves.

Four days' hard work on the ice-grotto where we proposed to camp saw the end of our hopes of a home. It was soon evident that thaw-water would be troublesome. When the temperature rose, streams welled up through the floor, drips fell from the roof, and rivulets gushed and gurgled from the walls. From our labours in excavation we reaped nothing but exercise. Then Wild hit upon the happy scheme of converting the two remaining boats into a hut. All hands were engaged in erecting low walls of stones, on to which the two boats were overturned side by side. The sails and the tent floor-cloths were next stretched over the boats to form a roof. These were secured with lashings and with thin laths of wood split from food cases; the extracted nails were used to tack them on. The sides were walled round with fabric from torn tents, and a tent doorway was sewn in on the side sheltered from the prevailing storms. The floor – which, by the way, was an old-established penguin rookery – was covered with gravel from the beach. The work occupied us for many days, for we had to improvise with sundry scraps and remnants, but finally the 'house' was voted weatherproof, and James and I, who in the meantime had occupied the only tent left intact, took up our quarters. I marked the occasion in my journal thus:

James and self take up residence in the boat shelter, which we have christened 'The Snuggery'. Night of terrific winds threatening to dislodge our new refuge. The wind is a succession of hurricane gusts that sweep down the glacier immediately SSW of us. Each gust heralds its approach by a low rumbling, which increases to a thunderous uproar. Snow, stones and gravel are whirled before it and any gear left unweighted by heavy stones flies seaward. The shelter is decidedly comfortable compared with tents and will ameliorate our existence considerably. The size of ground space enclosed is 18 feet by 12 feet and the height of our ceiling is only 4 feet 9 inches above the ground. The smaller blubber bogie radiates a pleasant warmth, does the cooking, and so fills the place with soot and smoke that our eyes run painfully and our lungs nigh choke. Still it is a step in the direction of making life more endurable under such fiendish conditions. The entire party of twenty-two sleep in this small space snugly packed like smoked sardines. Crude improvised stretchers are arranged between the boat thwarts, six sleeping in each boat, the remainder 'dossing' on the floor.

Light, or rather a faint glimmer, is shed over all this through two tiny windows – one, a tiny pane 8 inches across, made from the glass cover of a chronometer, and the other, from a small square of celluloid that at one time covered a home photograph. Further feeble flicker is provided by a couple of blubber lamps, made from discarded food tins with wicks of stranded clothing. They smoke and reek to such effect, that after a while the atmosphere is so dense that they choke their efficiency and us too.

When draughts drive the bogie fumes back down the chimney, it is impossible to see more than a yard or so, and the place croaks with coughs and compliments. Then one escapes out into the blizzard with a fervent 'Thank God!'

With meticulous precision Wild doles out the rations, which comprise all portions of seals and penguins except hair and feathers. We are just as hungry after meals as before; strictest economy has to be observed, and the climate produces prodigious appetites. Seals and penguins are exceptionally accommodating creatures to the polar castaway. Not only do they provide him with food, but their blubbery skins furnish sufficient fuel to cook all edible parts. Salt for cooking purposes speedily became exhausted, but we have discovered that 50 per cent of salt sea-water added to a stew or soup supplies an excellent substitute without ill-effects.

Our Life Beneath Two Boats

As time went on, it became evident that the blizzards which had assailed us at the outset were a chronic condition. In fact, had it not been for occasional brief lulls, the climate was nearly as evil as that experienced in Adélie Land with Sir Douglas Mawson. In Adélie Land, however, we had a warm, comfortable hut, and no dearth of foodstuffs. Now we were existing in a miserable hovel, and had to exercise the most stringent economy, for the spectre of starvation ever haunted us in our desolation.

Except for a few odd cases of 'palate-ticklers', which exasperated more than fed us, we were entirely dependent on the creatures that came to us from the sea. Many times, when the ice-packs sheathed the ocean for long periods, we were on the verge of starvation, but, just as desperate crises approached, blizzards invariably dispersed the ice-packs, and penguins and seals came from the open water. It seemed, indeed, that we were in the safekeeping of the Almighty. This happened not only once, but five times. When we were inclined to become apprehensive, Wild inspired us anew. 'Surely,' he said, 'the Almighty, who has already led us through great ordeals and hazards, has not guided us to this haven or refuge to let us die miserably of hunger.'

As we saw the wisdom of Wild's words, doubt left us, and a great faith took its place. Strangely, only sufficient penguins and seals came ashore to satisfy our wants. Until the end of our tenancy there was never a surfeit.

Though the bad weather kept us for days beneath the boats, there were brief spells, which atoned for all this savage cruelty, and I wrote the following effusion during such a respite, to describe the outlook from the summit of the pinnacle which we climbed each day to look for a sail:

The weather is delightful – bright, warm sunshine and dead calm. Cape Wild is a narrow neck of rock jutting out from the mainland at the base of a magnificent spire-shaped peak, where it is only 60 yards wide, is practically flat and about 9 feet above high tides. The ocean end rises to a precipitous rocky bluff about 120 feet in height which is guarded oceanwise by a rocky islet that presents a flat jagged face 300 feet in height, which we call 'The Gnomon'. To the east the coast stretches in glorious vistas of perpendicular peaks terminating at the exquisitely castellated Cornwallis Island, heavily capped with glaciers that hang like frozen cataracts over the sea. Looking west there is a gorgeous blue glacier down which from the interior roar SW blizzards and from which frequent avalanches debouch. Distant view is obscured by a noble rocky headland though one has glimpses of some islets known as the Seal Rocks. From my elevated lookout, seaward, there is a view beautiful beyond imagination, yet unwelcome, for it is over an ocean obscured by ice-pack – a vast impenetrable field, driving rapidly from east to west. On the eastern side of the spit there is at low tide a fine gravelly beach on which we secure seals and penguins. In fact it appears that Cape Wild is a penguin rookery during the breeding season.

For a fortnight after the departure of Shackleton and his companions, the days, filled with endeavours to make a habitable camp on this wind-blasted ledge, passed without any sense of dragging. Our minds dwelt constantly on the stout little craft, which we pictured winging its way across the waste of waters like the dove, to carry the news and bring help to us on our Ararat. We believed the *James Caird* to be sufficiently seaworthy in such capable hands to win through even such seas as we knew she must encounter. As the south-east winds brought up increasing masses of ice, and our bay frequently became packed with floes that reached away to the horizon, we began to realise that only a vessel built for navigation in the ice could possibly reach us, and then only if she came before the winter set in. We passed the day that marked the minimum time in which we calculated the *Caird* could reach the whaling grounds, and then, as day succeeded day, and no sign appeared on the horizon, we resigned ourselves to the inevitable. We must winter on this bleak, storm-swept spot, and await the coming of a vessel in the early spring. Life was still bearable. Hardship had inured us to weather conditions and had bred in us a measure of philosophy. We settled down to make the best of it. This was the camp routine, as recorded in my blubber-stained and soot-begrimed journal:

It is just daylight at 7 a.m. when the cook is called. His duties of preparing the breakfast of penguin steaks take till 8.45 a.m., when those who have not already risen and gone for a constitutional are awakened by a raucous cry from Wild of 'Lash up and stow.' 'Clearing decks' is effected by rolling up all gear and stowing it in the 'thwart' bunks overhead. The boxes which have served for the cook's bunk are then arranged in an eccentric circle around the bogie, previously set going by the messman, and all take their appointed places thereon. So that all may have their share of bogie warmth, the circle moves one seat round each meal. With the welcome cry of 'Hoosh-o!' the 'peggy' from each mess – there are four – takes his pot to the galley, where Wild officiates in the 'whacking out'. The steaks are divided into individual portions as accurately as possible and 'whosed'. After breakfast there is a break of fifteen minutes for 'smoke-oh' and Wild allots various occupations. These are neither arduous nor strenuous and are essential as exercise. 'Hoosh-o!' is again called at 12.30 and is a light meal, generally a palate-tickler such as paddies, fried biscuit, thin soup, hoosh, or the greatly appreciated yet seldom served nut-food. Afternoons are spent in nominal occupations – mending, snaring birds, skinning penguins, etc. The evening hoosh is served at 4.30. One can always be sure what it is going to be. Seal hoosh, although not admired for its flavour, is esteemed on account of its quantity. Extra blubber lamps are lit in the centre of the seated circle, lighting up grimy faces with their smoky flare. It is a weird sight – the light thrown up by the lamps illuminates smoke-grimed faces like stage footlights, and is reflected in sparkling eyes and the glint on the aluminium mugs. The stream of flickering light thrown out from the open bogie door makes weird dancing shadows on the inside of the boats, suggesting a council of brigands in a huge chimney or the corner of a coal mine, holding revelry after an escapade. I can imagine the look of surprise and bewilderment with which any visitor would regard this grizzly-bearded and unkempt assemblage could he be suddenly thrown among us. Bewilderment would speedily become aversion; for our blubbery emanations and the odours from twenty-two crowded and seven-month-unwashed men coupled with the blue tobacco smoke 'fug', must be productive of an atmosphere distinctly unsavoury.

Conversation after evening hoosh generally wanders back to the civilised world, to places, feasts and theatres; to what we intend doing – chiefly eating. Holidays such as we outline will be spent in ever-sultry climes, our dreams are of wanderings in equatorial lands and tropical isles. Travel in unexplored New Guinea is a favourite subject, and we all vow that if ever we escape from the frozen captivity we will forthwith embark upon an expedition to thaw out amid steaming swamps and jungles.

After 'smoke-o' the decks are again cleared by stowing the box seats to form the cook's bunk, the tenants of the attic bunks swing into their places of repose with monkey-like agility and the ground door is spread with sleeping-bags, into which the owners wriggle like gigantic slugs. Hussey generally treats us to half an hour's banjo serenade in which our choristers join their voices. Then we sleep. The dim rays from the blubber light, which is kept burning continuously to save matches, sheds a feeble glow over objects resembling mummies. Loud snores from our reindeer sleeping-bags mingle with the roar of the blizzard.

It was not astonishing that the unchanging diet of penguin and seal meat should produce a curious physical and psychological reaction. We slept for fifteen hours at a stretch. We dreamed dreams of wonderful banquets and fantastic dishes, which vanished with tantalising regularity just as we were about to devour them. Physically we grew fat and blubbery, but the least exertion produced a muscular weariness that tired us. The most annoying manifestation, however, was an epidemic of snoring. It was almost impossible to hear one's own snores above those of the others. Nevertheless there was one who easily outdid all and earned the title of 'the snorer'. His consistent efforts outrivalled those of a wandering minstrel with a trombone. He survived all efforts – and they were many and varied – at suppression. Wild laid a cord through eyelets past each man's bunk, and attached one end to the snorer's foot. When anyone was awakened, he hauled on the rope, with the result that up went the leg and down went the snores. But at the end of a week the snorer grew accustomed to these interruptions and took no notice of the leg-pulling. Topical verse relates how peace and quiet were eventually restored:

> *'Twas on a dark and stormy night,*
> *Much snow lay on the ground,*
> *Stealthily from my sleeping-bag –*
> *Casting furtive looks around,*

Our Life Beneath Two Boats

I groped towards the snorer;
His snores I vowed to wreck,
I took the cord from off his leg
And placed it round his neck.

And how we talked food! A doughnut would provide a topic for an hour's discussion; a five-course dinner would keep us arguing for an evening. The most popular book in the world for us was Marston's *Penny Cookery Book*. With watering mouths and straining ears we devoured every word of it. It was fortunate, indeed, that we had not to suffer the physical after-effects of the mental gorges which its pages offered us. Our minds, in fact, were obsessed with food. This strange phase was due, not to starvation, which sharpens the wits and quickens the mental faculties, but to the monotony of our blubbery diet. For amusement I jotted down a few scraps of typical conversation. The page from which I now transcribe it is black with sooty seal-grease:

Snatches of conversation while in sleeping-bag:

WILD: Do you like doughnuts?
McILROY: Rather!
WILD: Damned easily made, too. I like them cold with a little jam.
McILROY: Not bad, but how about a huge rum omelette?
WILD: Bally fine [with a deep sigh].

Overhead, two of the sailors are discussing some extraordinary mixture of hash, apple sauce, beer, and cheese. Marston is holding a debate with the cook as to whether all puddings should have breadcrumbs for their base. Farther down the room someone eulogises Scotch shortbread. Several of the sailors are talking of 'spotted dog' and 'sea-pie' with great feeling. Then someone reminiscently murmurs the praises of our nut-food sledging ration, upon which conversation becomes general.

Another entry in the diary reads:

Autumn's days are shortlived; for the sun, after describing his short arc
of four hours in the heavens, goes to rest in the ocean in a blaze of golden
glory. The landscape assumes once more a flame-red tinge, and then, like

the dying embers of a fire, takes on the cold, ashen tint of evening. The stars rush out and fill the sky with silver spangles, the waters lazily lap the shingly beach. Then, from out the Snuggery come the strains of Hussey's banjo and a well-remembered tune:

> *Soft o'er the fountain*
> *Lingering falls the silver moon,*
> *Soft o'er the fountain*
> *Breaks the day too soon.*

What a wild setting to a sweet song. For the moment I am home again in dear old Sydney, when I am suddenly brought to bearings by the glacier debouching an avalanche into the bay. The echoes roll and reverberate among the hills, followed by the wave-wash, then all falls silent. We turn into our bags, perchance to dream of home and familiar faces, and so our tiny world sleeps with this wild slumber of nature.

The month closed with winter hard upon us. The spit and the gravel beach were hidden beneath a deep layer of ice, and the reefs and outlying rocks wore ice-caps of frozen sea-spray. The frozen breath of the south poured its blizzard drifts seawards, and lashed the ocean into flying spume and spindrift. It streamed like a river down the glacier slopes, roaring over our home, serenading us with an incessant shriek, as its sweeping eddies played among the rocks. Terrific gusts flapped the thin canvas walls, and so shook the boat superstructure as to keep us in a constant state of anxiety. Nor dare we leave the shelter of the boats for fear of being cut with flying panes of 'window-ice'. This phenomenon is produced during a calm, when the sleet and rain freeze over the ground in a thin, glassy layer. The furious winds smash up this icy veneer, which is about half-an-inch thick, and whirl it in flying panes up to a foot square. Our shelter was subjected to a continual bombardment, which sounded like crashing glass and continued until the window-ice had all been swept seawards. Nevertheless, our position might have been infinitely worse. I felt especially comfortable when I remembered the fearsome blizzards of Adélie Land, with their temperatures of 30°F below zero, endured in a sledging-tent. And, as the month ended, I made an entry in my diary expressing thankfulness that we had at last arrived at a condition of filthiness in which it was impossible to become any dirtier. Inability to wash was our greatest hardship.

June opened with a threatened shortage of fuel. Six hundred and six penguins had been captured in the six weeks since we landed; but while we had cold-storaged the carcasses, we had used up the skins for the stove. Fortunately, I was able to construct a damper from an oil-drum, which saved 50 per cent of the heat from escaping up the chimney, though we all nearly choked and were smoke-blinded when making the experimental fitting. Then, in keeping with our usual good fortune, over a hundred birds came ashore on two successive nights, while I captured a huge bull seal – the equivalent in food-value of eighty penguins.

The event of the month was the celebration of Midwinter Day (22 June). The shortest day was further abbreviated by a dense fog, but we marked it with feasting, and we honoured the longest night with song.

The sea-elephant which I had captured was found to contain some thirty recently swallowed fish. This unexpected gift provided us with a fish and entrée course and we snared some seagulls for the poultry course; but the *pièce de résistance* was a pudding composed of twelve mouldy nut-food bars, twenty mouldy biscuits, and four mouldy sledging rations boiled together. In an extra-strong potion of dried milk we toasted 'The King', 'The sun's return', 'The Boss and crew of the *James Caird*', and 'Sweethearts and wives', with no lack of genuine sentiment. A single sea-bird remained after the feast, and Wild decided to allow our begrimed pack of cards to determine its ownership. The cut went round the circle until it narrowed down to James and myself. By the smoking flicker of the blubber lamps the bearded, sooty faces drew closer, as cut followed cut without decision. Wild shuffled the pack, but the even cutting remained unchanged. The cards seemed under a spell. At last, on the thirteenth cut, I won, only to find the bird an extremely tough proposition, in more ways than one.

I wonder if a popular concert was ever conducted under more peculiar conditions than that midwinter revel of ours. Take a glimpse through the chronometer glass that had recently been fitted into the wall of our hut, and through the haze from blubber lamps and bogie-stove, note the audience – which has, perforce, retired to its sleeping-bags; for the concert hall is but 4 feet 9 inches high, and for an assemblage of twenty-two provides only lying-down accommodation. At the far end, Wild, Dr McIlroy, James the physicist and myself are ranged on the ground. Being nearest the stove, I am alternately roasted by day and covered with frost-rime showers by night. In the foreground are five recumbent forms – Dr Macklin, Kerr, Wordie, Hudson and Blackborrow – the last two being invalids. The middle is occupied by cases (which do duty as the cook's bed), boxes of fuel, and a solitary mummy, who is Lees, in his reindeer sleeping-bag. Above this is our attic or second storey. In it recline some ten unkempt and careless lodgers. From every available point hang blubbery garments, which would reek to heaven but for the fact that competition is so keen that their smell is unnoticed. In the daytime we crawl through these hanging smells like a brood of incubated chicks in a 'foster-mother'; at the height of a concert, they are pulled down and stacked, to allow the music to percolate more readily through the thickened atmosphere.

The programme of that midwinter concert may not have been high art, but Covent Garden has held no more appreciative audience. How could it, when every member was also a performer? Of the thirty-odd items, fully half were topical songs, stories and recitations, on which the brains of members had worked overtime for days, and no body of undergraduates ever relished their own wit more keenly, or roared their topical choruses with greater fervour.

'The Village Blacksmith' was translated into 'The Snuggery Cook'. Whatever may be the merits of the song 'Solomon Levi' as a chronicle of biography, it has nothing on the substituted words 'Franky Wild-o!' in point of literal truth, for as the last verse beautifully expressed it:

O Franky Wild-o! Tra-la-la-la-la-la!
Mister Franky Wild-o! Tra-la-la-la-la-la;
My name is Franky Wild-o; my hut's on Elephant Isle,
The wall's without a single brick, the roof's without a tile;
But nevertheless, I must confess, by many and many a mile
It's the most palatial dwelling place you'll find on Elephant Isle.

As might be expected, food formed a fertile subject for topical wit, and the following ballad was soulfully rendered by James to the lilting melody 'Egypt, My Cleopatra':

Upon an isle whose icy shores are washed by stormy seas,
There dwells beneath two upturned boats in comfort and in ease,
A grimy crew of twenty-two who've drifted many a mile,
And oft at night within each bag a face beams with a smile.

CHORUS

It is dreaming of choice sweetmeats and rare confections,
Drowsy reflections of rich plum cake,
It is tucking into almond icing and duffs enticing,
Which mortal baker could scarcely bake!

Hussey, brightening the atmosphere with his sparkling repartee, leading the songs with his clear notes, and giving body to the choruses with his banjo, was the life and soul of the party. With 'the common tunes ... that make you laugh and blow your nose', yes, he 'tore our very heartstrings out with those'.

Constant danger and privation had infused into us a philosophy of toleration and unselfishness, enabling us to see the other man's point of view as well as our own. We learned, too, how to find fullness and contentment in a life which had stripped us of all the distinctions, baubles and trappings of civilisation, and had brought us all to a common level. Necessity compelled us to support life in the most primitive fashion conceivable, and to share with one another, not only material things, but the sorrows that ache and the joys that transcend. Only one fight occurred, between one of the sailors and myself. It was over a trifling incident, and took place in a blizzard, when all the others were inside, so no one knew about it. We were both of hot-headed Irish temperament, and after going at it with characteristic fervour, the fire died down as suddenly as it flared; we flung discord to the winds, shook hands and cemented a great friendship.

It was during this month of June that Dr McIlroy and Dr Macklin transformed our snuggery into an operating theatre, and amputated the frostbitten toes of our youngest member, Blackborrow, who had been suffering severely, and was a chronic cripple. Wild and I acted as hospital orderlies, and maintained the temperature of the 'theatre' at 50°F by stoking up the bogie-fire with penguin skins. In the dense smoke, by the feeble glimmer of blubber lamps, Macklin administered the chloroform and McIlroy performed the operation which saved Blackborrow's leg, if not, indeed, his life. It is worth noting that the general health of our party was good throughout, and scurvy, the bugbear of polar expeditions, did not manifest itself. On the *Endurance* we had sufficiently varied foods, and on Elephant Island our ample diet of fresh fats doubtless acted as an anti-scorbutic. Our palates so adapted themselves to our bodily needs that raw blubber, stripped and cut into thin slices, was eaten with relish, and half a cup of penguin oil could be quaffed like a draught of mellow vintage.

July was a particularly obnoxious month. The variable temperatures of early spring frayed our tempers and added to our discomforts. Warmer days were marked by increased humidity, in which we felt the cold more than in the actual winter. We now experienced occasional rain, and the stronger rays of the sun thawed the snow that had become heaped round our hut. Our floor, a mosaic of pebbles laid in penguin guano, became slushy and malodorous. I awoke one night from a dream of falling through a crevice into the sea, and found my hand in water, which was inches deep and rising. There was nothing to do but to turn out all the 'ground-floor' hands, dig a sump-hole, and bale out some 60 gallons of evil-smelling liquid – a performance that had to be repeated before morning came, and three times each day and night afterwards. The odour of this liquid was worse, if possible, than the mingled perfumes – distinctly not of Araby – which accompanied various experiments in tobacco substitutes. The last pipeful of genuine leaf was smoked by Wild on 23 August; but long before this we had been stifled with fumes of penguin feathers, rope-yarn, dried meat and other pipe-fuel, with which the confirmed smokers had endeavoured to satisfy their cravings. One evening I was awakened from a doze by the familiar smell of an Australian bushfire.

Rubbing my eyes, I beheld McLeod, one of the sailors, contentedly puffing out volumes of heavy smoke. The day before he had borrowed all the pipes and boiled them in a tin to extract the nicotine juice. McLeod then discovered that, by steeping the grass lining of his padded footwear in the concoction, and drying it before the fire, an aromatic 'tobacco' of exceptional flavour resulted. The unusual 'perfume' awakened everyone, and in a twinkling one and all were busy slitting open their boots to remove the padding. A few moments later clouds of this new incense were ascending into the upper regions of our hut, to fall again in an ever-thickening volume. That we had worn those padded boots continuously for seven long months was an unconsidered trifle. Then I discovered that cigarettes could be made with the India paper of the only remaining volume of the *Encyclopaedia Britannica*, and pages of this went up in smoke.

With spring firmly established, August found us daily looking out with growing eagerness for the expected relief. Wild was always a comforter. Each morning he encouraged us with: 'Lash up and stow, boys, the Boss is coming today.' Four times a day we would climb, separately or in groups, to the summit of Lookout Bluff, on which our flagstaff had been erected, and scan the horizon for some sign. Our supplies of concentrated food had long since disappeared, but as the beach became once more ice-free, we gathered limpets from the rocks and dulse from the pools, and these made a welcome change in the monotonous diet; but what we were most grateful for was that the return of the seals and sea-elephants rendered the ceaseless slaughter of penguins no longer necessary, for we had developed a great love for these beautiful creatures.

But we were still surrounded by dangers. The glacier, which extended from one side of the spit around the head of West Bay, suddenly became active under the influence of rising temperatures, and became a menace. Thousands of tons of ice constantly fell from its seafront into the bay, displacing great seas, which rolled ice-laden towards us like tidal waves, sweeping over the lower areas of the flat. On two occasions huge, ice-laden surfs surged across the entire spit into the bay on the opposite side and encroached to within a few paces of our home. In a few moments the spit had undergone a complete transformation, and was from then on heavily littered with stranded ice-blocks. The deep roaring of avalanches crashing into the bay, the tumult of jostling and splintering ice, and the reverberating echoes among the mountains, gave us many sleepless nights. We never knew what might happen next in this hostile place where all nature was at war.

Sometimes the ocean would open and become almost clear of ice except for some stray bergs, but more often the prospect was most dismal, with no water visible, even from the highest point, and the foreshore, owing to prevailing low tides, became littered with stranded floes. The horizon was always depressingly empty of sail or smoke-plume. The spit itself was covered with wet and sloppy snow, and walking was restricted to a tramping-track of a bare 80 yards. These were our circumstances until well past the middle of August. Almost without hope, we had begun to discuss the dispatch of a party to Deception Harbour in one of the other boats.

On 30 August 1916, the 137th day of our marooning, Marston and I were scanning the northern horizon, when I drew his attention to a long, curious-shaped berg. 'Been watching the infernal thing for a couple of months,' was his terse reply. Nevertheless, we continued to gaze at it, when, miracle of miracles, a vessel came in sight from under its lee. We immediately raised a cry, which was greeted from the interior – where the others were at lunch – with scoffing shouts of derision and mocking choruses. When at last we made them realise the truth of the joyful news, there was an astonishing display of energy. They came crawling through the roof and breaking through the walls, frantic with joy. Wild gave orders to kindle the beacon, and soon a goodly pile of penguin skins and seal blubber was sending a dense, oily smoke-signal across the sky. It was a worthy occasion on which to expend one of my three remaining spaces of film, and I am glad to say that, despite everything it had been through, it recorded faithfully that truly historic scene.

Suspense was over. The vessel, which proved to be the Chilian trawler, *Yelcho*, hove to, and a boat was dropped for the shore. Ringing cheers greeted its approach. Those on board returned our salvos. Cheer followed cheer, the mountains cheered back, the sun even burst momentarily through the clouds. It was not only the sight of relief that warmed our hearts, for as the little boat drew near, we recognised our long-absent and heroic comrades, Shackleton, Crean and Worsley. But there was no time to be lost in greetings and rejoicings; they could come later when we were safe on board. Our relentless gaolers, the ice-fields, were hurrying to close the portals. Scurrying clouds were drifting over the mountains and obscuring the sun; the wind began to pipe, bleak and gusty. A blizzard was coming; there was not a moment to lose. In less than an hour the marooned party were all safely on board the *Yelcho* and steaming north to those we held dear.

As we stood on deck, watching the gathering mists veil familiar peaks, there was not a man among us who did not feel, mingled with his gratitude, a touch of sadness. We were gazing for the last time upon the land which, though bleak and inhospitable, had taken us to its bosom and been the means of our salvation.

CHAPTER 12

EPILOGUE

I shall not attempt to describe our feelings at the reunion with the men who had made, first, a gallant bid for freedom, and then a series of untiring efforts for our rescue. As we listened to Shackleton's story of the eighteen weeks between their departure and return, there was a tinge of envy mixed with our admiration. Theirs was an achievement which, in spite of its almost incredible hardships, every one of us would have been glad to share. Over the cigars that followed our first civilised meal, 'the Boss' sketched it in outline; later talks filled in the details.

This was their fourth attempt to effect our rescue. After sixteen days of unspeakable privations, in a tiny, crazy boat, at the mercy of terrible seas, they reached the iron-bound coast of South Georgia. But the elements were still implacable, and gathered in a final effort \to defeat them. They were tossed in their cockleshell in the worst hurricane they had ever experienced, threatened with destruction on a lee shore, while searching hopelessly for a possible landing-place. At last, a narrow passage through foaming reefs was sighted and, thanks to superb seamanship, they made it. Seven hundred and fifty miles of turbulent sub-Antarctic ocean had been crossed in a small boat 23 feet long – a boat journey which will always rank with the noblest achievements in the epic of man's conflict with the sea. They landed, six gaunt, battered, spent, starving frozen men, more dead than alive.

They were still far from all human aid. Their way was barred by the unmapped mountains and glaciers of the interior. These had always been considered impassable, even to strong and well-equipped parties. It was impossible to put to sea again; their boat, badly damaged, could never weather the mad waves which storms were driving directly on to the coast. Yet stricken men on Elephant Island were awaiting relief which they alone could send. There was only one thing to be done. The impassable mountains must be conquered.

Epilogue

Several days were spent recuperating in a tiny cave before they dared attempt the journey. Then Sir Ernest, Worsley and Crean set out on the hazardous enterprise. Enveloped in mists, staggering perilously on the brink of precipices, they won their way doggedly. Their courage was rewarded. They reached Stromness whaling station – woebegone refugees, spectres from the Antarctic, surely the strangest wayfarers who had ever knocked at a civilised man's door.

Of the terrible perils encountered in that climb, Sir Ernest spoke scarcely at all, but, from what I afterwards saw, I say that nothing but unfaltering loyalty and the grimmest determination to save the lives of twenty-two starving comrades left behind on a storm-swept rock ledge, could have produced the desperate urge that impelled them to travel such damnable country by night and day without rest or equipment.

The first thing to be done was to dispatch a vessel to rescue the three men left in a cave on the opposite side of the island. Next, the *Southern Sky*, a steel whaler under the command of our old friend Captain Thom, was commissioned immediately, and made good speed for Elephant Island, but, after sighting the peaks and approaching to within 70 miles of the spit on which we were marooned, she could proceed no farther on account of dense pack-ice. Disappointed, but undaunted, they returned to the Falkland Islands. Sir Ernest appealed to the various South American governments.

The second attempt was in a steel trawler, generously equipped by the Uruguayan Government. This time the relief ship actually steamed to within 20 miles of our camp. A low fog veiled the sea at the time, otherwise we would have seen the vessel on the margin of the pack-ice which prevented her from reaching us. A desperate attempt to force a way through the ice ended in nearly stripping the blades from her propeller and, as coal was exhausted, once more our gallant comrades and their helpers were compelled to turn back. Sir Ernest then visited Punta Arenas, and the sum of £1500 was subscribed in a few days by the British residents to send a small auxiliary schooner, the *Emma*, to our rescue. After leaving the Falklands, bad weather was experienced throughout the whole voyage, which lasted a month. Life on board the cranky craft was a feat of anxious endurance, as, buffeted by heavy seas, she tossed about – a mere toy in the Cape Horn gales. Ice was met 100 miles from Elephant Island, and an attempt to force a way through was given up – the vessel becoming damaged and narrowly escaping being crushed. Limping north through the deep, furrowed seas, the little ship returned to the Falkland Islands in a battered condition. But Shackleton was still determined. He knew only too well the desperate straits of the men relying on his efforts. Each day was bringing them closer to starvation, and he dared not delay till the summer when the seas would be ice-free; he must try again in spite of storms and ice and the seventeen hours' daily darkness.

He appealed urgently to the Chilean Government. There was only a small, steel vessel, called the *Yelcho*, available. She was quite unsuitable for such a voyage, but on 25 August, with Shackleton, Crean and Worsley and a crew of Chilean officers and seamen, she left Punta Arenas on the fourth attempt. This time providence rewarded them. The sea was calm, and five days later Elephant Island came in view. There was a wide rift in the pack-ice, made by a recent gale, which allowed the rescue vessel to slip through. Worsley picked out the camping place, and the *Yelcho* was run as close in as reefs permitted. A boat was lowered and put off for the shore. The anxiety of those aboard the little boat can be imagined. The leader stood up and hailed Frank Wild, 'Are you all well?'

'We are all well, Boss,' Wild called back.

'Thank God,' replied Sir Ernest. Then there were cheers and greetings on either side as we recognised our three comrades, Shackleton, Crean and Worsley.

The three days' run across to the tip of South America was a period of new and renewed sensations. Our reception at Punta Arenas was something more than a welcome – it was a triumph that extended without interruption through the ten days which we spent in this southernmost town in the world, and through the following six weeks of our journey through the country.

The city was *en fête*. On the wharf a picturesque and dense assemblage had gathered, prepared to clasp us to its hospitable bosom. It cheered us wildly as we passed through its midst down a widening lane; for, in our Elephant Island husks of malodorous, blubbery clothes, our beards and hair grown long, and our bodies unwashed for ten months, we were indeed an unlovely group. Nevertheless, Punta

Arenas rose to us. Noble families, and families noble in deed if not in rank, carried off the rescued ones to their homes, except for four of us, who declined all pressing offers and made the chief hotel our home. Our appearance caused a stampede of waitresses from the hotel, and it was not until the next morning, when assured that the shaved, bathed and respectable fellows seated at table were actually the wild men of the night before, that the timorous maids would return to duty.

The 'wishing-game' had been a favourite sport in our Elephant Island shanty. In our sleeping-bags we had often speculated upon the sensation that would most poignantly appeal to our senses when, if ever, we enjoyed creature comforts again. We argued as to what would be the most delightful food, but on one point there was no argument; it would be magnificent to have a bath, for the encrusted grime of that smoky hut seemed to have penetrated to our very souls. The soaking tub, bars of soap, the tingling shower, the glow-infusing rub-down, the well-nigh forgotten rasp of the keen razor – these would represent to us paradise regained – and they did.

Social distinctions were forgotten in this overwhelming wave of hospitality, and I saw a greaser (one of the expedition's firemen) in borrowed finery, drinking champagne familiarly with millionaires, and puffing luxuriously the finest cigars with the complacency of a magnate. What a change from filthy, blubber-reeking garb! Yet how awkward it seemed to have to use knives, forks, spoons and plates again – what a useless lot of things there seemed to be on the banquet-table!

Only the bed-ridden and the blind failed to appear on the wharf when, at the end of ten days, we re-embarked. To the accompaniment of whistles and sirens, the *Yelcho* pulled out, dipping her ensign to the bunting that waved a thousand compliments and farewells from every masthead in the port and from every pole on shore.

Our programme was to push westward through the Magellan Straits, then northwards along the Chilean coast to Valparaiso, landing there to cross the Andes, take a train to Buenos Aires, then across the Atlantic to Europe and finally to London.

Let me pay tribute to the boat and crew who had rescued us from Elephant Island. Built for use as a British trawler, the *Yelcho* had, at the time of our rescue, seen twelve years' service – and she showed every day of it. In any kind of sea she behaved like a porpoise. In a blow, anchors, chains, deck cargo and a miscellaneous litter maintained a continual bumping. Paint had long since disappeared from her hull, and one picked the flakes of rust from her plates with uncomfortable speculation. Yet two days out from Punta Arenas she ran onto an uncharted bank, rose a couple of feet higher in the water, dented her plates badly and scraped over without leaking. It was as well; for, though fitted with pumps like all other craft, the pumps differed in one important respect – they would not pump.

And yet after all was she not the instrument of our relief from misery? *Yelcho*, we lift our hats to you – you and your crew and your cook. You were unkempt – but you did us an unforgettable service, and we shall ever remember you and your officers and crew with affection.

Those who have read this story must have marvelled that we survived the perils and ordeals without loss of life. Sir Ernest had absolute faith in providential guidance, faith in himself, and faith in his men. His unconquerable spirit inspired his team and made them invincible.

That we did not achieve the expedition's plans was no fault of the leader's nor of his team-mates. At the head of the Weddell Sea, fate erected a barrier which man could not penetrate. Had we been able to establish our base there as intended, the ambitious plans of the expedition would have matured successfully. Extricating the party from Weddell's 'white hell' was a far greater achievement, and one that has never been excelled in the epic deeds of the sea and of exploration. Our few specimens and scientific records, the boxes of negatives and cinematograph films, were all that we brought out of the Antarctic, which we had entered with high hopes and a well-found ship two years previously. That was all of tangible things; but in memories we were rich. We had pierced the veneer of outside things.

> *We had suffered, starved, and triumphed, grovelled down,*
>   *yet grasped at glory,*
> *We had grown bigger in the bigness of the whole.*
> *We had seen God in His splendours, heard the text*
>   *that Nature renders*
> *We had reached the naked soul of man.*